Reinventing the World Bank

Reinventing the World Bank

edited by
Jonathan R. Pincus &
Jeffrey A. Winters

CORNELL UNIVERSITY PRESS

ITHACA AND LONDON

First published 2002 by Cornell University Press
First printing, Cornell Paperbacks, 2002

Printed in the United States of America

Library of Congress Cataloging-in-Publication Data

Reinventing the World Bank / edited by Jonathan R. Pincus and
Jeffrey A. Winters.
    p.   cm.
Extensively revised and updated papers presented at a conference
held in Evanston, Ill. in the spring of 1999.
Includes bibliographical references and index.
    ISBN 0-8014-4037-8 (cloth : alk. paper) — ISBN 0-8014-8792-7
(pbk. : alk. paper)
    1. World Bank—Congresses.   2. Loans, Foreign—Developing
countries—Congresses.   3. Economic development—Developing
countries—Congresses.   I. Pincus, Jonathan.   II. Winters,
Jeffrey A. (Jeffrey Alan), 1960–
   HG3881.5.W57 R45   2002
   332.1′532—dc21

                                  2002005743

Cloth printing   10 9 8 7 6 5 4 3 2 1
Paperback printing   10 9 8 7 6 5 4 3 2 1

Contents

10. CONCLUSION 222
Jonathan R. Pincus and Jeffrey A. Winters

Preface

"Can the World Bank lend money without hurting the poor?" The question, posed in an August 2000 newspaper headline, is tinged with irony, mocking the Bank's widely publicized rededication to the fight against world poverty. Recounting the failure of a major coal project in India to resettle 10,000 displaced farmers, the article highlights the continuing disjuncture between the Bank's antipoverty rhetoric and the real impact of its lending operations. "Evidence from the field," the author concludes, "suggests that despite five years of reformist talk from Bank President James D. Wolfensohn, the institution is still having trouble figuring out how to finance big development projects in poor countries while protecting the poor themselves" (Phillips 2000, 1).

This is well-charted territory for the World Bank's many critics. The conclusion that the Bank's internal efforts at reform have failed is echoed routinely in publications such as the *New Internationalist* and on countless antiglobalization websites. But, appearing as it did in the conservative pages of the *Wall Street Journal,* the Coal India story is emblematic of the predicament confronting the World Bank as it seeks to adapt to a rapidly changing world. No longer able to count on the political and economic certainties that underpinned its rise to preeminence among the international development organizations, the Bank has been left to cast about for new sources of legitimacy and political support.

The response of the Bank under James D. Wolfensohn was to launch a torrent of initiatives designed to restore the institution's sense of mission, shore up confidence among recipient and donor countries, and reinvigorate its lending operations. The Strategic Compact, announced at the 1996 annual meeting, includes commitments to pay greater attention to social issues and improve the performance of the lending portfolio. It was followed by the Partnership Initiative in 1997, which aspires to "put committed governments, and the people of developing countries, in the driver's seat" through greater involvement of governments, donors, civil society, and the private sector in devising development strategies (World Bank 1998k). The 1998 *World Development Report* redefined the institution as a "knowledge bank," harnessing new information technologies to spread information about development (World Bank 1998o). These ideas were reiterated in the

Comprehensive Development Framework (CDF) introduced in the form of a presidential working paper in January 1999. The CDF stressed the need for "a long term, holistic approach to development" based on a two-dimensional matrix of issues and stakeholders (Wolfensohn 1999). In practice, CDF documents have moved institution-building and governance issues to the center of the Bank's antipoverty strategy (World Bank 2000c). Country-level Poverty Reduction Strategy Papers—introduced at the end of 1999 as a condition for debt relief and concessional lending—were intended to ensure country "ownership" of antipoverty strategies and improve donor coordination (World Bank 2000a).

The overall thrust of the changes introduced thus far is to broaden the Bank's role from lender and economic adviser to include aid coordinator, political organizer, social reformer, law enforcer, and even the voice of the world's poor (see Narayan, Chambers et al. 2000; Narayan, Patel et al. 2000). Yet, as the Coal India story shows, serious questions remain unanswered. Does the Bank possess the operational capacity to take on these new tasks? Indeed, is the World Bank the appropriate vehicle to lead the fight against world poverty? Does the Bank possess a viable conceptual framework for the analysis of poverty and broader development issues? Has the Bank, in trying to please everyone, pleased no one? If it is as unpopular on Wall Street as on the streets of Seattle, Prague, and Genoa, where will it draw the political legitimacy and support it needs to retain its status as the world's pre-eminent development institution?

These are important questions because the World Bank is an important institution. It has a staff of 10,587 people originating from 160 countries. In FY2001 it made 225 loans valued at $17.3 billion and guaranteed investments worth an addition $2 billion in twenty-eight countries. The Bank also boasted a large research budget and published numerous books, journals, and papers. In 2001 its website tallied 18 million hits, averaging nearly 50,000 per day. Vilified by some as an imperialist plot and by others as a socialist giveaway, it is an organization that inspires strong emotions, although usually for what it symbolizes rather than for what it actually does. It is also a consciously and intensely political organization, keenly aware of the image it projects to the world.

The original idea for a book on World Bank reinvention developed from the observation that World Bank staff—whether of the permanent or the intermittent variety—accounted for a surprisingly large share of the published materials on the topic of the World Bank and World Bank reform. We thought it would be useful to organize a conference on possible directions of institutional change that was neither funded by the Bank nor dominated by speakers presently or previously employed by the World Bank. Although we did not want to exclude representatives of the Bank, we felt that such a conference would be more productive if a majority of participants had no institutional loyalties to the World Bank.

We were very fortunate that the J. M. Kaplan Fund also liked the idea and agreed to provide financial support for the conference. However, very early in the planning process it became clear that the World Bank was less than enthusiastic. When we contacted the Bank to invite the people we felt could best engage the issues we wanted to examine, we were referred to the Public Relations office, which expressed considerable surprise and dismay that a conference had been organized on the Bank without involving the institution from the start. "It's like having all your neighbors gather to talk about what's going on in your house," a senior staff member in the office complained. "Perhaps so," we responded, "with the small difference that all your neighbors pay your mortgage." We invited President Wolfensohn, but his travel schedule did allow him to attend. Although reluctant to participate, the Bank did finally agree to send a small delegation. A (leaked) confidential memorandum on the conference by the most senior Bank official in attendance amounted to a rant about the event: "a meeting organized with little reference to Bank inputs, and in many respects those of us from the Bank attended as 'listeners' more than integrated participants." The memorandum continued, "Striking in this meeting was the range of criticisms tabled, coming from virtually every direction: left and right, operational and intellectual, political and social, legal and environmental." "[T]he very willingness [of the Bank] to participate and listen was plainly respected by many" (Marshall 1999). It was as much an education trying to engage the Bank constructively on these issues as it was exploring the issues themselves.

All of the chapters in this volume were extensively revised and updated following the gathering in Evanston, Illinois, in spring 1999. For those who presented excellent papers that could not be included here because of space limitations, we are deeply grateful for your important intellectual contributions.

We also thank a number of people who made the conference and this book possible: the J. M. Kaplan Fund and especially Mary E. Kaplan, President Henry Bienen of Northwestern University, the University of London's School of Oriental and African Studies, Northwestern's Center for International and Comparative Studies, the Allen Center at the Kellogg School of Management, and the team of fifty bright and energetic Northwestern undergraduates whose commitment of time and effort made the 1999 conference possible. A special word of thanks goes to Steve Berkman, an inspiring individual and the World Bank's most dedicated reformer. We express our gratitude to Arif Arryman, Binny Buchori, Bruce Cumings, Russell Dilts, Edward Gibson, Béatrice Hibou, Peter Kenmore, John Kurtz, Rizal Ramli, Peter Riggs, Barbara Upton, and Meredith Woo-Cumings, as well as to our editor at Cornell University Press, Roger Haydon, two external readers who provided useful feedback on the manuscript, and Todd Gluckman for his careful editing of the notes and bibliography. Together with our contributors, we take full responsibility for any errors or shortcomings this volume may contain.

CHAPTER ONE

Reinventing the World Bank

Jonathan R. Pincus and Jeffrey A. Winters

The World Bank has a long history of adaptation to changing global circumstances and demands.[1] From its humble beginnings as a funding agency for postwar reconstruction, the Bank transformed itself in stages into a development bank, an aid agency, an antipoverty crusader, and a leading proponent of state retrenchment under the rubric of structural adjustment. More recently, the Bank has taken on issues as diverse as postconflict reconstruction, biodiversity, crime, governance, and public participation in development planning (Pincus 2001). Each new operational initiative has led the Bank to take on new functions; add new agencies, offices, and programs; collaborate with a wider range of institutions; and address new constituencies. Yet, like most large bureaucracies, the Bank has found it easier to expand than to retrench: archaeological remnants of previous Bank reforms are readily apparent within the Bank's labyrinthine organizational structure and in its portfolio of lending operations.

Although the Bank's tendency toward mission creep is in part attributable to bureaucratic inertia, the problem also reflects a conscious political containment strategy (Einhorn 2001). Confronted with increasing demands from member countries, pressure groups, and business interests, the Bank has attempted to accommodate these demands through ever more inclusive and wide-ranging consultation mechanisms. This, in turn, has led to longer lists of operational targets and development objectives, more demands, and yet more consultation. Overwhelmingly, the Bank has responded to political challenges by growing and taking on more.

For several decades, this strategy of institutional stretching, incremental change, goal proliferation, and wider consultation allowed the Bank to operate with relatively little dysfunction and political friction. Resources were made available to tackle the Bank's growing inventory of functions and spe-

---

1. What was to become the World Bank Group began as the International Bank for Reconstruction and Development. The International Finance Corporation (IFC) was added in 1956, the International Development Association (IDA) was created in 1960, the Operations Evaluation Department (OED) was formed in 1983, and the Multilateral Investment Guarantee Agency (MIGA) was founded in 1985.

cializations, if for no other reason than the fact that creditor countries lacked a politically viable alternative. However, two changes in the external environment have reduced the likelihood that the United States and other major donors will continue to underwrite new attempts to extend the Bank's mandate. The first is the end of the Cold War and the attendant shifts in the political alliances that underpinned the Bank's rise from minor player in postwar reconstruction to the world's premier development agency. The second, of equal importance, is the widespread perception that the integration of global capital markets has undermined the rationale of public sector development lending. The argument that investment decisions should be left to the market has gained support as the volume of private capital flows to developing countries has increased. Accommodating these new political and economic realities will require more than a continued process of adjustment at the margins.

The importance of these developments is evident in the advent of two key political challenges to the Bank's preferred strategy of incrementalism. In March 2000, a report of the International Financial Institution Advisory Commission—a committee of experts appointed by the U.S. Congress—sharply criticized the Bank for overstepping its mandate and failing to direct resources to the poorest developing countries (Meltzer et al. 2000).[2] The report gave voice to conservative legislators' demands for more selectivity in the allocation of aid flows and increased reliance on private capital markets. At the opposite end of the political spectrum, populist campaigners have been remarkably effective in forcing the issue of the democratic accountability of the Bretton Woods institutions onto the international agenda. Efforts on the part of the Bank to increase the involvement of nongovernmental organizations in all aspects of its work have been met with increasingly strident calls for a fundamental restructuring of the World Bank, International Monetary Fund (IMF), and World Trade Organization (WTO). Despite their ideological differences, aid skeptics and antiglobalization activists share in common a deep suspicion of the Bank and therefore constitute a powerful, if unlikely, coalition opposed to further attempts at incremental reform.

THREE DIMENSIONS OF REINVENTION

The World Bank as we know it bears little resemblance to the institution envisaged at the Bretton Woods conference in 1944. Moreover, if the Bank did not exist, it is unlikely that a similar conference held today would design anything remotely similar to the present-day World Bank Group. Six decades of incremental change have spawned an institution of immense size and com-

2. The International Financial Institution Advisory Commission was set up in 1998 as part of the legislation authorizing additional U.S. funding for the International Monetary Fund (IMF). Chaired by Allan Meltzer, the commission included prominent economists, business people, and politicians.

plexity, driven by grandiose ambitions and operating well beyond its core areas of competence.

Predictably, calls for greater focus and accountability have provoked yet another round of piecemeal reforms. Under the leadership of James D. Wolfensohn, the Bank launched a torrent of initiatives such as the Strategic Compact, Partnership Initiative, Knowledge Bank, and Comprehensive Development Framework (CDF). These represent the latest series of internally managed efforts to redefine the Bank's mission and restructure its relationships with creditor and debtor countries. As did previous attempts at internal reform, these proposals seek to broaden the Bank's mandate even further. Indeed, we would be hard pressed to think of an issue or constituency that does not in some way fall under the "long term, holistic approach to development" envisioned by the CDF (Wolfensohn 1999, 30).

This book takes as its point of departure the premise that it is unrealistic to expect an institution that has grown to unmanageable proportions on the basis of internally driven change to manage its own reform program. The World Bank cannot be reformed and certainly cannot reform itself: it must be reinvented. Moreover, the Bank's demonstrated failures of self-redesign in fact mask a larger failure on the part of the institution's most powerful shareholders to confront the daunting task of reinvention. Reinvention in this book denotes a thoroughgoing and externally controlled process of transformation, starting from basic principles and encompassing three closely related, yet distinct dimensions: *operations,* by which we mean the fit between the Bank's lending program and its development objectives; *concepts,* which are the institution's vision of development; and finally *power,* which includes the relationship between the Bank, member countries, and the wider public as well as structures of internal governance and accountability.

These three dimensions of reinvention inform our critique of the Bank as it exists and also provide us with a framework for the analysis of competing visions of reinvention that have been proposed by the Bank or by external observers of the institution. In this chapter we consider four possibilities for a reinvented World Bank and examine each in terms of its likely operational, conceptual, and political-power implications, as well as the internal coherence among these three dimensions of reinvention. This framework also helps us to move beyond normative questions concerning what the Bank should do and address the positive issue of which alternatives for reinvention are likely to succeed. In different ways, all of the chapters in this volume engage these same elements of operations, concepts, and power.

Several lessons emerge from the analyses set forth here and elaborated by our contributors. First, the need for a public sector development bank remains as strong as ever. Although private sector investment in developing countries increased during the 1990s, these flows are highly volatile and are therefore a poor substitute for public lending. Moreover, evidence of strong complementarities between public and private sector investment indicates that development banks play a crucial role in creating the conditions necessary for capital accumulation and growth in poor countries. If the World Bank did not exist, there would be a pressing need to create one. The problem is not having a World Bank, it is having this World Bank—a point largely overlooked by those who respond to the dysfunctions of the Bank by demanding that it simply be shut down.

Second, the World Bank can no longer be allowed to be both author and object of its own reinvention. As discussed earlier, the Bank's consistent response to criticism has been to acquire additional objectives and functions, each with its own external and internal constituencies. The World Bank has also shown an eagerness to acquiesce to demands emanating from donor countries—particularly the United States—to serve as a global dustbin, a convenient receptacle for expensive, politically risky, or otherwise irresolvable international problems. Tasks as diverse as lubricating the transition to capitalism in Russia and underwriting the peace processes in the Middle East and the Balkans have fallen to the Bank, despite the fact that the institution lacks the resources and political clout to deal with them effectively.[3] The discipline needed for reinventing the World Bank must be imposed. It will not come from within.

But who will impose this discipline? As Ernst Haas has noted, international regimes thrive when hegemonic states define, control, and fund them and falter when they do not (Haas 1980). This is clearly the case for the World Bank, which has responded with drift to conflicting signals from Congress and successive U.S. administrations. For the present, the United States appears content to treat the World Bank as an extension of the U.S. Treasury, an arrangement that will remain attractive as long as U.S. dominance remains unperturbed by its declining relative capital contribution and voting shares. Although aid skeptics in Congress favor a downsized Bank in principle, most realize that any course of radical reinvention will impose significant short-term costs on the United States. For both the executive and legislative branches, the political risks of allowing the World Bank to continue with the business of bungling its own reforms are low relative to the potential risks associated with a more activist stance. Barring a new global economic crisis, this is unlikely to change soon. The need to reinvent the

3. In May 1997, the major shareholder states issued a policy statement entitled, "Conflict, Peace, and Development Co-operation on the Threshold of the 21st Century," by the Development Assistance Committee of the OECD. "This statement signalled a new determination to link development assistance to preventing deadly conflict," according to Stremlau and Sagasti (1998, 4). Also in 1997, the Bank established a new unit devoted to postconflict situations, as well as a special new fund to expand the Bank's capacity to consolidate peace processes (see Stremlau and Sagasti 1998).

World Bank is urgent and will remain so for the foreseeable future. But the prospects for reinvention are as dim as they have been at any time in the institution's history.

CHANGING POLITICAL AND ECONOMIC CONTEXT

Earlier we noted that the end of the Cold War and an upsurge in private capital flows to the developing world have combined to create strong pressures for change at the World Bank. As we see in the following section, these pressures have mostly been in the direction of a smaller Bank with a more limited mandate (Mikesell 2000). The Cold War had provided the Organization for Economic Cooperation and Development (OECD) countries with a powerful justification for foreign aid budgets, and following the collapse of the Soviet Union these began to decline, first as a share of GNP and then after 1992 in absolute terms (Hjertholm and White 2000, 85). The volume of World Bank lending continued to increase for a time, largely in response to successive macroeconomic crises. By 2000, however, International Bank for Reconstruction and Development (IBRD) and International Development Association (IDA) lending totals were also falling sharply, down by nearly 50 percent in one year (figure 1.1). Although the Bank attributes this abrupt decrease to the tailing off of emergency lending in the wake of the financial crisis in Asia, lending was in fact down across most sectors, including agriculture and transportation.

One of the most significant changes in the post–Cold War period is the rise of governance as a salient factor in Bank lending decisions. Throughout the Cold War, the strategic objectives of the Bank's major shareholders

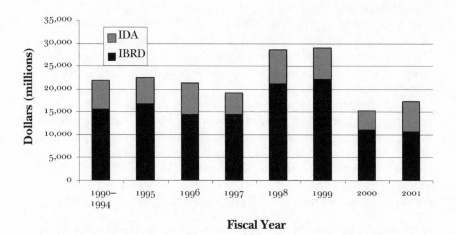

Figure 1.1 World Bank Lending Operations, FY1990–FY2001
Source: World Bank (1999a, 2000a, 2001a).

outweighed these concerns. U.S. allies such as Indonesia, Turkey, Mexico, Congo, and the Philippines enjoyed consistent backing from the Bank despite repeated noncompliance with loan provisions, unpredictable policy shifts, and endemic corruption (Gwin 1997, 252–63). In each of these countries, Bank staff developed close working relationships with predominantly U.S.-trained technocrats who shared the Bank's neoliberal worldview and who represented the greatest hope for sustained reform along the lines advocated by the Bretton Woods organizations. U.S. pressure was also decisive in curtailing or blocking loans to states outside of the U.S. orbit such as Gamal Abdel Nasser's Egypt, Salvador Allende's Chile, postwar Vietnam, or Nicaragua under the Sandinistas. Although national security motives are still relevant—the United States, for example, is still eager to enlist Bank support in the former Soviet and Yugoslav republics—they no longer provide a blanket justification for large-scale programs in much of Asia, Africa, and Latin America. U.S. ambivalence in part reflects the growing role of Congress and nongovernmental organizations (NGOs) in setting the terms of the Bank-U.S. relationship, a development that the administration of President Bill Clinton did not resist.

The second major change in the international context is the rise in private capital flows to developing countries during the 1990s. When the Bretton Woods institutions were founded, and throughout most of their existence, aid was seen as an important instrument for relaxing capital and foreign exchange constraints in industrializing countries. Indeed, the Bank's original mission emphasized the role of public-sector capital transfers in stimulating private investment. This had changed by the early 1990s. The share of net multilateral lending in total capital flows from OECD to developing countries fell from over 20 percent in the late 1980s to less than 10 percent in 1997 (see table 1.1).[4] The declining share of development assistance in total capital flows led many observers to claim that public sector lending was no longer necessary and that it was more likely to distort than to supplement international capital markets (e.g., see Meltzer et al. 2000; Krueger 1998; Gilbert, Powell, and Vines 1999).

Stripped of its ideological content, however, the argument against public-sector capital transfers is vastly overstated. As many commentators have noted, a small number of countries account for the majority of private capital transfers received by developing countries. Sixty percent of private resource flows from Development Assistance Committee (DAC) member countries to developing countries in 1997 were received by countries with per capita incomes greater than $3,000 (table 1.2).[5] Poor countries (those

4. This figure includes all capital flows from members of the Development Assistance Committee (DAC) of the OECD.
5. Including the former Soviet republics. Figures are in U.S. dollars unless otherwise indicated.

Table 1.1

Net Flow of Financial Resources from OECD Development Assistance Committee Countries to Developing Countries and Multilateral Organizations, 1982–83 to 1999[a]

	1982–83 (average)	1987–88 (average)	1994	1995	1996	1997	1998	1999
Official development assistance	26,904	43,834	59,152	58,926	55,438	48,324	51,888	56,435
Bilateral grants and grant-like flows	12,908	23,479	35,185	36,184	36,506	31,246	32,396	33,910
Bilateral loans	4,796	6,956	6,115	4,444	2,585	1,147	2,729	3,952
Contributions to multilateral institutions	9,199	13,339	17,852	18,299	16,347	15,932	16,764	18,573
Other official flows	6,098	3,022	10,456	9,872	5,562	6,113	13,785	15,477
Private flows at market terms	41,007	21,491	90,238	90,411	128,881	129,136	109,926	110,525
Direct investment	9,319	21,202	48,459	52,484	59,873	80,910	82,869	89,493
Bilateral portfolio investment	18,671	1,723	37,384	33,145	68,662	50,601	27,228	24,934
Multilateral portfolio investment	4,948	2,033	−3,018	−790	−948	−6,126	−2,043	−5,768
Export credits	8,070	−3,468	7,413	5,572	1,295	3,751	1,873	1,866
Net grants by NGOs	2,317	4,123	6,046	5,973	5,568	5,191	5,375	6,715
TOTAL NET FLOWS	76,327	72,470	165,893	165,182	195,449	188,764	180,974	189,151

[a]In millions of dollars. OECD DAC members include the major bilateral donor countries. Data from OECD, www.oecd.org/dac.
[b]A transaction in which the donor country retains formal title to repayment but has expressed its intention in the commitment to hold the proceeds of repayment in the borrowing country.

Table 1.2

Private Capital Flows from OECD Development Assistance Committee Member Countries and Net World Bank Transfers to Developing and Transitional Countries, 1995–1999[a]

	1995	1996	1997	1998	1999
Foreign direct investment					
Low income	5,607[b]	7,425	9,984	5,924	5,265
Middle income	11,298[c]	13,087	17,339	18,336	14,543
Upper income	21,639[d]	17,090	31,500	34,204	50,506
Other CEEC/NIS[e]	7,230	5,655	7,221	11,592	12,941
Total Bank					
Low income	410	1,686	4,420	−3,353	−2,424
Middle income	9,163	6,655	7,689	1,064	−153
Upper income	6,643	10,458	16,024	8,076	1,645
Other CEEC/NIS	1,852	2,992	3,088	217	−4,553
Total non-bank					
Low income	457	1,341	1,187	3,219	1,783
Middle income	3,254	10,324	4,730	3,990	6,853
Upper income	−225	6,952	10,009	9,564	16,727
Other CEEC/NIS	−1,147	−128	2,200	7,716	6,269
Total private[f]					
Low income	6,341	10,269	15,332	5,502	4,527
Middle income	23,263	28,484	29,703	23,323	21,234
Upper income	27,640	34,487	57,532	51,843	68,877
Other CEEC/NIC	3,032	8,501	12,508	19,437	14,657
IBRD and IDA (net flows)					
Low income	4,732	5,686	5,556	4,799	4,480
Middle income	260	−679	−471	617	1,850
Upper income	−287	477	519	2,280	1,140
Other CEEC/NIS	1,660	1,754	3,579	1,288	1,107

[a]In million of dollars. Data from OECD, www.oecd.org. CEEC/NIS; IBRD, International Bank for Reconstruction and Development; IDA, International Development Association.
[b]Per capita income less than $765 in 1995, at prevailing exchange rates.
[c]Per capita income greater than $765 and less than $3,035 in 1995, at prevailing exchange rates.
[d]Per capita income greater than $3,036 and less than $9,385 in 1995, at prevailing exchange rates.
[e]Central and eastern European countries and countries of the former Soviet Union not classified as DAC Part I developing countries.
[f]Net of offsetting entries for debt relief.

with per capita incomes below $765) received only 15 percent of the total. Moreover, private long-term net resource flows to the forty-eight least developed countries recorded in 1998 were only approximately one-half of the total for 1993 (UN Conference on Trade and Development [UNCTAD] 2000, 54).[6]

The late 1990s financial crises in Latin America and Asia also demonstrated that the shift from official to private capital in the 1990s did not

6. Long-term capital flows have maturities equal to or greater than one year. "Least developed countries" is a category established by the United Nations.

come without costs. Portfolio capital, a particularly volatile form of invest-ment, increased from just 2 percent of total net financial flows to developing countries in 1987 to nearly 50 percent by 1996. In just two years, however, the figure again plunged to 25 percent of capital flows. Given volatility on this scale, increasing reliance on forms of capital such as short-term com-mercial bank loans entailed a redistribution of risk from rich to poor coun-tries. Motivated largely by strategic concerns, official flows could, in theory, be used in a countercyclical manner to support client states experiencing external shocks (Carnegie Endowment for International Peace [CEIP] 2001).[7] But during political and economic crises, private capital crowds the exits and new sources quickly dry up (see Winters 1999a, 1999b; Armijo 1999).

The Bank has internalized the logic of its critics to a surprising degree. Rather than defend the role of public sector lending, the Wolfensohn Bank has chosen instead to emphasize the institution's pedagogical, nonfinancial role. This partly reflects the dominance of neoliberalism within the Bank it-self, but also an awareness that aid skeptics are gaining influence in both the U.S. Congress and Treasury. Whatever the reason, the Bank's failure to mount an aggressive defense of its development bank functions has left the institution vulnerable to attacks from both the Left and Right of the ideo-logical spectrum.

COMPETING VISIONS OF REINVENTION

The evolving external context has created intense pressure for change. But what sort of change? Wolfensohn's first presidential term was marked by the emergence of several competing visions of a newly reinvented Bank, each containing an implicit view of the operational, conceptual, and political power dimensions of reinvention. This section examines the main con-tenders. We begin with the Knowledge Bank, an idea closely associated with Joseph Stiglitz, former chief economist of the World Bank, and strongly en-dorsed by management during his tenure. The second option—the niche bank—reflects the views of Right-wing critics of the institution, who argue that the private sector has rendered the World Bank's lending role redun-dant. A newly reinvented Bank by this vision would focus exclusively on the world's poorest countries and would provide loans or loan guarantees se-lectively even within this group. We then consider the Left populist view that the Bank cannot be reformed and therefore should be shut down.

Finally we put forward a fourth option, which has not received much at-

---

7. However, a later UNCTAD report demonstates that in practice aid flows in the least-de-veloped countries (LDCs) are positively correlated with domestic financing. "Foreign aid by and large," the report concludes, "has not alleviated the effects of short-term external shocks in the LDCs, and has, if anything, reinforced the effect of such external shocks" (UNCTAD 2000, 181).

tention in the literature—the World Bank as a development bank. This proposal runs directly counter to the conventional wisdom, which holds that development banking is passé in an era of vibrant international capital markets. We argue that the conventional wisdom is wrong and that the World Bank should build on its comparative advantage in development banking and surrender unrelated tasks to existing or newly created institutions better suited to carrying out these ancillary functions. The question is not whether development banking is still relevant but instead whether the U.S. government as the hegemonic power that must drive World Bank reinvention is prepared to accept the political risks associated with restructuring the World Bank and, if it is, whether the executive and legislative branches are prepared to act pragmatically rather than ideologically.

The Knowledge Bank

Since the 1970s, the World Bank has thought of itself as a global development agency rather than as a financial institution in the strict sense. In contemporary parlance, the Bank's size, experience, and expertise allow it to "bundle together" services such as loans, technical assistance, policy advice, and aid coordination. Christopher Gilbert, Andrew Powell, and David Vines, for example, offer this prosaic description of the Bank as development agency:

> [T]he Bank is rather like an Oxbridge college, or a private American
> university, which uses endowment income to subsidize its research
> and teaching. The IBRD provides subsidized loans to its clients while
> the IDA provides highly concessional loans with a grant component.
> The Bank also invests in the production and dissemination of devel-
> opment knowledge and provides direct development assistance.
> It simultaneously combines the activities of financial intermediary,
> development research institution, consulting company and inter-
> governmental agency. (1999, 612)

This is a vision of the Bank that current management strongly endorses; it informs the knowledge bank, CDF, and development partnership concepts put forward by the Wolfensohn Bank. A common thread running through these initiatives is the need to find a convincing rationale for the Bank's leadership role that is not dependent on public sector lending.

Three arguments have compelled the Bank to deemphasize its financial role. As already discussed, private capital flows to middle-income developing countries increased sharply in the 1990s, leading some commentators to claim that capital market imperfections no longer provide a persuasive justification for large-scale public sector lending. Second, the Bank has often noted that the success rate of individual projects is closely associated with the overall management of the economy in developing countries. Even good projects are unlikely to achieve their objectives if the appropriate incentive structures, administrative capacity, and ancillary infrastructure and services are not in place. Finally, foreign aid is fungible. Even in the absence of external loans, governments would fund the best projects from their own resources, implying that external funds only serve to free up domestic spending for more marginal projects or for consumption.

In the 1980s these three propositions led the Bank in the direction of program lending and hence greater use of loan conditionality—that is, tying the delivery of resources to the implementation of specific policy changes in recipient countries. Increasingly, the Bretton Woods institutions identified poor or inappropriate policies rather than savings or foreign exchange constraints as the chief obstacles facing developing countries. Getting policies right meant creating an environment conducive to private investment and trade, controlling government expenditure to eliminate marginal or low payoff activities, and in general improving the state's capacity to manage the resources at its disposal. Recurrent macroeconomic crises since the 1970s and the attendant need to provide large quick-disbursing loans to countries facing short-term balance-of-payments deficits intensified the Bank's shift away from investment projects and toward program lending and conditionality.

By the 1990s, conditionality was under attack, not only from critics of the Bretton Woods institutions, but from within as well (World Bank 1998d; Stiglitz 1998c, 1998d). Attaching extensive and detailed conditions to structural and sectoral adjustment loans had neither changed borrowers' economic policies nor improved macroeconomic performance (Mosely, Harrigan, and Toye 1995; Killick 1998). This theme was enthusiastically picked up by Joseph Stiglitz, who, during his three years as chief economist of the Bank, initiated a wide-ranging rethink of the dominant economic development strategy pursued by the Bretton Woods institutions. In a series of papers and public lectures, he attacked the so-called Washington Consensus—the neoliberal stabilization formula that came to prominence in the 1980s, consisting of trade and financial liberalization, deregulation, privatization, and fiscal restraint.[8] Stiglitz's critique centered not so much on the content of the policies themselves but rather on the prior need for institutional reform and an adequate regulatory framework in support of market-oriented reforms. The main problem of the Washington Consensus was, according to Stiglitz, "a failure to understand the subtleties of the market economy, to understand that private property and 'getting prices right' (that is liberalization) are not sufficient to make a market economy work" (1998d, 9). What is needed is a thoroughgoing transformation of society that extends beyond

8. The term was coined by John Williamson (1993, 1334), who set out ten axioms that constitute "the common core of wisdom embraced by all serious economists."

tinkering at the margins to encompass institutional change and the creation of new institutions in the private and public sectors, including corporations, states, local communities, and families. This Herculean task cannot be achieved by "imposing change from the outside" but requires local ownership, participation, inclusion, and consensus building (24–29).

Whatever the merits of Stiglitz's post-Washington Consensus as a development theory, his views, to the extent that they have filtered into the Bank's conception of its own role, pose a serious dilemma for the reinvention project.[9] Stated simply, the post-Washington Consensus aggressively widens the scope for policy intervention from economic issues to the political, social, and cultural spheres while at the same time narrowing the range of acceptable leverage points needed for effective intervention. In terms of the three dimensions of reinvention, Stiglitz has provided a new conceptual framework, but has failed to link it up with a viable operational strategy.

Both the Bank in its official publications and Stiglitz in his own writings have sought to bridge the widening gap between objectives and instruments by recourse to the knowledge bank, development partnerships, and Wolfensohn's own CDF. The knowledge bank would no longer enforce policy change through conditionality but would instead teach poor countries how to transform themselves, encourage participation in the process of change through partnerships, and encourage commitment and "ownership" through the vehicle of the CDF.[10]

This is a strategy for a kinder, gentler Bank, but one that entails sizeable risks for an institution that is already under fire for failing to live up to its own internal performance standards. Knowledge may be important for development, but the Bank's alarmingly frequent attacks of "institutional amnesia" raise the legitimate question, posed most forcefully by Bruce Rich (chap. 2 of this volume), of whether this is an area in which the Bank's comparative advantage lies. The Bank's track record in knowledge generation is not much better.[11] The poor performance of public-sector reform programs also casts doubt on the Bank's capacity to promote, design and implement activities related to institutional reform.[12] Creating new institutions, im-

9. For a critique of the different facets of the post-Washington Consensus, see Standing (2000) and Fine (2001).

10. Or as Ben Fine succinctly puts it: "What the new consensus does analytically is to strengthen and widen the scope for discretionary intervention under the guise of good governance and the imperative to moderate both market *and* non-market imperfections, and wrap it up in terms of local ownership" (2001, 26).

11. Gavin and Rodrik put it bluntly: "It is difficult to pinpoint a single important idea or method in development economics that has its origins in the World Bank" (1995, 333).

12. Elliot Berg attributes the failure of these programs to the Bank's deficiencies in designing and implementing institutional reform. "One factor," he writes, "is the well-known organisational inclination in the World Bank to give much greater weight to analytic issues than to the softer matters of process such as concern with ownership and nurturing of local ca-

proving governance, and fostering participation must surely mean redistribution of political and economic power if it means anything at all. But the Bank—forbidden from engaging in political activity by its own rules and ideologically opposed to the redistribution of wealth and income—has precious few operational levers to achieve much of an impact in these areas.

The history of structural adjustment lending and conditionality is itself an important case of internal failures of knowledge and governance. That the Bank persisted so long and spent so many billions of dollars promoting a single, demonstrably unsuccessful approach confirms that the Bank, like most large bureaucracies, is a rather slow learner. It also raises fundamental questions about what the proposed transformation from conditionality bank to knowledge bank would mean in practice. Whether conditionality is ex post, as in the old form, or ex ante, as implied by the partnership model, control over loan conditions has gone hand in hand with control over knowledge or at least the authority to decide what is knowledge and what is not. World Bank and IMF economists have clear ideas about what counts as knowledge, but no governance procedures exist within these institutions to ensure that these officers are rewarded for distributing good advice and penalized for their errors. Guy Standing makes the important point that until the Bank and IMF surrender hegemony over knowledge and embrace a pragmatic experimental approach to policy making, knowledge and conditionality will continue to act as complements rather than substitutes. Citing the example of the Russia, he writes:

A community of economists, many linked to the Bank or IMF, visited the region with "knowledge" and sold their wares. As Larry Summers, a predecessor of Stiglitz as World Bank Chief Economist, said approvingly in 1994, there was a "striking degree of unanimity" on the standard reform prescriptions. . . . What transpired in Russia and other parts of the region has surely demonstrated that the knowledge of that community was wrong. (Standing 2000, 752)

Herein lies the central problem of the Wolfensohn Bank's partnership rhetoric. According to the Bank, the first pillar of partnership states that "the government and the people of the developing countries must be in the driver's seat" (World Bank 1998k, 1). The third pillar, however, reads, "assistance must be selective, with the type of assistance—financial or technical, for example—to be determined by country circumstances and delivered by appropriate partnerships." Despite the use of the passive voice, it is clear that the *Bank* will determine the type and amount of assistance and the appro-

---

pacity. . . . Awareness of institutional weakness should permeate all reform activities in low-income countries. But sensitivity to country specific institutional constraints has never been a strong point in World Bank operations" (Berg 2000, 495).

priate forms of partnership. This suggests a taxicab approach to partnership, in which the country is in the driver's seat, but no one is going anywhere until the Bank climbs in back, gives the destination, and pays the fare.

Ironically, Stiglitz in the end received a firsthand lesson in the political dimension of knowledge banking. His confrontations with the IMF during the financial crisis in Asia won him few friends in the U.S. Treasury, a fact that was revealed in dramatic fashion when Lawrence H. Summers, by then U.S. Treasury secretary, made Stiglitz's resignation a condition for Wolfensohn's reappointment (Stiglitz 2000; Wade 2001a). Stiglitz was followed in May 2000 by Ravi Kanbur, director of the *World Development Report* on poverty of the same year. Again under pressure from the U.S. Treasury, the Bank substantially altered Kanbur's draft report, assigning greater emphasis to growth and softening Kanbur's emphasis on social protection and his criticisms of financial liberalization (World Bank 2000f; Wade 2001a). These episodes illustrate the narrow political and ideological confines within which intellectual work at the Bank takes place, limits that effectively undermine the knowledge bank concept. They also explain why the concept is politically appealing to U.S. policy makers, who significantly control the range of acceptable knowledge to be created, stored, and lent by the knowledge bank.

These are not new issues for the Bank, which, since the Robert McNamara years, has grappled with the operational dimension of reinvention—that is, the mismatch between its own lofty ambitions and its capacity to achieve results on the ground. Much of the problem springs from vague notions regarding what development agencies are and what they should do. Surely they must promote development and use all available means to do so. But the definition of what constitutes development is poorly specified, its causes are imperfectly understood, and the range of practical policy measures has repeatedly shown itself to be sorely inadequate to the task. In a prescient remark written in 1973, Edward S. Mason and Robert E. Asher identified the problem when the Bank attempted for the first time to transform itself from a development bank into a development agency:

> If we are to take seriously the various pronouncements of management and discussions in the board of directors, there have also been significant changes in the Bank's conception of how the development process is to be promoted. It is not enough to transfer capital to an increasing range of viable projects, to contribute foreign exchange to development programs through local expenditure financing and program lending, and to assist in the building of institutions. If development is to be understood as a sustained increase in the capacity of member countries to satisfy social preferences, then a reduction of unemployment and underemployment, a

more equitable distribution of income, and wider participation by the citizenry in decision-making may need to be considered as necessary inputs. . . . It must be said that, to date, there continues to be a sizeable gap between the public pronouncements of some of the Bank's spokesmen and its day-to-day practice. (1973, 732)

The gap between rhetoric and performance has continued to widen since Mason and Asher first identified the problem. Ironically, the Bank's repeated admonition that "the state has to move away from doing many things badly to doing its few core tasks well" (World Bank 1996m, 110) has so far failed to provoke many horrified moments of self-recognition on H Street (of the "we have seen the public sector and it is us" variety). In this, the knowledge bank is best viewed as a continuation and perhaps intensification of a long-term process in which rising political demands have been quelled through heightened rhetoric and goal proliferation. But it is an idea that is deeply flawed conceptually and operationally. Unfortunately, its attractiveness to the U.S. government and current Bank management means that it is among the most likely outcomes of the reinvention process.

The Bank as Niche Player
The acceleration of private net capital flows to the developing world in the 1990s has led some observers to conclude that the public sector should no longer have a direct role in development financing, at least so far as middle-income countries are concerned. Long associated with libertarianism in the United States (e.g., see Bandow and Vasquez 1994), this view gained credibility in the mainstream with the publication of the sharply critical Congressional commission report on the international financial institutions. According to the report, eleven countries that already enjoy easy access to private capital markets still account for 70 percent of World Bank nonaid transfers (Meltzer et al. 2000, 9). Although the financial crises in Asia and Latin America in the 1990s have underlined the risks involved in relying on private lending in moments of global financial turbulence, the authors argue that countries normally enjoying adequate access to private capital markets can effectively manage these risks through improved monitoring, regulation, and, as a last resort, recourse to short-term IMF credits.[13] Moreover, middle-income countries have already developed sufficient technical capabilities to formulate and implement projects and are thus no longer in

13. The opposite conclusion was reached by another influential commission, this one formed by the Carnegie Endowment for International Peace (CEIP 2001) and including among its members former Federal Reserve Chairman Paul Volcker, former U.S. Treasury Secretary Nicholas Brady, and former World Bank President Robert McNamara. The Carnegie panel points out that lending by multilateral development banks to emerging economies has tended to be countercyclical and thus support, rather than replace, private sector flows.

need of technical assistance or well-executed showcase projects that provide opportunities for learning by doing. This suggests that the Bank should, in Anne Kreuger's words, "become more of a 'niche' player," phasing out lending to middle-income countries and focusing instead on the poorest countries in sub-Saharan Africa and in south and central Asia (1998, 2009). Citing the fungibility problem, this author also urges the Bank to steer clear of "soft issues" such as the environment, gender equality, labor standards, and support for NGOs (2006).

Aid selectivity, both in terms of geographical coverage and project focus, was very much in vogue among bilateral donors in the 1990s as funding levels declined prior to the Asian financial crisis (see U.S. Agency for International Development [USAID] 1997; Department for International Development [DFID] 1997; Canadian International Development Agency [CIDA] 1997). For these creditors, however, strategic considerations, trade and migration patterns, and historical links have always factored prominently and explicitly in aid decisions. What is new is not the idea of selectivity itself, but the counterintuitive claim that rationing aid is somehow in the interests of the recipients as well as the donors. As already discussed, this theme dovetails with the Bank's increasingly critical stance on conditionality as a means of achieving policy reform, a view expressed most forcefully in the publication *Assessing Aid: What Works, What Doesn't and Why* (World Bank 1998d). The report argues that aid can only be effective in a good policy environment, with "good policies" defined as low inflation (which is in fact an outcome rather than a policy), fiscal surplus, trade openness, and an index of institutional quality. If the objective of aid is to reduce poverty, then the efficiency of aid allocations can be increased by focusing deliveries on countries with high levels of poverty and good policies. Countries with poor policies can best be helped with knowledge and encouragement rather than large amounts of money (117).

Several critics have identified the report's numerous and serious conceptual and methodological shortcomings, which, taken together, undermine the proposed link between policies, aid, and growth (Lensink and White 1999; Hansen and Tarp 2000).[14] Of greater relevance to Bank reinvention, however, are the report's policy conclusions, above all the claim that the high failure rate of structural adjustment programs can be attributed to

---

14. The results of cross-country growth regressions of this sort are notoriously fragile (Levine and Renelt 1992). Curiously, *Assessing Aid* omits the share of investment in GDP, one of the few variables that is consistently associated with growth. The omission of this variable means that the coefficients for variables included in the model are biased. Another crucial problem is the construction of the policy index from the four variables previously mentioned. As Lensink and White point out, the individual components of the index are poorly specified and not closely associated with economic growth. Combining these indicators in a linear fashion, while omitting more detailed policy variables, only compounds the misspecification problem (Lensink and White 1999, 5–7).

poor policies and weak institutions in recipient countries. The assumption made throughout the report is that the failure of orthodox adjustment policies has nothing to do with their content, design, and implementation, which are, apparently, beyond criticism. This assumption is unwarranted. Robert Lensink and Oliver Morrissey (1999) argue that conditionality is itself a major source of macroeconomic instability in poor countries that are dependent on aid to finance current expenditures. The stop-go financing associated with loan conditionality leads to greater uncertainty, thus reducing the effectiveness of both aid and changes in policies (Lensink and Morrissey 1999, 22). UNCTAD argues in a similar vein that the fiscal austerity demanded as part of IMF and World Bank adjustment programs routinely undermines the capacity of the state to implement reforms. The report concludes:

> The move to the more market-based strategy of development, since the early 1980s particularly, actually involved *additional* administrative and organizational functions for these States in order to create the preconditions for the proper functioning of markets and the strengthening of civil society organizations and institutions. During such reform periods, an increase rather than a decline in the financial and administrative resources of the Government is required. The erosion of those resources of Governments during this critical period would affect not only aid effectiveness but also the efficiency of resource use in the economy as a whole, and in extreme cases could lead to the unravelling of the social cohesion and national integrity of the country. (UNCTAD 2000, 185, emphasis in the original)

As John Sender (chap. 8 in this volume) argues, the uncritical stance toward structural adjustment programs taken in *Assessing Aid* leaves the Bank open to the charge that it is attempting to shift the blame to borrowers while ignoring the substantial theoretical and empirical literature linking orthodox policies to economic instability, low rates of investment, and slow growth.[15]

The argument for policy-based selectivity is also politically naïve. Thandika Mkandawire (1994) makes the point that there is no reason to assume that democratically elected governments will pursue policies deemed acceptable to the World Bank. A latent conflict therefore exists between the Bank's desire for both good governance and orthodox stabilization policies (Mkandawire 1994, 165). The Bank is also susceptible to the same political factors that shape aid allocation decisions made by the main bilateral donors (Gwin 1997, 252). It is unlikely that policy-based selectivity could withstand,

15. See Mosely, Subasat, and Weeks (1995) for a comprehensive critique of the Bank's orthodox adjustment policies in Africa.

for example, U.S. pressure for new loans to Egypt or French support for Francophone Africa. Much the same can be said for reducing disbursements to middle-income countries, many of which (e.g., the Latin American and southeast Asian countries) fall within the spheres of influence of the largest donors. Selectivity on the basis of per capita income at the national level also runs counter to the Bank's 1990s emphasis on decentralization and attempts to reach beyond the central state to address problems at the regional and local levels. It is not clear, for example, that poverty in regions like Northeastern Brazil is less intense, and therefore less deserving of international attention, than poverty in countries with lower average incomes. Nor is it clear that creditor countries would be prepared to make up for the loss of income that the Bank receives from middle-income countries and uses to subsidize loans to poor borrowers. Finally, the experience of the Asian financial crisis suggests that the Bank would find it difficult to remain aloof when middle-income countries suffer sudden external shocks owing to the welfare implications of internal adjustment and the likely impact on major creditors and trading partners.

The niche bank has substantial support in the U.S. Congress, primarily because it implies a smaller financial burden on the World Bank's main shareholders. It has less appeal to the U.S. foreign policy establishment, which understands that the Bank delivers substantial support to friendly states at relatively low cost to the United States. The response of the World Bank and the U.S. government to the east Asian financial crisis demonstrates that aid selectivity—however fashionable at the moment—quickly falls off the donor agenda during periods of emergency.

The Bank's Dissolution—Fifty Years Is Enough?

Pressure for World Bank reform intensified during the 1980s as U.S. environmental groups joined forces with Congressional critics of aid to challenge U.S. contributions to IDA. In response, the Bank launched a series of initiatives to strengthen its environmental, resettlement, and social policies. However, patchy implementation of the new policies—manifested most painfully for the Bank in the case of India's Narmada dam project—fueled suspicion among activists that the Bank was beyond reform. This theme was joined to parallel criticisms of the social impact of IMF stabilization programs in a spate of popular books on the Bretton Woods institutions (e.g., Danaher 1994; Cavanagh, Wysham, and Arruda 1994; Oxfam 1995; Caufield 1996; Chossudovsky 1997). "Fifty Years Is Enough" became the rallying cry of an increasingly strident movement seeking to restructure and democratize these institutions and, in some cases, to reduce or discontinue new funding.[16]

16. The World Bank and IMF, which believe they work to reduce poverty not worsen it, have responded to this upsurge in protests with what one Indian editorial termed "a mark of injured innocence." The Bank has launched a dizzying flurry of new patches and fixes, ac-

Despite the provocative sloganeering, these groups do not for the most part advocate the immediate closure of either the World Bank or the IMF. That turf has with few exceptions been reserved for populists of the Right-wing variant, who regard the Bretton Woods institutions, in the words of U.S. Congressman Ron Paul, as "a socialist giveaway that hands out American tax-payers' money to foreign dictatorships" (Caplen 1999, 177). Environmentalists, human rights groups and antipoverty campaigners, wary of allying themselves too closely to aid skeptics, have instead argued for reforms such as greater accountability, a reallocation of voting rights, and more attention to employment generation and poverty alleviation in the context of structural adjustment lending (e.g., see Oxfam 1995, 45). Rather than shut the Bank down, these groups now appear to favor measures to increase accountability in tandem with greater diversification within a multilateral system in which the Bank surrenders its leading role to NGOs, U.N. agencies, and bilateral donors.

The Bank under James Wolfensohn responded to some of these demands. His intervention in 1995 to cancel Nepal's Arun III dam project against the advice of senior management was a landmark concession to the Bank's environmental critics. The institution also increased the role of NGOs in development projects and policy analysis, emphasized public participation in project design, adopted a more liberal information disclosure policy, stepped up environmental assessment, and launched showcase projects in new fields such as biodiversity conservation.

Yet as Bruce Rich (chap. 2 in this volume) points out, these are largely symbolic efforts that have not yet had a demonstrable impact on project quality. Compliance with new operational directives relating to resettlement, the environment, and social impact has been patchy, contributing to a widening gap between proclaimed goals and achievements on the ground. Wolfensohn himself came under fire for backing a controversial resettlement project in China despite a finding by the Bank's Inspection Panel that staff had violated internal regulations in the course of project appraisal (Dunne and Sanghera 2000). For Rich, a prominent critic of the Bank's environmental policy, the desire to be "all things to all people" has resulted in a loss of focus as political accommodation is given priority over the hard work of more careful design, supervision, and evaluation of lending operations.

It should also be said, however, that the Bank's loss of focus, in part, reflects inconsistent positions put forward by the Bank's more vocal opponents. Giving greater voice to poor countries in the Bank's internal governance procedures, for example, is unlikely to result in more stringent

companied by an aggressive public relations campaign that has made linguistic accommodations to protesters by admitting for the first time the downside of globalization and stressing the need for a "human face" as market liberalization widens ("What Are They Protesting About?" 2000, 1).

environmental and resettlement safeguards. The saga of India's Narmada dam illustrates the point that standards in poor countries are often much lower than the Bank's. As Jonathan Fox (chap. 6 in this volume) makes evident, many of these countries would also resist greater involvement of NGOs in decision making and implementation of projects, full disclosure of information, and measures to ensure public consent for new loans. It is also not clear that the involvement of NGOs would lead to more efficient delivery of services: NGOs are subject to the same pressures that undermine government efforts in areas such as credit allocation and health services. Specific demands, such as the proposed moratorium on large infrastructure projects, reduced support for export-oriented agriculture, and an end to structural adjustment lending, have not been accompanied by realistic alternative proposals for poor countries seeking to generate employment, raise productivity, and finance necessary imports.

Activist groups demand that World Bank reinvention address the problem of the organization's democratic deficit—in other words, the creation of mechanisms to strengthen accountability and encourage greater sensitivity to public opinion (Nye 2001). But accountable to whom and sensitive to which publics? As Devesh Kapur (chap. 3 in this volume) argues, the issue of the Bank's internal governance structures cannot be separated from the problem of the institution's operational loss of focus. An institution that is at heart a development bank makes for a rather unlikely "voice of the poor": we would not expect the former to mount a political challenge to the status quo nor the latter to raise money cheaply on the international capital markets. Similarly, the governance apparatus appropriate to a development bank is entirely unsuited to that of an NGO. The fact is that the Bank is a membership, not a representative organization, and its members are nation-states, not people or local communities. If the Bank limits its operations to development banking, this should not pose too much of a problem as long as the rules under which it operates are clear and procedures are in place to ensure accountability locally, nationally, and internationally. But when the Bank begins to imagine that it is a representative body and speaks for the poor, the oppressed, and the nationally disenfranchised, then perhaps fifty years really is enough.

The Bank as Development Bank

Proponents of the Bank as a niche player draw support from critics of the institution who note that the Bank has lost control over its agenda and that the long-term trend toward mission creep and goal proliferation accelerated under Wolfensohn (Einhorn 2001; Kapur, Lewis, and Webb 1997, 1216). Goal proliferation is due in part to conflicting signals from member countries and activist groups and, as noted earlier, to three assumptions relating to the impact of the Bank's lending operations: the diminished role for public sector lending in an era dominated by private sector capital flows, the increasing weight attached to macroeconomic management relative to the design and implementation of individual projects, and loan fungibility. These assumptions have led the Bank to deemphasize its role as a development bank—the niche that it was originally intended to fill—in favor of activities such as knowledge dissemination, consensus building, governance, and quality improvement of public and private institutions. The Bank, for example, now justifies investment projects not on the basis of their direct effects on incomes and welfare but rather in their pedagogical impact as examples of best practice (World Bank 1998d, 3).

The danger inherent in this line of thinking is that the conventional wisdom is wrong and that an unwarranted pessimism regarding the benefits of investment projects will discourage the Bank from performing its core responsibilities as a development bank. From this perspective, the experience of the financial crisis in Asia is instructive. Low-income countries around the globe suffered a sudden reversal of commercial bank lending originating in OECD countries from a net inflow of $4.5 billion in 1997 to a net outflow of $3.4 billion in 1998 (table 1.2). Net flows from the World Bank to these countries, however, actually declined in the same year.

This severe and unexpected shock serves as a timely reminder that private capital flows are not a perfect substitute for public sector lending. Nor is there a strong empirical basis for the assumption that loan fungibility negates the positive effects of aid financing. Robert Lensink and Howard White argue that the relevance of empirical tests of fungibility is open to question given the lack of information on sectoral allocations of aid (1999, 8). The degree of fungibility is likely to vary by country, sector, type of aid (loans, concessional loans, and grants), and donor (Feyzioglu, Swaroop, and Zhu 1998, 54). Howard Pack and Janet Rothenberg Pack, for example, find that in Indonesia foreign aid neither substituted for domestic development expenditures nor reduced local revenue raising (1990, 193). For the least developed countries, UNCTAD argues against the mainstream view that fungibility results in reduced aid effectiveness. World Bank and IMF targeting of current government expenditure in a context of fiscal austerity and rising debt-service obligations has reduced the capacity of poor countries to sustain public services and support the administrative capacity of the state. "The proliferation of unsustainable aid projects," the report concludes "was almost an inevitable outcome of this situation, as the cash-starved line ministries scrambled for new aid projects and the disbursement-driven donor agencies competed to download their funds, with little time to worry about the recurrent cost quagmire they were creating" (UNCTAD 2000, 190). This is not to say that fungibility is not a real problem at certain times and in certain places but rather that it will not do as a blanket justification for decreased aid deliveries or ex-ante conditionality.

The Bank's pessimism with regard to the impact of development projects cannot be separated from the growing evidence of aid fatigue among donor countries. Official development assistance received by poor countries in 1998 was equal to just 1.3 percent of the average national income in these countries, precisely one-half the figure recorded in 1990. Meanwhile, according to World Bank statistics public spending on education and per capita consumption of electricity in these countries declined over the same period. The mortality rate for children under five remained above 10 percent and the vast majority of people lacked access to clean drinking water. The demand for public sector investment in poor countries remains high, but donor countries are increasingly skeptical about the capacity of development projects to address these problems.

As in the case of conditionality, however, the Bank's attempt to explain the poor performance of development projects in terms of knowledge, institutions, and governance effectively shifts the blame from aid donors to recipients. The Bank, for example, reports that fewer than one-half of all evaluated projects and only 30 percent of projects in Africa are likely to have a sustained impact (World Bank 2000b, 37). Mismanagement and malfeasance on the part of the recipients are surely part of the problem, but the Bank in its internal documents also recognizes that the incentive structure within the Bank has emphasized new lending and lending volumes over project quality and supervision (World Bank 1992). As Jeffrey Winters (chap. 5 in this volume) argues, if more attention to project design and intensive project supervision do have a positive impact on project outcomes, improving the Bank's performance as a development bank is partly a problem of internal governance and institutional reform (see also Kilby 2000). It is here that the inherent conflict between the Bank as knowledge bank and as a development bank is most apparent. A knowledge bank seeks to bundle a wide range of services, including research, analysis, development strategy, consensus building, project design, implementation, and evaluation into one institution. But these overlapping functions create an environment rife with moral hazard, thus impeding the effective execution of the institution's responsibilities as a development bank.

Guy Standing picks up this theme in his critique of the knowledge bank concept. What kind of knowledge will an institution that conducts its own research without benefit of peer review, evaluates its own projects, and sets up think tanks around the world that subscribe to its worldview produce? And should this kind of institution also be assigned responsibility for selectively disbursing enormous sums of money? "The issue," Standing writes, "is governance":

Who determines what is a knowledge gap? Who determines whose knowledge is to be taken into account? And who determines the

chosen few to sit in judgement over the knowledge? An alternative
view is that the World Bank should not be a knowledge bank. It
should be a bank. When you go into your bank, the clerks do not
tell you that you have a knowledge gap and they are going to fill it.
You would regard this as impertinence. (2000, 751, emphasis in the
original)

Reducing the scope for moral hazard thus implies a need for a radical decentralization of the Bank's functions. But in place of the Bank's interpretation of decentralization—which entails a shift of operations from
Washington, D.C., to regional offices or subagencies—what is needed is the
decentralization of key functions to external organizations that can provide
outside knowledge, increase transparency, and enforce accountability. Separate institutions could be established for research, banking, concessional
lending, technical advice, and evaluation, all with governance structures appropriate to the task.

From the perspective of our three dimensions of reinvention, unbun-
dling, rather than the proposed bundling of the Bank's current activities,
carries with it the greatest chance of success. In terms of operations, the
World Bank—first and foremost a development bank—would be free to focus on the tasks for which it was designed, namely making public sector loans
to promote economic development. The separation of the research and project evaluation functions into not one but many competing institutions
would reduce the scope for moral hazard and create a more intellectually
dynamic research environment. Knowledge about the development process
and the impact of development efforts would no longer be tied to the operational agenda of one powerful agency. There would be a greater likelihood that unfashionable or otherwise "off-message" research would see the
light of day, thus reducing the current tendency toward faddishness and institutional solipsism in World Bank research.[17] Politically, a decentralized,
more pluralistic Bank would appeal to debtor countries insofar as pluralism
implies some diffusion of the Bank's bargaining power and greater scope
for operational experimentation. In political terms, populist campaigners
would be deprived of an easy target because both the Left- and Right-wing
variants have relied on the the Bank's size and the absence of competitors
to portray the institution as an evil monolith.

Yet politics is also the main weakness of the development bank model of
reinvention. A decentralized, pluralistic World Bank is antithetical to the interests of the United States, which has underwritten the Bank's rise to pre-

17. Ben Fine (chap. 9 in this volume) identifies a number of weaknesses in World Bank research, including poor quality, ideological rigidity, an emphasis on dissemination over research capacity, overgeneralization, and a lack of self-criticism and rigorous assessment
procedures.

eminence in large part because the Bank is highly centralized and ideologically predictable. Promoting a market in development thinking and practice would most likely generate a number of ideas and projects beyond the carefully delineated boundaries of the Washington Consensus. The internal management of the Bank would also object to any form of decentralization that implies a diminution of the institution's bargaining power vis-à-vis debtor countries or a loss of status relative to the IMF, WTO, and regional development banks.

Conceptually sound and operationally feasible, the development bank is our preferred model of reinvention. Politically, however, we recognize that we are sailing against the prevailing winds. The United States, as the Bank's dominant shareholder, is less concerned about the moral hazard problems endemic to the knowledge bank idea than the potential loss of control associated with meaningful decentralization of World Bank functions. Committed to the concept of economies of scale in its own operations (if not in those of its clients), the World Bank itself is unlikely to voluntarily surrender key tasks such as research, evaluation, and policy advice or to subject these subagencies to more stringent accountability mechanisms.

STRUCTURE OF THE BOOK

Each of the chapters in this book addresses the operational, conceptual, and power dimensions of World Bank reinvention in relation to a specific set of issues or institutional context. In chapter 2, Bruce Rich argues that the Bank reforms as presently constituted have failed to address the problem of disconnect between the institution's publicly stated goals and its operational performance. In trying to be all things to all people, the Bank has squandered an important opportunity to take decisive action to restructure internal incentives and thus fundamentally change the way in which lending operations are selected, designed, and implemented. In chapter 4, Jonathan Pincus views the problem of development effectiveness from the project level and argues that the design, implementation, and evaluation of World Bank projects are biased toward simplification and standardization and against local knowledge and contextual specificity. Citing examples from individual projects, he concludes that the Bank as currently constituted is unsuited to the task of institutional development and should focus its efforts instead on areas where it is better able to demonstrate its comparative advantage in operational terms.

Three chapters concentrate mostly on the power dimension of reinvention. In chapter 5, Jeffrey Winters explores the World Bank's efforts to reduce corruption in its lending operations. Using case material from Indonesia, he argues for an explicitly political approach to the issue that situates Bank operations within the web of domestic power relationships that allow corruption to flourish. Winters demonstrates that the Bank violated its own *Articles of Agreement* when it failed for decades to ensure against the accumulation of Criminal Debt. The Bank is bound under international law, therefore, to share the financial burden of the many billions in losses. In chapter 3, Devesh Kapur asks whether changes in internal governance have made the Bank a more effective or more democratic organization. Although the question of who governs the Bank is an important one, he argues that changes in internal institutional mechanisms by themselves will not move the Bank closer to its expressed goals of greater accountability, development effectiveness, and inclusiveness. The Bank must also have a clearer and more modest vision of its role in the development process. In chapter 6, Jonathan Fox focuses his attention on the World Bank Inspection Panel, assessing the impact of the panel and its implications for the relationship between the Bank, member states, and civil society groups. Although the panel is a precedent-setting institution, he finds it has achieved very little in the way of accountability.

Three chapters have as their dominant focus the conceptual dimension of reinvention. In chapter 9, Ben Fine examines the Bank's approach to the relationship between economy and society through the lens of work on social capital. Under the Washington Consensus, markets were understood to work well, with the implication that the goal of policy was to reduce social impediments to the market. The post-Washington Consensus, in contrast, views social factors as a remedy for market imperfections using nonmarket means. Both approaches, however, posit an artificial separation between the social and the economic, leaving existing policy priorities largely undisturbed. In chapter 8, John Sender examines the Bank's record in Africa. He concludes that the Bank's uncritical attachment to neoclassical economic theory has prevented it from developing an effective program to promote investment and growth and to reduce poverty on the continent. The Bank's internal criticisms of Washington Consensus policies, he argues, retain the institution's traditional antistate bias and thus do not represent a decisive break with the failed policies of the past. Mushtaq Khan echoes these themes in his chapter on the Bank's approach to governance issues. He argues that the Bank's ideological resistance to studying the political economy of capitalist transitions in historically specific contexts gives rise to an overly idealistic treatment of the issue and policy recommendations that are unlikely to reduce corruption or promote growth in developing countries.

CHAPTER TWO

The World Bank under James Wolfensohn

Bruce Rich

When he assumed his position in 1995, the World Bank president had a unique opportunity to choose priorities for the institution. By trying to be all things to all people and not choosing among what may be fundamentally irreconcilable priorities, current management has not closed the gap between the World Bank's publicly stated goals and its performance. Indeed, in critical areas the gap—or "disconnect," to use a favorite Bank expression—may be growing.

From his first day in office, James Wolfensohn promised to revolutionize the Bank and finish the unfinished business of internal reforms long overdue. He promised to change the institution's embedded internal culture from one of loan approval—in which staff were rewarded above all for pushing money—to a culture of "development effectiveness" and "accountability," in which economic, social, and environmental results in the field would be top priorities (World Bank 1995c). Making the World Bank more effective in helping the poor while protecting the environment would mean putting a priority on more intensive preparation, monitoring, and supervision of Bank projects, as well as a much greater willingness to halt loan disbursements to governments—the Bank's major borrowers—that do not comply with Bank policies and loan conditions. But an effect of many of Wolfensohn's changes has been to make the Bank more amenable to its official governmental and corporate clients and weaken internal mechanisms for quality control. A number of promising initiatives to improve development effectiveness—for example to mainstream participation in Bank operations—that Wolfensohn personally promoted with great public relations fanfare have languished in bureaucratic limbo because of lack of continuity and follow-through. The most rapidly growing areas of Bank operations since the late 1990s have been in direct support of the private sector and in huge nonproject emergency bail-out packages. Both priorities have even less connection to directly helping the poorest of the poor than do more traditional Bank project loans.

There is disturbing evidence that management efforts to change the Bank's loan approval culture have been largely ineffective and that a never-ending chaotic internal reorganization has reinforced it. Publicly available reports of the Bank's Operations Evaluation Department (OED) on development effectiveness paint an upbeat picture of progress that is difficult to reconcile with confidential internal Bank reports. More and more evidence is coming to light that the loan approval culture fosters systematic graft and the diversion of billions of dollars by corrupt politicians and bureaucrats in major Bank borrowers such as Indonesia and Russia.

AN INSTITUTION IN CRISIS

James Wolfensohn inherited an institution in crisis. From the early 1970s every World Bank president—starting with Wolfensohn's mentor, Robert McNamara—proclaimed that the Bank's overarching objective, its ultimate goal, was the alleviation of poverty. But since the early 1980s, nongovernmental organizations (NGOs) concerned with poverty alleviation and the environment have criticized the Bank relentlessly for financing development disasters in numerous countries. The new Bank policies on environment and poverty alleviation and its increased staff did little to mute the criticism because many Bank operations in the field appeared to go forward in violation of these policies. This was documented in countless reports of the Bank's internal OED and ignored for a over a decade by the World Bank's management and Executive Board.

In 1991 and 1992, international controversy over the environmental and social impacts of the Bank-financed India Narmada River Sardar Sarovar dam became so acrimonious that one of Wolfensohn's predecessors, Barber Conable, created an independent review commission to conduct a special investigation of the project. The principal finding of the 1992 Independent Review report was that the Bank and the Indian government were culpable of "gross delinquency" in their implementation of the project, particularly concerning the forced resettlement of over 200,000 poor farmers. The commission concluded that "the Bank is more concerned to accommodate the pressures emanating from its borrowers than to guarantee implementation of its policies" (Morse and Berger 1992, 234). Indeed this is the central dilemma facing the World Bank in its entire $170 billion portfolio of outstanding loans, one which was Wolfensohn's most urgent and difficult challenge to address.

Another study released in 1992, known as *The Wapenhans Report* after Willi Wapenhans, the Bank vice president who directed the study, confirmed that a "culture of loan approval" deeply embedded in senior Bank management had caused a relentless decline in the performance and quality of Bank operations (Wapenhans 1992, 12). The report found that over one-third of completed Bank projects were failures by the Bank's own criteria and that well over half of ongoing operations were not of "likely sustainability," meaning likely to deliver their promised benefits during a project's duration. For the poorest countries in sub-Saharan Africa, the Bank's own internal audit office estimated that less than one-quarter of Bank projects were of likely sustainability. The implications of these statistics were enormous: poor countries especially were highly indebted to the World Bank, but the chances that a World Bank loan would support an investment with sustainable benefits were less than one-half on the whole, and for the poorest, often most indebted countries, less than one in four. But by its very nature the World Bank's only answer to the growing economic difficulties of many of its most indebted client countries is to loan more money.

These deep-rooted institutional problems had been brewing for the better part of two decades and were unresolved when Wolfensohn began his tenure. At the same time the Bank also faced a crisis of relevance concerning its financial role and influence. Private capital flows to developing countries increased explosively in the early 1990s, more than quintupling, from $40.9 billion in 1990 to $256 billion in 1997 (Multilateral Investment Guarantee Agency [MIGA] 1998, 5). In the same period, multilateral and bilateral foreign aid declined in relative importance from 57 percent of all net financial flows to developing countries to only 15 percent (World Bank 1998f). The Bank faced not only the threat of becoming an increasingly marginal international player, at least terms of moving money, but also a growing loss of faith in "aid" and "development" as coherent, believable approaches to the economic and social quandaries of poorer parts of the world. Moreover, evidence of the growing gap between the Bank's proclaimed goals and the floundering performance of its projects was a major factor contributing to this loss of faith.

Thus, Wolfensohn started his tenure by confronting two external challenges that would be difficult, if not impossible, to reconcile. On the one hand, the growth of private sector capital flows to developing countries made all the more urgent the complaints of borrowing governments and private business about the Bank's cumbersome, time-consuming processing procedures for loans and about conditionality—the requirements in loan agreements to carry out and report on implementation of Bank-required policies and procedures. On the other hand, nongovernmental groups and parliamentarians in many countries continued to remind the Bank of its self-proclaimed mission of poverty alleviation and environmentally sustainable development, pressuring the Bank to better ensure that its lending operations actually complied with its politically correct rhetoric and policies.

The Bank under Wolfensohn responded by trying to address all of these concerns simultaneously. He and Bank management maintained that there was no inherent contradiction in what amounted to promising all things to all constituencies. Rather than recognizing that hard choices had to be made among conflicting priorities and goals, he appeared to proceed as if all variables the Bank faced in its operational and institutional choices could be maximized. He promised to change the Bank's internal culture to better implement policies and to deliver better developmental results on the ground, but also to streamline the Bank's lending procedures to shorten loan processing and to increase the volume of lending. He proclaimed the Bank's recommitment to helping the poorest, gave greater emphasis to the involvement of NGOs and organizations of civil society, and repeatedly invoked the image of putting smiles on the faces of the world's impoverished children (World Bank 1995a). But he has overseen an unprecedented expansion of the Bank's financing of private corporations, to the point where it is the most rapidly growing operational activity.

THE CULTURE OF CHANGE

At first, there was much hope that Wolfensohn would indeed change the culture of the Bank to one of development effectiveness as opposed to loan approval. There could be no better example of the challenge he faced than the controversy he inherited from his predecessor concerning the proposed Arun III dam in Nepal. This case illustrates how little progress the Bank has made in reforming the perverse institutional culture that had bankrolled so many development disasters in the 1980s and early 1990s. On his first day at the Bank, Wolfensohn was confronted with a potential public relations disaster that had been brewing for over two years.

This was a project that was so ill-advised that the Bank's chief manager for health, education, and population projects in Nepal, a Bank veteran of twenty-nine years, took early retirement and publicly lambasted Bank management for ignoring his protests against the project for over three years. The project was so costly for Nepal—more than the entire annual budget of the country—that it would crowd out other investments (Martin Karcher, interview, 9 Sept. 1994). Much of the power generated, some 201 megawatts, would not go for domestic use but to one potential customer, India. The Nepalese would be burdened with a large loan relative to the size of their economy and with the maintenance costs for an infrastructure project on a scale unprecedented in the country's history and would be dependent on the good will of their largest neighbor for much of the revenue stream the project would generate. Sources as disparate as the *Economist* ("Nepal" 1993) and the German Federal Audit Office (1994) advised against the project on purely economic grounds. Yet the Bank's senior management persisted in stonewalling on Arun III, such that it risked becoming the Dien Bien Phu of infrastructure projects. The then vice president for south Asia, Joe Wood, proclaimed that if the Bank did not push ahead with Arun, "the signal we'd send out is that the Bank can no longer support infrastructure projects like this" (Lachica 1994). It was only the direct intervention of Wolfensohn that finally halted the project.

A number of Wolfensohn's other first initiatives showed potential for transforming the Bank into an institution that might begin to deliver on its promises. Following the murder of Nobel Prize nominee Ken Saro-Wiwa by the Nigerian military junta, Wolfensohn personally intervened to stop a proposed International Finance Corporation (IFC) liquefied gas project in Nigeria. He did much to encourage greater Bank consultation with non-governmental groups; he initiated a debt-relief initiative for highly indebted poor countries—the inadequacies of which were not the Bank's fault but more a function of the parsimony of some G-7 countries (Shepard 1996; Bread for the World Institute 1996)—and he supported a joint NGO-Bank review of structural adjustment lending. "I was being hit over the head with the words 'structural adjustment' as though this evil was the principal cause of all the evils in the world," Wolfensohn told reporters at a press conference held at the end of the Bank-Fund 1996 October annual meeting. He added, "I am anxious to get the criticism" (Bureau of National Affairs 1996, 1).

Wolfensohn publicly addressed a problem plaguing all development assistance, which Bank presidents in the past for all practical purposes virtually had ignored: corruption. He launched an initiative to conduct periodic spot financial audits on Bank lending programs in selected countries. In fact, the Bank under Wolfensohn also announced it would put more emphasis on "good governance," encouraging greater respect for the rule of law, including human rights and the environment.

He also backed investigations by the newly created World Bank Independent Inspection Panel in the face of growing opposition from developing-country representatives on the Bank's Executive Board. The India Narmada River Sardar Sarovar dam controversy, and in particular the precedent of the creation of the Independent Review of the Sardar Sarovar Projects (the Morse Commission), catalyzed the creation of a World Bank Independent Inspection Panel. The panel is a three-member commission charged with investigating complaints of violations of Bank "operational policies and procedures" that directly have, or threaten to have, a "material adverse effect" on the "rights or interests" of parties and groups (not single individuals) in borrowing countries (Shihata 1994, 131–32; Bradlow 1996). The subject of the panel's first complaint and investigation was the Nepal Arun III dam.[1]

But many of these efforts aged poorly because of lack of continuity and

1. Although the creation of the Independent Inspection Panel was an important precedent for greater accountability in multilateral organizations, it is also important to remember that it originated under the Damocles sword of the U.S. Congress, which threatened to withhold funding if the panel were not established.

follow-through by Wolfensohn and Bank management. A particularly relevant case in point was the Bank's much heralded initiative on "mainstreaming" participation in Bank projects. In fact, this was an initiative that actually began before Wolfensohn's tenure, but which was to be implemented and received considerable publicity under his watch. A Bank-wide Participatory Development Learning Group (PDLG) was established in 1991, and in May 1994 the Bank established a $4.24 million Fund for Innovative Approaches in Human and Social Development (FIAHS) "to support and build capacity for participation and social assessment I operations." In 1994 the Bank issued the final report of the PDLG, which committed the Bank to a Participation Action Plan to mainstream participation in Bank operations (World Bank 1999i, 12).

It should be noted that mainstreaming participation was viewed as critical in changing the Bank's internal culture from one of loan approval to a culture of results. Participation was seen by the OED as a key element in increasing borrower commitment and ownership and, thus, Bank development effectiveness (World Bank 1997c, 2).

The rest of this story is, alas, all too typical for current Bank management and is best told by an ongoing review of the OED:

> Bank work on participation expanded dramatically after the release of the strategy paper [the Participation Action Plan]. In 1995 the operations units (regions) of the Bank completed regional participation action plans, identified participation coordinators, and designated 20 projects (about three per region) as participation "flagships." The central participation unit sent quarterly reports on the flagship projects to the Bank President. The Bank initiated two participation networks with external partners: the Interagency Group on Participation (IGP, composed of multilateral and bilateral agencies) and the NGO Working Group (NGOWG), a subcommittee of the NGO-Bank Committee. In February 1996 the Bank officially launched *The World Bank Participation Sourcebook.* . . . Several units launched participation training and learning program. The Bank expanded analytical work with a series of papers on participation in various sectors. . . . In fact, President Wolfensohn integrated much of the Bank's work under the rubric of "inclusion" in his speech at the 1997 Annual Meeting in Hong Kong.
>
> In 1997 the institutional focus on participation appeared to diminish. The IGP ceased meeting. The Bank discontinued quarterly "flagship" progress reports. The senior management committee overseeing the implementation of the participation action plan disbanded after its chairman left the Bank. The system of regional participation focal persons faded away. . . . The Bank terminated

funding for the FIAHS. In essence, the Bank declared victory and
moved on. Many of the most important institutional structures,
processes, and incentives for promoting participation were allowed
to disappear. No one could document if participation had indeed
become mainstreamed. . . . (World Bank 1999i, 24–25)

Indeed, what preliminary data exist suggest that very little mainstreaming
of participation occurred after the Participation Action Plan was launched
in 1994. In fact, in terms of what the Bank characterizes as high-level stake-
holder involvement, none occurred at all (27–28).

All of these initiatives, even if they had been followed through, were of
marginal importance for increased development effectiveness when compared with new forays under the Wolfensohn administration to reorganize
and change the culture of the Bank. These measures were fraught with fa-
tal contradictions from the outset. Bank management initiated critical institutional changes that, if anything, appeared to reinforce the culture of
loan approval rather than dismantle it. First, management streamlined business procedures to promote speedier preparation and approval of loans. Senior Bank officials claimed that it would be simultaneously possible to speed
up loan approval while devoting more quality time up front in project preparation to implementation of Bank policies—but it was not clear how. Second, the Bank engaged in a process to convert existing, detailed, binding
Bank policies, known as Operational Directives, into a simpler, shorter, less
rigorous format. Nongovernmental groups such as Oxfam, the Bank Information Center, and the Environmental Defense Fund found that the re-
issued directives (in three separate parts, two of which are binding) were in
fact weakening key policies in areas such as energy and the rehabilitation of
forcibly resettled populations. The official Bank response was that no weakening of mandatory Bank policy was intended, only a clarification to assist
Bank staff in better implementing the policies. A leaked internal memorandum authored by one of the Bank staff in charge of the policy conversion process revealed one of the main motivations: "For the Bank to be held
accountable for following its policies, as we are now, it is essential that we be
able to distinguish between the 'bottom line' of what is mandatory policy
and the 'would it not be nice to have' statements of intention. . . . Our experiences with the Inspection Panel are teaching us that we have to be increasingly careful in setting policy that we are able to implement in practice"
(World Bank 1996g). In other words, it appeared to many that Bank management was backpedaling to water down existing policies relating to the
developmental quality of projects once it became apparent that the Independent Inspection Panel might actually hold management accountable for
carrying out the policies.

The response to all of this, as NGOs and some executive directors of the

Bank voiced their concern, was for the Bank's Environment Department—itself losing staff and budget—to establish in 1998 a compliance unit to ensure that several key safeguard policies in the environmental and social area would be monitored more closely for implementation. Budgetary constraints on the Environment Department have delayed the functioning of the unit, but as of May 1999 it was operating with a staff of three. More important, its very existence is a rearguard reaction to deal with the overall strengthening of the approval culture in the Bank in the late 1990s. A May 1998 internal Bank memo to Bank operational vice presidents announcing the initiative notes that "compliance with policies was variable and poorly monitored and accountability was diffuse" (Sandstrom 1998). Yet at this same time (in spring 1998), a new Bank Human Resources Policy Reform rewarded staff for operating in teams, moving projects through the approval process at a faster pace, and having a client (borrower) orientation—not for policy compliance (World Bank 1998g).

THE NETWORKS

In 1996, Bank management hired a consulting firm to promote a major restructuring. Its main feature was the creation of four Bank-wide Technical Networks that would incorporate the vast majority of Bank staff. The four networks purportedly embodied the Bank's four major self-proclaimed priorities: Human Development, Poverty Reduction and Economic Management, Private Sector Development and Infrastructure, and Environment, Rural, and Social Development; a fifth network, Core Services, was added later (World Bank 1996k, 2). The Bank's numerous regional country departments would be downsized, but the Bank's fifty-five to sixty country managers, (as the country directors were now called) would command over $600 million of the Bank's operating and administrative budget, which averaged approximately $750 million in the period 1995–97. Bank staff, organized into the networks, would compete with one another to sell their services to the country managers, under whom project directors (called task managers) would put together teams to prepare and appraise loans. In the words of a Bank vice president at an internal meeting of Bank managers, "[o]nly a small fraction of the budgets of the networks will be their own budget. *CMs* [country managers] *will have a tremendous say and this will create a more fluid environment*" (World Bank 1996f, emphasis added).

In any bureaucracy, there is no greater institutional lever than the control of internal resources and budgets. Before the creation of the networks, the regional technical departments responsible for technical clearance of projects (including environmental clearance) had an independent core budget, but also had to solicit the remainder of their budgets, more than 50 percent, by selling their services to the country departments in their respective regions. Rather than strengthening these technical departments (which included environmental review staff), the institution of the networks weakened still further their independence. The budgetary reallocations that accompanied the creation of the networks removed their last vestiges of budgetary autonomy by putting almost all ultimate power for quality control in the hands of the very people under the most pressure to promote loan approval, the country managers and task managers. The Bank had made a choice—it was certainly turning itself inside out to be more responsive to and flexible for its clients: government bureaucracies and big business. This meant nothing else than embracing and reinforcing the loan approval culture while claiming the opposite.

The bureaucratic rhetoric of initiatives to change the Bank's culture escalated. Wolfensohn created a Change Management Group, headed up by three of the Bank's five managing directors, and a new Department of Institutional Change and Strategy with its own director. Public and external relations was elevated to the level of a vice presidency, which launched an in-house Change Bulletin that attempted to explain to the bewildered staff what was changing.

The thrust of the cultural change Wolfensohn claimed to promote was contradictory—improved project quality (i.e., better development results on the ground) and, simultaneously, more responsiveness to the Bank's clients (World Bank 1996h). The Bank's clients have always been, and will in large part remain, borrowing governments and government agencies; private business is also a growing part of the Bank's clientele, through the IFC, the Multilateral Investment Guarantee Agency (MIGA, which provides political risk insurance for the investments of private corporations in developing countries), and the increasing use of the World Bank's main lending capital to guarantee commercial bank loans for private investment. The crisis of the culture of loan approval had become so overwhelming precisely because of the Bank's desire to not offend its government borrowers. In many past development debacles, the Bank had continued to disburse funds despite the systematic violation by borrowing government agencies of major environmental, social, and economic policies and loan conditions.

THE FAILURE OF ENVIRONMENTAL AND POVERTY ASSESSMENTS
Wolfensohn's institutional changes proceeded as increasingly disturbing information became available to Bank management on the Bank's failure to carry out its self-proclaimed goals of poverty alleviation and environmentally sustainable development. In summer 1996, two OED studies revealed the massive failure of the Bank to effectively implement its key policy environmental and poverty alleviation policy instruments—Environmental Assessments (EAs) and Poverty Assessments. The environmental report's main findings were damning, concluding that most full EAs (required for Category A projects) "generate massive documents that are of little use in proj-

ect design and during implementation" (World Bank 1996d, 24, 25). Most EAs were undertaken too late in the project cycle, so that "very few EAs actually influence project design"; as a result, public consultation and information disclosure, also required by the Bank's public information policy, were also weak and, when it did occur, often happened too late in the project cycle to be effective (37). Moreover, "most Category A project EAs have failed to give serious consideration to alternative designs and technologies as called for in the [Operational] Directive, and those that do often explore weak, superficial or easily dismissed options" (6–7). The recommendations and environmental action plans contained in EAs were often not implemented, and Bank supervision of the environmental components of projects was often lax or nonexistent. EAs, the report continued, "are often not understood by project implementation staff and, in many instances, not even available in project offices" (6). Eighty percent of the borrowing country representatives polled by OED "thought that EAs were not conducted effectively. In contrast, 54 percent of Bank staff respondents thought that they were" (76). This was a situation that OED characterized with its favorite term, "disconnect," meaning the lack of connection between the perceptions of Bank staff and the rest of the world.

Finally the report pointed out that because the single most important problem undermining the effectiveness of the EAs was their tardy preparation in the project cycle, Wolfensohn's efforts to speed up loan approval would worsen the problem: "if the Bank continues to reduce the number of days available for project preparation and appraisal, finding time for meaningful consultation (and quality control of EA reports) will be increasingly problematic without procedural modifications in the timing of EAs" (World Bank 1996d, 37).

Beginning in 1988, the Bank began to conduct Poverty Assessments of its borrowing nations, to serve as a basis for better incorporating poverty reduction elements into the Bank's main country lending-strategy documents, the Country Assistance Strategies (CASs). The Poverty Assessments were supposed to promote increased collaboration between the Bank and its borrowers in poverty reduction and to identify specific poverty reduction lending initiatives. The Bank's major donor governments made the preparation of these Poverty Assessments a condition of the $18 billion funding replenishment of the International Development Association (IDA) for the period 1994–96. IDA is the part of the World Bank that makes low-interest loans to the poorest countries, and it accounts for approximately one-third of the Bank's lending volume. Bank staff prepared a voluminous *Poverty Reduction Handbook* to guide staff and management in carrying out Poverty Assessments and poverty reduction lending. By the end of 1994, forty-six Poverty Assessments had been completed (World Bank 1996i, 3–7).

The OED review concluded that the Poverty Assessments were not any more effective than EAs in influencing lending priorities and project design. The Poverty Assessments had little impact on CASs, this impact supposedly being the single most important reason for their existence. The OED report found that "CASs focused overwhelmingly on broad macroeconomic stabilization and structural reform issues, with few references to the status or causes of poverty, or to approaches to poverty reduction" (World Bank 1996i, 8). Not surprisingly, "Poverty Assessments have so far had little influence on the volume of lending targeted on reducing poverty" (42). The OED report indicated that many of the Bank's borrowing governments did not, in any case, view poverty reduction as a goal or priority.

Perhaps the most interesting insight into the real role of concern for poverty in the Bank's institutional culture can be gleaned from the report's characterization of comments by Bank staff familiar with the Poverty Assessment initiatives. They were able to express their opinions anonymously on Bank electronic meeting software:

> Poverty Assessments are believed to lack influence with borrowers because poverty reduction is often not the overarching operational objective. . . . Within the Bank, Poverty Assessments are not influential because they are believed not to be taken seriously by senior management. . . . The Program of targeted interventions [increased loans to reduce poverty] (PTI) defined in the Bank's operational directive on poverty reduction, has little support and generates a degree of cynicism. Too often the PTI designation is merely a label applied to projects that have little genuine poverty-reducing influence to meet an imposed requirement. (World Bank 1996i, 68–9)

As with other OED reports, the analysis was devastating, but effective follow-up by Bank management was virtually nonexistent. The only response to this state of affairs appears to have been the formation in 1998 of the exiguous Compliance Unit already referred to, whose ability to promote improved implementation of key EA and poverty policies in the face of enormous countervailing pressures and currents appears to be very limited indeed.

Thus it comes as no surprise that a 2000 OED report, *Poverty Assessments: A Follow-up Review* continued to find "many Poverty Assessments wanting as an aid to country strategies" (World Bank 2000e). A 2001 OED review of IDA's performance found that "despite the Bank's poverty reduction mission, poverty has been a relatively minor explicit consideration in [internal administrative] budget allocations" (World Bank 2001c, 75).

The July 2001 *OED Review of the Bank's Performance on the Environment* makes for lugubrious reading, documenting a marked deterioration in the Bank's environmental performance directly linked to the misguided reorganization launched by Wolfensohn in 1996. OED itself concluded belatedly what NGOs had warned Bank management about from the beginning: the creation of the networks and the budgetary weakening of the technical departments had the direct—and completely foreseeable consequence— that "the quality of the EA process deteriorated" (World Bank 2001d, 20). Wolfensohn's botched decentralization "changes diminished the Bank's capacity both to mainstream the environment into country programs and to implement its [environmental and social] safeguard policies effectively" (23). The EAs still had little or no impact on project design, the Bank's across-the-board failure to deliver environmentally sustainable results worsened, and the responsibility started at the top:

> The findings of this evaluation [July 2001] are not new. Many are based on internal and external studies done over the past decade. . . . the structure of incentives, priorities, and direct processes of accountability from senior management down the line have not been supportive of strategic inclusion of the environment, of adequate monitoring and evaluation, nor of positive recognition of activities and staff in this area. (24–25)

CORPORATE WELFARE OR POVERTY ALLEVIATION?

The Bank under Wolfensohn at times appeared to be trying to be all things to all people. In addition to reiterating the Bank's commitments to poverty alleviation and to the environment, Wolfensohn simultaneously strengthened the institution's shift to supporting private corporations through loan guarantees, risk insurance, and direct financing. These priorities were not new; poverty alleviation, environment, and encouraging the private sector had been the three self-declared priorities of the Bank from the late 1980s. The key question was whether the growing use of the Bank's financial resources to support corporate investment was really a good or optimal use of public funds to help the poor and conserve the environment. Already in its 1995 *Annual Report,* the Bank had claimed that it was directly supporting, insuring, or guaranteeing at least 10 percent of all private sector investment in the developing world (some $25 billion annually) and that this proportion would increase (World Bank 1996c, 30).

The Bank's key argument was that by supporting private sector investment in capital intensive areas, especially infrastructure, "fiscal space" would be opened up for governments to devote proportionally more resources to social and environmental services. In practice, however, this was often not the case—in many countries where the Bank promoted privatization and helped finance private sector investment, governments had cut social expenditures under Bank-supported structural adjustment programs. The promised land of export-led private sector growth that would raise the living standards of the poor often receded further into the future with each new Bank loan. Mexico had been a model pupil through the 1980s and early 1990s, and the living standard of more than one-half its population was lower in 1996 than it had been in 1980.

In any case, Wolfensohn's private sector strategy was straightforward: he committed the Bank to increasing the scale of the IFC and MIGA and to devoting increasing amounts of International Bank for Reconstruction and Development (IBRD) capital to guarantee private sector investment, as opposed to direct lending to governments. He promised stronger environmental and social policies for the IFC and MIGA to ensure that the Bank's private sector operations were promoting the same goals of poverty alleviation and sustainable development as the rest of the Bank.

To a significant degree the Bank under Wolfensohn at least began to deliver on the promise of putting long-overdue policies on EA and public disclosure of information in place for the IFC. In 1998, the IFC put out new draft policies on public disclosure of information and EA, posted the drafts on its website, and solicited comments from the public around the world—certainly an unprecedented and praiseworthy procedure for a public international financial institution supporting private sector investment. The new policy on information disclosure was finalized (and posted on the IFC website) in September 1998, and on EA in December 1998. Whatever weaknesses the policies embodied, they were a major step forward. The IFC's ability to implement the new policies remains, however, an issue still to be tested. And MIGA continues to resist the elaboration of more rigorous environmental and social policies that would be coherent with the rest of the World Bank Group.

But many environmental and grassroots development groups had a more fundamental criticism of both the IFC and MIGA, seeing the growing focus on the private sector as little more than corporate welfare with little direct connection to improving the lot of the poor. Improved environmental and social assessment policies would do little to improve, from the standpoint of development effectiveness, portfolios of fundamentally ill-chosen and ill-conceived investments. For one thing, the Bank's private sector financial services principally helped larger corporations, including some of the largest multinationals on Earth. MIGA and the IFC approved loans and insurance for Coca Cola bottling plants in Kyrgyzstan in 1996 and Azerbaijan in 1997 and 1998. Since 1997 the Bank has been preparing a huge IBRD-IFC project to assist Elf Aquitaine of France Royal Dutch Shell, and Exxon in oilfield development and pipeline construction in Chad and Cameroon. MIGA guarantees had helped to support huge gold-mining operations in Indonesian Irian Jaya and Papua New Guinea run by giant multinational mining operations with execrable environmental records, Freeport McMoRan and Rio Tinto Zinc.

According to Devesh Kapur, who coauthored the fifty-year official history of the Bank, "the IFC has this habit of financing someone who is already a dominant player. . . . Look at all the liquor companies being funded [by the IFC] under the rubric of 'agro-industrial.' If you're a financial institution, that's where the money is." In Mexico, a September 1997 *Wall Street Journal* article noted, "over the past 18 months the recipients of IFC money have been a who's who of the country's publicly listed blue chips." Among several examples, the article cited a 1997 IFC investment in a fund sponsored by Carlos Slim, a multibillionaire who is one of the developing world's richest men. In Brazil, the IFC's investments include stakes in multibillion-dollar companies that are partners of large U.S. multinationals such as Wal-Mart Stores and GTE Corporation (Millman and Friedland 1997, A16).

Another area of dubious developmental benefits for the poor that has attracted IFC (and MIGA) investment is four- and five-star luxury hotels of well-known international chains such as Inter-Continental, Westin, and Marriott. One would assume at the very least that IFC investments in such hotels would be financially sound, but surprisingly, the IFC *Annual Portfolio Performance Review* for 1998 lists two such investments that have performed so poorly they have required major restructuring. The first, the Camino Real hotel in the beach resort of Ixtapa, Mexico, "made losses for the past eight years, primarily owing to the failure of Ixtapa to become a popular tourist destination as well as high operating costs." The second, two hotels in Zambia operated by Inter-Continental Hotels, performed poorly "Due to poor management of the project implementation: (i) project implementation was delayed; (ii) a cost overrun of U.S. $9 million (30% of estimated project cost) was incurred; and (iii) the quality of the work done was borderline" (International Finance Corporation [IFC] 1998, 79).

MIGA's 1998 *Annual Report* includes guarantees of about $29 million each for a Dutch beer company to build breweries in Moscow and near Bucharest and guarantees totaling $34.3 million to construct a Marriott hotel in Miraflores, the richest, most expensive residential district of Lima, Peru—indeed, one of the most expensive and richest residential neighborhoods in all of Latin America. In 1998, MIGA issued four guarantees totaling $75 million to expand Citibank operations in Turkey and the Dominican Republic; four guarantees totaling $64 million to expand operations of the two biggest banks in the Netherlands, the ING and ABN Amro groups, in Turkey and Ecuador; and a $90 million guarantee to expand the branch bank of the Banque Nationale de Paris in St. Petersburg. Banco Santander, one of the biggest banks in Spain, was the beneficiary of three guarantees totaling $64.1 million to expand its operations in Uruguay and Peru, and Lloyd's Bank of London also received a guarantee of $13.9 million to expand lending in its Argentine branch office (MIGA 1998, 21–28). These operations accounted for nearly one-half (48 percent) of MIGA's 1998 commitments.

MIGA's 2000 guarantee approvals included a total of $28.64 million for still more Coca Cola bottling plants in Turkmenistan and Bosnia, and a $34.2 million guarantee to Rabobank International of the Netherlands to expand its banking operations in Moscow, "to be used for financing commodities . . . through purchase and repurchase agreements with the Russian subsidiaries of global commodity traders" (MIGA 2000, 19, 28–29). The FY2000 *Annual Report* boasted of MIGA's first operation in Albania: a guarantee of $1.6 million to an Italian Bank for a "tourist marina—including a lodge, a restaurant, a supermarket, a yachting club, and moorings for leisure boats" (23). In 2000, MIGA continued its trend of guaranteeing the operations of banks based in the Cayman Islands, including a $33.8 million guarantee to Scotiabank of the Cayman Islands for a loan to construct the Acropolis/Citibank Tower in Santo Domingo, Dominican Republic: "The tower consists of 15 stories of office space and four stories of retail and shopping stores. The shopping section will feature two or three anchor stores, 30 to 40 boutiques, two restaurants, an eight-screen multiplex theater, and an entertainment center" (23).

How indeed were projects like these helping the poor or protecting the environment? The Bank's standard response, apart from the fiscal space rationale, was that they promoted growth and created employment—an assertion that could justify almost any project. But even on these grounds the record is suspect. In 1997, MIGA claimed that the seventy guarantees it approved facilitated some $4.7 billion in foreign direct investment, creating 4,000 jobs in host countries (MIGA 1997, 17). This amounts to $1.175 million dollars in investment per job. If the goal is job creation for the poorest of the poor, this is a bankrupt strategy.

Ironically, a number of private banks around the world have also protested that the IFC and MIGA were offering unfair competition, providing financial services that they could provide except that the World Bank had discriminatory competitive advantages because of its access to insider government-provided information and its taxpayer-subsidized charges.[2]

At the same time, it became increasingly clear that using more and more

2. The U.S. General Accounting Office reports the following: "According to the firms we interviewed, the World Bank inhibited efforts to invest in a limited number of developing country markets. . . . More than one-quarter of the private sector officials we spoke with [a total of sixty-five] cited instances in which the IFC's presence conflicted with their participation in a given project. These instances occurred in commercially viable sectors, including pulp and paper, oil and gas, power generation and telecommunications. . . . We were also told that IFC's nonlending services (e.g., advisory services) have displaced commercial and investment banks that wanted to provide these services for development projects. . . . Several commercial banks in Hong Kong and Japan also noted that the IFC displaces the private sector by arranging financing, a service they would like to provide" (General Accounting Office [GAO] 1996, 30).

Bank resources for private sector finance was pushing the institution into an area where its record of poor project quality and inability to carry out its environmental and social policies was even worse than in its main lending operations to governments. The Hair report was one alarming wake-up call among several. This was a 1997 independent audit of a controversial IFC project, the Pangue dam on the Bio-Bio River in Chile, conducted by Jay Hair, president emeritus of the U.S. National Wildlife Federation and past president of the World Conservation Union (IUCN). Chilean NGOs had brought a complaint about the project before the Independent Inspection Panel, but the panel has no mandate to examine the Bank's private sector projects. To Wolfensohn's credit, he called for Hair to conduct an independent review.

Hair accused key IFC staff of "fail[ing] to disclose key documents to the IFC Board of Directors (and perhaps senior management). . . ." "At each stage of the project approval process, key decision-support documents often did not faithfully or accurately reflect the contents of underlying environmental studies." In fact, "there was no evidence that specific standards or criteria had been established by the IFC or discussed with Pangue S.A. as to what levels of environmental and social impacts for the Pangue Project were 'acceptable to the World Bank' or IFC" (Hair et al. 1997, 3). Thus,

> from an environmental and social perspective IFC added little, if any value to the Pangue Project. Its failure to adequately supervise the project—from beginning to end—significantly increased the business risks and diminished the public credibility for both the World Bank Group (particularly IFC) and its private sector partner. There is no indication at this time (April 1997) that IFC has in place the necessary institutional operating systems, or clarity in its policy and procedural mandate, to manage complicated projects such as Pangue in a manner that complies consistently with World Bank Group environmental and social requirements. . . . (4)

The conclusions of the Hair report were an indictment not just of the Pangue project, but of the IFC's ability to contribute to the World Bank Group's stated developmental goals. Certainly a reconsideration of the Bank's private sector financing would be in order, but the Hair report did nothing to staunch the accelerating pace of Bank private sector lending. Although, as already mentioned, the IFC has clarified its environmental and public disclosure policies, there is no evidence that its ability to adequately implement these policies has changed since the completion of the Hair report. Whatever the theory, under Wolfensohn the Bank's poverty alleviation and private sector priorities in practice grew more contradictory.

THE STRATEGIC COMPACT

Meanwhile, the "change process" careened ahead. In early 1997, Wolfensohn proposed the single biggest internal budget increase in the institution's history. The premise of the request—known as the Strategic Compact —was that without an additional $570 million increase in administrative expenses over 1998 and 1999 he and management would not be able to complete the promised institutional and cultural changes. After Wolfensohn submitted the proposal to the Bank's board in February 1997, controversy erupted. After a decade and a half of preaching adjustment and downsizing to borrowing governments around the world and in a time when all of its industrialized donors were slashing government spending and social safety nets, the Bank was now announcing that it needed an 11 percent increase in operating costs (some $420 million) over two years to deliver the changes that it already had been promising for nearly five years since *The Wapenhans Report,* twenty months of which were under Wolfensohn's tenure. In addition, $150 million would go for golden parachutes to get rid of an estimated 500–700 staff members.

The Strategic Compact claimed to be nothing really new—rather, it would be a one-time effort to "deepen and accelerate the renewal effort" that was already ongoing. It reiterated the same contradictory goals of being more responsive to the Bank's governmental and corporate clients and claiming it would finally deliver on better "development effectiveness" while simultaneously increasing private sector operations. A greater proportion of staff would be allotted to operations, the so-called "front-line," as opposed to research and policy. The Bank's "knowledge base" would be "retooled," through strengthening the information base and creating a "first class knowledge management system" (World Bank 1997e, 4).

Some of the reasons that Bank documents cited for the Strategic Compact were not reassuring: "There are complaints from our clients . . . our processes are seen as slow and cumbersome, and our products as static and inflexible. . . . Demand for the Bank's standard loan product is flat . . . income is on a declining path" (World Bank 1997e, 4). What did this have to do with overcoming the infamous culture of loan approval? "Deflecting expected criticism that the new restructuring would be no different from previous ones," the London *Financial Times* reported, "the Bank said: 'This one will work because it's different'" (Waldmeier 1997, 6).

THE BANK THAT LIKES TO FORGET

"The lessons from past experience are well known, yet they are generally ignored in the design of new operations. This synthesis concludes that institutional amnesia is the corollary of institutional optimism" (World Bank 1997h, 15). One of the ironies of the Strategic Compact was its emphasis on the comparative advantage of the World Bank in the future as the knowledge bank. According to the compact, the Bank's future influence would lie not so much its relative financial clout—diminishing in many respects because of the rapid growth of private sector financial flows to some developing countries in the 1990s—but in its supposedly unique ability to share decades of learning about economic development with clients around the world. Only weeks after the Bank's board approved the compact (giving Wolfensohn only one-half of his original request, some $250 million over two years), in April 1997, a new internal review entity called the Quality Assurance Group (QAG) concluded a year-long review of key areas of the Bank's ongoing lending portfolio. It examined 150 projects in detail across in fourteen major areas.[3] The methodology for the fourteen-sector reviews varied—some were biased toward poorly performing projects at risk, others looked at a broad sample, and others examined every single project in the sector. The Synthesis report summarizing these reviews was an indictment of the Bank's chronic, institutionwide inability to learn from past experience, the lessons of which were "well known but generally ignored," the report noted, in new lending operations. What was behind this pervasive institutional amnesia? According to the Synthesis report:

> The weaknesses in assessing government commitment, local capacity, and the more general risks involved in project implementation have their roots in the Bank's culture. . . . [there is a] disconnect between the usually accurate assessment of the real prospects for the project by the staff and the generally more optimistic assessment that appears in the appraisal report. Many factors are at work: pressure to lend; fear of offending the client . . . fear that a realistic, and thus more modest, project would be dismissed as too small and inadequate in its impact . . . and more generally, a conviction held by many staff members that the function of the Bank is to help create the conditions for operations to go forward, not to "sit around and wait." (World Bank 1997i, 20)

One of the sector reviews noted that the higher up one went in the Bank's management, the more lending volume became "a proxy or surrogate for development contribution" (World Bank 1997i, 20). The portfolio review's characterization of technical assistance projects—an area where we might think that the knowledge bank would be particularly strong—concluded that "there is a sense of boredom and fatalism in this sector, which is well

3. The fourteen reviews of sector portfolios covered adjustment lending, agricultural research and extension, financial intermediary lending, forestry, highways, irrigation, natural resource management, oil and gas loans, power, public enterprise reform and privatization loans, social funds, human development (including education and health), technical assistance loans, and water supply and sanitation.

known for its poor performance" (20). Indeed, only 19 percent of technical assistance projects were performing satisfactorily (World Bank 1997j, i). The reasons? "The Bank's inability to handle institutional and capacity development persists" (iii). Technical assistance loans

> cannot compare in size and importance to other resource flows. . . . most operational staff perceive technical assistance as having a lower professional status when compared to Structural Adjustment Loans and Sector Adjustment Loans. This view of technical assistance loans as a second class activity seems to have changed little during the 1990s. Few task managers . . . see much of a connection between technical assistance work such as supervision and recognition from senior management. (20–21)

The news concerning some other sectors where the Bank purported to have a comparative advantage in experience and leadership was also disconcerting. For human development projects (including education and public health) the Synthesis report concluded, "there are reasons for concern. The portfolio has been rapidly growing. . . . Human development projects do not age well" (World Bank 1997i, 20).

Bank management touted the Quality Assurance Group as one of the key institutional changes that would bring about the much heralded "culture of development effectiveness." When the report finally was leaked to the public, they claimed that its conclusions were based on a sample of projects that were intentionally selected as risky and thus not valid for the Bank's whole portfolio. But the Synthesis report itself noted that "few of the findings of these reviews are surprising or new, which raises the question of why improvements were not made earlier. . . . while a finding (for example, quality at entry) *made 20 years ago might look remarkably similar to the one made today,* it relates to a very different development context and Bank environment" (World Bank 1997i, 25, emphasis added).

The full text of the QAG reports was never officially shared with the Bank's executive directors, despite repeated efforts and demands by the U.S. executive director's office that this take place. Instead, the QAG review was reduced to a two-page, significantly sanitized summary in an annual portfolio report to the board known as the *Annual Review of Portfolio Performance* (*ARPP*).

Was there any chance that this exercise would finally result in change? The main Synthesis report concluded that "None of the reviews, however, includes what could be regarded as an action plan . . . and it is unclear if, how, and when follow-up on these action recommendations will take place. The lack of specificity with regard to follow-up is the shortcoming of these reviews" (World Bank 1997i, 24).

THE FAILURE TO DELIVER SUSTAINABLE RESULTS

The 1997 QAG reports never did result in action plans or systematic follow-up, nor were the reports ever officially shared with the Bank's board, let alone the public. But the *ARPP*, prepared by the QAG for wider distribution to the board, with circulation of the findings to the public, did record some signs of improved performance of completed projects in the portfolio in 1997 and in 1998—in fact, right on target with the goals of the Strategic Compact. These results were made public in the 1998 *Annual Review of Development Effectiveness* (*ARDE*), which recorded that in 1997 the percentage of projects with satisfactory outcomes (i.e., achieving the stated objectives of the project) reached 75 percent, up from the level of around 64 percent that the Bank appeared to have been stuck at ever since *The Wapenhans Report*. Indeed, the 1998 *ARDE* noted that if the trend continued the Bank would meet the goal set out in the Strategic Compact of a satisfactory rate of 80 percent for completed projects (World Bank 1998c, 7). But these estimates subsequently turned out to be overly optimistic, and the 1999 *ARDE* showed a regression, with much more pessimistic conclusions. The overall success (satisfactory outcomes) rate for Bank projects declined to 72 percent (World Bank 2000a, xiii). The 2000 *ARDE* recorded a 73 percent successful outcome rate for projects exiting in FY1999 and FY2000, but resumed the tone of optimism, proclaiming that the success rate for 2000–2001 would rebound to over 75 percent (World Bank 2001b, xiv).

The rate of satisfactory outcomes is only one of three main indicators of development effectiveness, the two others being sustainability and institutional development impact. Here the results are much more disquieting. The 1999 *ARDE* recorded a dismal 51 percent failure rate in achieving sustainable results in FY1998–99, a performance that had not changed appreciably in the previous decade (World Bank 2000b, 7). "Sustainability" is defined simply as "the likelihood, at the time of evaluation, that a project will maintain its results in the future" (36). In the 2000 *ARDE*, overall sustainability increased to 57 percent, but it is difficult to evaluate whether this indeed indicates a real turnaround or is simply a statistical fluctuation that may be reversed in future years (World Bank 2000a, 51). This failure rate is even more acute in the poorest countries and in the developmentally most critical sectors. In Africa, for FY1999–2000 only 39 percent of evaluated projects are of likely sustainability and only 31 percent of likely "institutional development impact" (51). In the social sector, the OED found sustainability declined from 25 percent in 1994–97 to 20 percent in 1998–99 (World Bank 2000b, 42). For population, health, and nutrition lending, sustainability declined from 55 percent in 1994–97 to 50 percent in 1998–99 (42). In the environment sector, sustainability also declined from 55 percent in 1994–97 to 50 percent in 1998–99 (42). Again, the 2000 *ARDE* showed what appears to be a bottoming out and reversal of these trends, but it is too early to judge whether a real improvement in long-term project quality is in the offing or whether the apparent improvement is a statistical fluctuation in a decade-long pattern of dismal results.

Part of this low sustainability level is associated by the Bank with the external economic environment (e.g., the east Asian crisis), but a significant part is indeed associated with low long-term development impact in terms of building institutional and social capacity to sustain the putative benefits of projects the Bank finances. The 1999 *ARDE* records this, noting that "only 39 percent of the exiting projects in FY1998–99 show substantial institutional development impact" (43 percent in 2000) (World Bank 2000a, 51; 2000b, 8).

Hence, during the first four years of Wolfensohn's tenure, an already abysmally low performance in the social and environment sectors became even worse. This is particularly significant because if a project does not produce lasting benefits beyond or even during its lifetime, the increased debt burden that borrowing from the Bank incurs is nothing more than a drag on the economies of poor countries. From the borrowers' standpoint, the Bank thus becomes as much a contributor to their problems as a solution.

THE CULTURE OF CORRUPTION

The internal culture of loan approval has had much more far-reaching effects than the Bank's supporting too many projects of dubious quality: it has been a major factor in supporting the systematic diversion of funds and corruption in a number of the Bank's major borrowers. Once again, this was a problem that Wolfensohn inherited and that was well known to Bank senior management. One of the most astounding aspects of *The Wapenhans Report* in 1992 was its finding that the Bank's auditing and accounting of the use of its funds was a shambles. Indeed, Wapenhans reported that nearly four-fifths of the financial conditions in World Bank loans—78 percent—were not adhered to, a figure he characterized as "startlingly low" (Wapenhans et al. 1992, ii).

In late 1993, a World Bank Financial Reporting and Auditing Task Force reported that "less than 40% of audited financial information is received by its due date, making it inconsequential for project management purposes" (World Bank 1993c, 1). It found that the format of the financial information that is received often does not allow for "1) comparison with information in the staff appraisal report and 2) linkage of physical achievements with project expenditures and reconciliation with Bank disbursement records." Moreover, "financial statements and reports rarely address specific requirements of the loan agreements and rarely make reference to accounting principles and auditing standards applied." Finally, the report found that the Bank "rarely 1) reviews the borrower country's reviewing and auditing standards and 2) reviews the auditors' independence and capabilities. Financial statements received by the World Bank frequently are not reviewed by Bank staff or are reviewed by staff without the necessary skills to identify significant problems and initiate appropriate action" (1). One reads with amazement the major conclusion of the report, coming as it does from the planet's largest public international financial institution: "As a general principle the World Bank should promote the concept that accounting is the foundation of financial management." After more than one-half century of operations and $170 billion in loans, the Bank had learned the following: "Without efficient accounting and financial auditing arrangements project management itself is not under control" (2).

Like *The Wapenhans Report,* the Financial Reporting and Auditing Task Force report disappeared into the bowels of the Bank bureaucracy with no effective follow-up.[4] "It is perhaps noteworthy," Wapenhans himself wrote in 1994, "that the Bank's management response to the Wapenhans report does not yet address the recommendation concerning accountability. The 'cultural change' required is, however, unlikely to occur unless the performance criteria change" (Wapenhans 1994, C-304 n. 22). And the Bank under Wolfensohn, although proclaiming a more visible World Bank role in fighting corruption in developing countries, has done little to address the fundamental source of that corruption associated with World Bank lending, namely the internal pressure to keep lending in spite of poor compliance with World Bank policies—not just concerning poverty alleviation and the environment, but concerning the Bank's most basic fiduciary duty to ensure that its funds are not misappropriated from their intended uses. If the Bank is serious about knowing—and changing—how its money is really used, much more is needed than Wolfensohn's initiatives to hire a private accounting firm to conduct spot audits in a handful of countries and, later, firing a few staff members caught in acts of flagrant corruption and disqualifying the few companies that are caught red-handed in procurement irregularities (e.g., see World Bank 1999m, 1999n).

In summer 1997, the consequences of years of Bank complicity in the corruption of its major borrowers finally began to surface in Russia and Indonesia. *Business Week* alleged that "at least $100 million" from a $500 million Russian coal sector loan was either misspent or could not be accounted for. Noting that the Bank was preparing a new one-half-billion-dollar loan for the Russian coal sector, *Business Week* observed that "World Bank officials seem surprisingly unperturbed by the misspending. They contend offering loans to spur change is better than micromanaging expenditures" (Matlack 1997, 52, 54). A little over a year later, the *Financial Times* estimated the

---

4. The follow-up was, in 1993, an eighty-seven-step action plan entitled "Next Steps," which Bank management proclaimed within a year to be "92 percent either . . . completed or at an advanced stage of completion" (World Bank 1994c, ii).

amount stolen in the coal sector loan to be much higher, as much as $250 million (Lloyd 1998, XXVI).

In the Indonesia case, U.S. political economist Jeffrey Winters alleged in a July 1997 Jakarta press conference that shoddy accounting practices by the World Bank had allowed corrupt Indonesian officials to steal as much as 30 percent of Bank loans over a thirty-year period—a mind-boggling total approaching $10 billion (Winters 1997, 29; Loveard 1997). At about the same time, the Bank's Jakarta office commissioned an internal study of corruption in World Bank lending programs to Indonesia. The findings and recommendations of the study, which confirmed many of Winters's charges, were never acted on by World Bank senior management, and Wolfensohn learned of the existence of the report only in July 1998, a year after its completion (anonymous member of World Bank management, personal communication, 17 Sept. 1998). The internal Bank report, known as the Dice memorandum (Simpson 1998, A14), after the Bank staffer who authored it, directly contradicted the assertions of the Bank's vice president for east Asia, Jean-Michel Severino, who, in response to Winters's charges, stated that "this [systematic corruption in World Bank lending to Indonesia] is demonstrably untrue. We know exactly where our money is going" (World Bank 1997g).

In the fifteen months subsequent to the Dice memorandum, the Bank committed and disbursed over $1.3 billion more to Indonesia without any effective measures to contain the "leakage" detailed in the memo. In October 1998, with plans to commit and disburse $2 billion more over the next nine months, a second Bank mission, headed by Jane Loos, recorded the following:

> Our mission confirms earlier reports on corruption in Indonesia: that it is pervasive, institutionalized, and a significant deterrent to overall growth of the economy and effectiveness of the Bank's assistance. . . . We cannot rely on probity of audits both from BPKP [government internal audit agency] and local associates of international audit firms. . . . Despite apparent compliance with World Bank guidelines and documentation requirements for procurement, disbursement, supervision and audits, there is significant leakage from Bank funds. . . . Bank procedures/standards are not being applied uniformly. . . . The [World Bank] auditing requirements have been allowed to deteriorate into a superficial exercise; even an agency with overdue audits was not excluded from receiving new loans. (Loos 1998, 1–2)

In mid-December 1998, Severino, the vice president for east Asia, responded to correspondence of 126 NGOs from thirty-five countries (Environmental Defense Fund 1998) on the continued systematic corruption in Bank's lending to Indonesia by asserting that the Dice memorandum was "one person's view based on informal interviews" and that "following up on the work by Jane Loos and her team" the Bank was "implementing actions to address the identified shortcomings and opportunities." As for the blatantly false (in comparison with what was known and documented in the Bank Indonesia country department and Jakarta office for years) denials in 1997 of corruption in the Bank's lending to Indonesia, the response was "my 1997 press statement was based on our knowledge at the time. Since that date, the Bank's view, including that expressed by senior management, has consistently and been informed by, and in line with, internal memoranda and reports" (Severino 1998, 3–4).

The full consequences for development effectiveness of the inability to root out the culture of loan approval were spelled out in an unusually candid reevaluation of the entire thirty-year record of the Bank in Indonesia conducted by the OED and circulated internally (and leaked to the press) in February 1999 (Sanger 1999b, 1999c). The OED *Indonesia Country Assistance Note* of February 4, 1999, is remarkable in that it presents a major revision of the Bank's development effectiveness in Indonesia over the previous three decades (World Bank 1998h). The Bank for years had touted Indonesia as one of its great success stories ("widely perceived within the Bank to be a miracle and a symbol of the Bank's success" [World Bank 1999f]), but the OED report concludes that reluctance to offend a major borrower, a refusal to address corruption, and a dysfunctional internal Bank culture that punished staff for identifying problems that could slow down lending contributed to the propagation of what the original draft of the OED report called the "myth of the Indonesian miracle." The final report omitted this phrase in response to the objection of the Indonesian government. The OED report rates the Bank and Indonesian government as only marginally satisfactory for the previous three decades, contradicting numerous previous evaluations of Bank involvement in Indonesia as a leading example, at least relatively, of development effectiveness (World Bank 1999f).

One of the more revealing analyses in the report describes how the culture of approval and perverse Bank career incentives that punished staff who contradicted the party line led to disastrous consequences in lending for the financial sector. As the Indonesian melt-down was brewing, supervision reports indicated the Bank's single biggest financial sector project, the Financial Sector Development Project, was riddled with problems. Then,

A thorough supervision effort in August 1996 not only found the project outcome to be unsatisfactory on all counts, but concluded that Indonesia's State Banking Sector was in disarray, riddled with

insolvency. . . . the Bank downplayed the evidence presented in the
supervision report and rejected the proposed cancellation of the
loan for several months (cancellation was postponed until a new
Banking Reform Assistance project was approved in November,
1997), arguing that such action would do serious damage to the
Bank-Government relationship. This process also triggered perceptions of unjustified penalties to career prospects of some Bank staff
who had brought the issues to light. The staff proposals for in-depth
[financial] sector work were shelved; ESW [economic and sector
work] in the finance sector dropped from 1.76 staff years in FY95, to
0.55 in FY96, and 0.10 in FY97. Coverage of financial sector issues in
the July, 1997 CAS was minimal. The Bank's readiness to address the
subsequent financial crisis in Indonesia was seriously impaired.
(World Bank 1999f, 20)

The report also recounts how the reorganization of the Bank under Wolfensohn and the Strategic Compact further undermined the ability of the Bank
to respond to the Indonesian crisis in 1997–98: "An unfortunate combination of staff turnover, some of it the result of policy disagreements, and the
1997 reorganization complicated the ability of the Bank to respond to the
crisis. . . . The far-reaching 1997 reorganization detracted attention from
economic development issues" (9).

The major recommendations of the February 1999 OED Indonesia study
echo the conclusions of countless reports past, particularly the 1992 Morse
Commission and Wapenhans reports. If country monitoring is to be effective, there must be "major changes in the Bank's internal culture." Once
again "warning signals were either ignored or played down by senior managers in their effort to maintain the country relationship. Some staff feared
the potential negative impact on their opportunities that might result from
challenging mainstream Regional thinking" (World Bank 1999f, 26). One
of the biggest obstacles to improved development effectiveness and a major
factor in the culture of loan approval, again flagged in the Morse Commission and Wapenhans reports, is the chronic "clientitis" of the Bank, the desire to keep lending to maintain the country relationship often to the direct
detriment of the poor that the Bank purports to be trying to help. The current Bank reorganization is making this clientitis worse, not better. The OED
Indonesia report makes clear that in many cases a choice has to be made:
"Bank strategy should look at the importance of the issues to the country's
development, and not whether the country relationship may be jeopar-
dized" (26).

CONCLUSION
The key word for understanding the World Bank since the 1990s is disconnect—the disconnect between its alleged purposes and its record and the

disconnect between Wolfensohn's proclamations to change the Bank's culture and the actual reforms needed to address the Bank's systematic failure to implement its most basic policies concerning poverty alleviation and environmental assessment. There is also the disconnect between speeding up loan approval, thus weakening Bank policies, and claiming to root out the culture of loan approval. There is a widely noted disconnect between claiming to use public funds and guarantees to help the poor and the rapid growth of the IFC and MIGA, whose preponderance of clients are large multinational corporations and international money center banks whose activities provide little direct economic benefit for—and too often a negative environmental and social impact on—poor populations in developing countries. There is the disconnect between Bank staff's majority view that the environmental assessment process was effective and the 80 percent negative evaluation of borrowing country representatives. There is the disconnect between Wolfensohn's promise to strengthen accountability and his reorganization of the Bank, resulting in the systematic weakening of accountability from top management downward in the implementation of the Bank's most basic social and environmental policies. There is, finally, the disconnect between the Bank management's proclamations that the future of the institution lies increasingly in being the incubator and repository of experience and expertise as the knowledge bank, and the pervasive reality of institutional amnesia documented so alarmingly by the latest in a long series of internal portfolio and country reviews.

Since 1997, the external pressures put on the Bank to funnel large quick disbursing nonproject loans to major borrowers as a consequence of the financial crisis in Asia have heightened still further the tension and contradiction between development effectiveness and the loan approval culture. The October 19, 1998, Jane Loos memorandum identifies the contradiction clearly: "There is an inherent tension not only between volume/speed of commitments/disbursements and the quality of our work, but also between these and potential leakages" (Loos 1998, 2).

In this light, the trends are troubling. In FY1998 nearly 40 percent of new IBRD-IDA commitments were large, nonproject, quick-disbursing loans and credits (World Bank 1998b, xii). In FY1999, 63 percent of the Bank's new commitments were nonproject, quick-disbursing loans and credits; this fell back to 41 percent in FY2000 (World Bank 2000a, 9). It appears that in the future nonproject adjustment lending will, after declining from the all-time high in 1999, continue to be a more important component of the Bank's lending portfolio than in the past. The Bank cannot promote improved development effectiveness and simultaneously be an automatic teller machine for the much criticized bail-out deals of the International Monetary Fund (IMF). Claims that such loans are effective tools for promoting needed policy reforms in crisis situations are hollow, indeed disingenuous. This is evident from the convincing assertion in the 1999 OED *Indonesia Country*

Assistance Note with respect to the $1 billion Policy Reform Support Loan (PRSL) approved in July, 1998:

> In retrospect, even if there had been evidence of political will, it appears questionable whether the PRSL was an appropriate vehicle to address Indonesia's systemic problems in the financial sector. Although the financial conditionality in a SAL [Structural Adjustment Loan] may provide greater credibility for Board approval, a quick-disbursing loan generally provides a poor vehicle for implementing and monitoring needed reforms that require both political and institutional changes as all-encompassing as those needed in Indonesia. In addition, a quick-disbursing loan provides little opportunity to track disbursements. . . . What is needed in the financial sector is not quick-disbursing assistance, but dialogue and technical assistance if there is evidence of commitment at the highest level. (World Bank 1999f, 9–10)

In the final analysis, the Bank's prospects in promoting greater development effectiveness turn not on trying to be all things to all people but on choosing priorities—particularly, given its current managerial resources, on choosing to focus on quality instead of quantity in its lending, rewarding staff first and foremost for ensuring that its policies relating to poverty alleviation, participation, and environment are carried out in the design and implementation of operations.

To make this choice, the question of who the Bank's real clients are is critical and decisive. In a March 1996 session between Wolfensohn and three hundred senior managers, a Bank manager identified the fundamental contradiction in the entire cultural change that Wolfensohn is trying to promote:

> Mr. President, the second-most recurrent theme in your appeals, after today's theme of cynicism and lack of trust [of Bank staff vis-à-vis management], is client responsiveness, which can be rephrased as "Why can't we be more like merchant banks, which are quick in providing what their customers ask. . . . " We keep assuming the client is the government. . . . we can't have our cake and eat it too. We have to make a choice. *Either we treat our governments as clients and we behave like merchant banks, in which case we owe it—again, to ourselves, in the first place, and to our counterparts, second—to stop talking about the environment, about women in development, about poverty alleviation, and so on, as priorities.* . . . If the government is not our client . . . the client is the people of the countries we work with, and the governments are agencies, instruments, with whom we work to meet our clients' needs. (World Bank 1996e, 17, emphasis added)

Wolfensohn did not have a coherent rejoinder, because the contradiction is real, and perhaps insurmountable:

> I, obviously, have perceived the task of moving from investment banking to development banking in a too-simplistic fashion . . . there are no generalizations about governments and their relationships with people. . . . we have a legal client that is the government . . . by law the Bank can lend only to governments. . . . We're ultimately serving the people. Ultimately. But our instrument is to work with government. . . . So it is a process of persuasion, of discussion, of ca-joling, of advice and, in some cases, agreeing not to agree and doing no lending. . . . to help a government and not help the people is not going to come through, in terms of economic stability, political sta-bility, social stability. . . . And I still go back, as I said before. . . . I judge our effectiveness by the smile on the child's face in the village. I would extend it to the mother. (17–19)

The World Bank's *raison d'être*, in its own words, is environmentally sustain-able poverty alleviation; it is really the only reason why taxpayers in the in-dustrialized world, already faced with a shrinking domestic social safety net, should support such an institution. The smiles of poor children notwith-standing, World Bank actions under Wolfensohn increasingly have revealed a pattern. The charismatic, passionate president makes spectacular personal gestures and supports worthy but peripheral institutional commitments to please the Bank's politically correct constituencies. Often there is little fol-low through and virtually no significant impact on operations. These are side-currents and eddies, swept aside by the broader tide of the continuous change process Wolfensohn inherited and intensified.

Meanwhile, the deepest, strongest bureaucratic pull in the direction of the culture of loan approval is fatally reinforced. The octopus-like bureau-cracy emits an immense ink cloud of reports that for twenty years have iden-tified the same problems, but the reports, like all their predecessors, have no lasting operational consequences. The Executive Board is mollified be-cause the turnover rate and lack of institutional memory and continuity are high because most directors leave after two or three years. Steadily, the in-stitution mutates into an entity for which public support becomes harder and harder to justify: a merchant bank, but one that is government subsi-dized and completely insulated from the financial, political, and moral con-sequences of its actions.

CHAPTER THREE

The Changing Anatomy of Governance of the World Bank

Devesh Kapur

A puzzling feature of the World Bank (and indeed most international organizations) is the question of who is in charge, who has power. This chapter examines the principal actors that shape the governance of the Bank and focuses on two competing theses. Is the governance of the World Bank essentially an international variant of C. Wright Mills's (2000) thesis, in which a power elite is at work, encompassing the interests of the U.S. and global financial markets? Or is it more in line with Dahl's (1999) pluralist view of multiple open and competing groups? The chapter examines the changing contours of governance through the growing influence of new groups that are affecting the Bank's governance: legislatures, nongovernmental organizations (NGOs) and the academic/policy community. These actors have defended their greater role in the World Bank's governance as necessitated by their desire to at least minimize the damage the World Bank inflicts on the poor in less developed countries (LDCs) and, if possible, to leverage their influence within and over the institution to improve the welfare of the poor in developing countries. But has the presence of a greater number of actors in the Bank's governance improved its effectiveness? And if so, for whom? Has it mitigated United States dominance of the institution or has it, paradoxically, amplified it? And what are the consequences of these changes for poor people, as distinct from poor countries?

BRIEF HISTORY

The International Bank for Reconstruction and Development (IBRD) was almost an afterthought at Bretton Woods, where the focus of attention was the International Monetary Fund (IMF). (This section draws heavily from Kapur, Lewis, and Webb 1997.) The institution almost collapsed shortly after its establishment and was resurrected by a new management brought in from Wall Street, led by John McCloy. Although McCloy's stint was short, he began to lay the foundations of the IBRD. It was under his successor, Eugene Black, president for thirteen years until 1961, that the IBRD established itself as a premier multilateral institution, its foundations firmly secured by four principal anchors.

Foremost of these was the exceptional nurturing role of the United States, whether as godfather or provider of insurance through its guarantees. The direct financial contributions of the United States (in the form of paid-in capital) were the overwhelming fraction of the IBRD's usable equity. This, together with sizeable contingent guarantees that reassured Wall Street about the viability of the institution's bonds, was crucial in securing the Bank's financial base. Despite its overwhelming potential power, U.S. interventions were selective. The evident self-restraint not only helped build institutional reputation, but was also important in building confidence among borrowing members about the institution's relative impartiality.

Second, and crucially, certain financial traits were skillfully sculpted into the institution's persona. In principle, at least, the institution was organized as a financial cooperative. The nonborrowing shareholders endowed the institution by direct cash contributions in the form of paid-in capital, but especially by assuming large contingent liabilities in the form of callable capital. The borrowers also contributed to capital, albeit in quite modest amounts. More important, they faithfully serviced their financial obligations, granting preferential treatment to the institution. The cost-plus pricing formula of the IBRD's loans (over market borrowing costs) ensured both healthy profits for the institution and a steady growth of its equity while avoiding the psychological baggage that this was aid.

These financial traits affected the third anchor of the institution: its governance. McCloy's condition for accepting the presidency of the Bank—that the board cede effective power to management over the day-to-day operations of the Bank—ensured managerial autonomy and became a cornerstone of board-management relations for the next four decades. The autonomy from governments was enhanced by the institution's dependence on financial markets (effectively Wall Street during its first two decades). The strong support of the United States notwithstanding, the IBRD's management was leery of the fickleness of state support, a sentiment expressed early by McCloy, who insisted that "the necessity [for the IBRD] of going to private investors for funds, in addition to keeping the Bank's management in touch with financial markets also insures that its operations will be free of political influence" (Kapur, Lewis, and Webb 1997, 1112).

Finally, the fourth trait that served the institution well was a keen sense of institutional comparative advantage. Although recognizing to a considerable extent the importance of many factors later considered as a *sine qua non* for development, the Bank made a sharp distinction between these variables and its own comparative advantage. In part, of course, this was making virtue out of necessity. Although a remarkably successful institution enjoying the position of a quasimonopoly in long-term segment of international capital markets, the 1950s Bank was a small affair in the early phases of the institutional life cycle. In addition, with management ranks drawn from Wall Street, Wall Street's then-conservative financial practices were also imbedded in the institutional culture. Lending operations intended for direct production were confined to the private sector (although its articles required government guarantees); the bulk of lending was, however, to governments for hard and visible infrastructure projects, with conditions on tariffs and the like that would ensure healthy income streams.

The tension between institutional policies and practices thought to advance development objectives, on the one hand, and the vital need to project the image and reality of financial probity, on the other, became a recurrent theme in the Bank's history, albeit of varying intensity, disappearing only at the end of the 1980s. Another recurrent tension was direct support for the private sector, as opposed to markets where its position was always strongly supportive. Early on, the Bank's management began to chafe at its constitutional inability to lend to the private sector without government guarantees. The result was the creation of the International Finance Corporation (IFC), but with shareholder enthusiasm muted, particularly from the United States, its size was quite modest well into the 1980s.

Since the 1950s, every decade has been punctuated by a change of such significance as to leave a lasting impact on the institution. Curiously, it was the first such change, the accession of the International Development Association (IDA)—a soft-loan window funded by government monies—in 1960 that was to prove the single most important event in transforming the institution. For a decade, the Bank's management had opposed IDA, fearful that a dependence on government funds would undermine institutional autonomy. It relaxed its opposition when it became clear that a concessional fund being mooted in the international community might otherwise be placed with the UN. At the same time, the IBRD was facing rising creditworthiness problems, especially in India and Pakistan, then among its largest borrowers. IDA helped alleviate the debt burden of low-income countries and rescued the IBRD's financial chestnuts in south Asia in the 1960s and 1970s and later in Africa and parts of Latin America, both by helping finance repayments to the IBRD and by mitigating pressure on the IBRD to make loans to countries with low creditworthiness.

IDA fundamentally transformed the nature of the World Bank, affecting both the scale and the content of the institution's operations. It became much less risk averse and willing to experiment especially in sectors with a direct impact on the poor, beginning with agriculture and education in the 1960s. At the same time IDA expanded the institution's administrative budget, further softening an already pliable budget envelope. The institution now had the administrative resources to undertake a plethora of studies, analyses, reflections, retrospectives, and conferences—all of which leveraged it head and shoulder above any alternative by the mid-1970s.

Unfortunately, in the long run IDA was to prove a Trojan horse for the Bank. Before that, the Bank was struck by a second seismic shock in the form of a new president in 1968. Few presidents have arrived at the World Bank as seemingly unqualified as Robert McNamara. Except perhaps for Eugene Black, no other Bank president has demonstrated the institutional leadership, strategic thinking, and sheer energy of McNamara.[1] Even though his home country never quite forgave him for Vietnam (both during his tenure and subsequently), the outside world remembers him—ironically, with high regard—for his leadership at the World Bank. His leadership was pivotal in reorienting the Bank to focus on a direct attack on poverty. And, in what was perhaps his shrewdest move, McNamara translated his conviction that knowledge is power by positioning the institution as the leading research institution in development. The resulting emergence of the Bank as the preeminent development guru gave it a larger-than-life image—but also made it an easier target to attack. The poverty thrust had mixed results, partly because the rapid expansion of lending undermined quality, but more because of the onerous nature of the problem, the weak commitment of many LDCs and the turbulence engendered by the oil shock. The latter, resulting in substantially greater dubious lending by private financial institutions and governments, undermined government discipline in a wide array of settings.

It has become a well-worn cliché that the McNamara Bank was preoccupied with money pushing. In reality, although the absolute levels of the Bank's financial intermediary role increased rapidly, in relative terms its share barely budged during his tenure. Instead, two of his other legacies haunted the Bank in later years. One was a virtual negation of the idea of trade-offs, in McNamara's case between quantity and quality. The second was that, like its chief, the institution began to take itself too seriously—and the distinction between what the institution could and should do and what was good for development began to blur.

The end of the 1970s saw another major change—the introduction of structural adjustment lending. Originally intended to help mainly middle-income LDCs restructure their economies to become more outward oriented as well as reduce the degree of state intervention, it burgeoned into a much more expansive and ambitious exercise as a result of a sharply deteriorating external environment for LDCs, pressures from major shareholders, and weakening management inhibitions about what the institution could do. Structural adjustment lending and the debt crisis both further increased the institution's salience—but also made it an even more prominent target for the variety of ills afflicting LDCs. Association became causality and the plight of Africa and some well-publicized project fiascoes with major eco-

---

1. The legacy of the current World Bank President Jim Wolfensohn is as yet uncertain. For one assessment, see Fidler (2001).

logical and human consequences—Polonoreste in Brazil, Narmada in India, transmigration in Indonesia—suddenly turned the tide of public opinion fiercely against the institution. From being seen as having a hitherto carefully nurtured mystique, the institution had suddenly become an ogre. The sense of demonization, drift, and demoralization was exacerbated by the major changes in the global environment in the first half of the 1990s: the end of the Cold War, an explosive growth in capital flows, a bear market in the fortunes of state actors, and a bull market in the fortunes of nonstate and market actors.

In the late 1990s, there appeared to have been a shift in the Bank's persona. The financial, economic, and natural shocks afflicting many LDCs have given it a new lease. Although its role as a financial intermediary has been stagnant (indeed declining in relative terms), other functions, notably the Bank's information intermediary role, didactic role, global insurance role, role as an "agency of restraint," and role as a networking hub, have become more important.

WHO GOVERNS?

As in any institution, the framework of the Bank's governance is guided by its charter, the *Articles of Agreement*. The articles of the Bank have served both as an anchor and a shield, limiting the degree to which the institution responds to external pressures. Changes to its charter requires super-majorities that are not easily achieved. The super-majority required for a formal amendment to the articles of the World Bank or for a capital increase effectively gives veto power to one country, the United States, and is one reason why the articles have been amended just twice since it was established.[2] However, the substantive change in the scope and substance of the institution's work also means that the original articles themselves were not very confining (and when they appeared so, the institutions' lawyers were skillful in their creative interpretation). In later years, when even creative interpretation was not possible, the institution managed to skirt the spirit if not the letter of the articles, largely because the issues involved only affected developing countries while the voting rules were heavily weighted in favor of industrialized countries.

Formally, the articles of the Bank provide that the shareholders are the principals of the World Bank and exercise oversight over the institution through their agents, namely the executive directors. In turn, the executive directors of the World Bank select its president, who is simultaneously the chairman of the board. In that capacity, he conducts the business of the in-

2. Indeed one of the two amendments in 1989 to the World Bank's articles was to increase the voting majority for approving a capital increase from 80 percent to 85 percent to ensure that the United States retained its veto power even as its share in the capital declined; see World Bank (1999c).

stitution under the direction of the executive directors, who in turn represent the member countries of the institution. This, in turn, sets forth complex principal-agent relationships that shape the institution's governance. The World Bank is both the principal for the borrowing country and the agent of its shareholders, especially its major shareholders. Although there is little doubt of the paramount power of one shareholder, the United States, even that has its limits. Not only do other shareholders, especially other G-7 countries, impose significant bounds, but U.S. interests themselves are a complex amalgam of diverse economic, financial, security, and ideological interests. The Bank itself has competing interest groups in its bureaucracy, as well as institutional interests separate from its shareholders (in so far as the latter can be clearly defined). The borrowing country similarly has diverse and often competing interests, both bureaucratic and political. The outcome of loan negotiations between the Bank and borrowing countries can be seen as the bargaining equilibrium resulting from these complex and competing agendas in an embedded principal-agent framework.

The influence of the Executive Board on the institution is quite limited. Unlike the IMF, management's upper hand in board-management relations was established early. This meant that over time, the stature of executive directors nominated by industrialized countries declined. In any important issue, the Bank's presidents began to go directly to their parent governments rather than deal with or through their representatives in the board. In the case of borrowers, the board members were preoccupied with issues concerning their own constituency, with little time to focus on broad institutional matters. Two other factors have enhanced management's autonomy vis-à-vis the board. First, the sheer range and complexity of issues engaged by the Bank overwhelms most executive directors unless their offices are buttressed by strong analytical support from their parent ministries. Second, the frequent rotations of the executive directors means that by the time learning occurs, it is time for an executive director to leave and the replacement has to begin the process anew (Naim 1996).

The Bank's Executive Board has inherent structural weaknesses, but is its governance dominated by its president? The degree to which the leadership of international organizations matters is an issue of considerabe analytical dispute (Young 1999). In general, international organizations are plagued by severe agency problems. The accountability mechanisms covering the leadership of international organizations are weak except in cases of the renewal or denial of another term—it is virtually impossible to sanction the leader of an international organization until his or her term is completed. But does such leadership really lead or does it lead only to the extent it is allowed by an international organization's principals? The bitter disputes over the leadership selection in international organizations in the 1990s (the IMF and the World Trade Organization, WTO, are prominent examples), the U.S. insistence on retaining its prerogative in selecting the World Bank's president, and historical evidence suggest that the leadership of the World Bank shapes the institution's governance.[3]

What is the effective power of the World Bank's president? For one, the visibility of the position allows it to be used as a bully pulpit, be it for broad consciousness raising or the deft manipulation of the "politics of shame." More important, the Bank's president has considerable agenda-setting power, which affects not just which issues are brought to the table but, critically, when. In a rapidly changing world, timing can be critical in advancing or thwarting national interests. In the World Bank, shareholders acting through the executive directors can turn down a loan proposed by management. However, the decision whether to bring a loan before the Executive Board, and if so when, rests exclusively with the president of the institution. The president of the World Bank also has considerable discretion in shaping organizational ecology, ranging from budgetary procedures and priorities to financial controls, personnel, and procurement policies.

The nature of the Bank's work is such that judgment and discretion, as opposed to a strict rule-based approach, are integral to its work. And it is here that the president's proclivities are crucial. Thus, the World Bank's decisions to not lend to Vietnam in the 1970s and 1980s, to not lend to Iran in the 1980s and 1990s, to reduce lending to India and Pakistan after their nuclear tests in 1998, and to continue lending to Russia despite staff concerns about the country's reforms were all given a veneer of plausible justification. Yet, in all cases, if the political biases of the president had leaned differently, the decisions could easily have gone the other way.

However, in other cases the evidence is more equivocal. The World Bank under the leadership of Wolfensohn has undertaken actions that have been projected to be those of a dynamic proactive leadership. On the other hand, these actions could easily be interpreted as liberally dispensing patronage, whether it was committing the institution to bankroll the foreign policy objectives of the G-7, coopting NGOs, or committing substantial budgetary expenditures to public relations to enhance the image of and member support for the president in his individual capacity rather than the image of and support for the institution he represents. Wolfensohn's renomination as president of the World Bank, reportedly after he agreed to remove Joseph Stiglitz, the institution's chief economist, who had not endeared himself to the U.S. Treasury, is another instance of the subtle influence of the president in shaping the institution's governance (Moberg 2000).

As with any other organization, the World Bank's organizational structures and processes play a role in its governance. Furthermore, as a public

---

3. On leadership battles in international organizations, see Kapur (2000d). For a detailed examination of the role of the World Bank's presidents, see Kraske (1996).

organization, the World Bank also faces the constraints that all public organizations are subject to. Since the 1980s, a standard charge against the institution has been that it is a bloated bureaucracy, obdurate and resistant to change—the implication being that the staff of the institution plays an important role in its governance.[4] An equally standard response of the Bank's presidents during this period has been to launch expensive reorganizations that are then redone by their successors.

Although the Bank's bureaucracy has indeed been a formidable force in its governance, its relative influence has declined in the 1990s. The flab in the institution has increased because of—and not despite—external pressures; operational front staff spend nearly half their time on reviews and responses to the multitudes of queries from the Executive Board and stakeholders. As for obduracy, the opposite is often the case. Terrified of losing their substantial benefits and (for many) their visa status, the staff are supine, prone to jump at the smallest presidential twitch. And the charge of being an obstructionist can be a convenient cover for the removal by a chief executive of senior managers who have dared voice dissent (Fidler 2001).

FINANCIAL TRAITS SHAPING INSTITUTIONAL GOVERNANCE

A critical factor that has shaped the World Bank's governance have been the nature of the institution's finances. The financial design of the Bank, relying as it did on Wall Street initially and global financial markets in later years, was critical in establishing a degree of political autonomy for the institution, although this came at the expense of greater reliance on the preferences of financial markets. Over time, the institution became a mature financial institution. Its reputation in financial markets became firmly established and net borrowings and lending stagnated. At the same time, it became hooked on budgetary transfers. This transformation is fundamental in explaining shifts in the institution's governance.

The Bank's initial paid-in capital from its shareholders, especially the United States, helped jump-start the institution as a going concern. The callable capital plus cautious management ensured growth. Over the decades, the institution's equity grew fairly steadily, partly through additions of paid-in capital but largely through additions to reserves out of the substantial net income. In effect, the Bank's equity has been tantamount to an endowment whose value is apparent when the institution's fortunes are compared with another pillar of the postwar multilateral system, the UN. Al-

---

4. The optimum size of an institutional bureaucracy can only be gauged relative to its roles and functions, not by some abstract yardstick. The World Bank's staff would fit into the annex of a large commercial bank, with room left over. If a bureaucracy of this small size seems too large to manage effectively, we wonder about the quality of the advice the institution imparts to LDCs about reforming their administrative structures, which are several orders of magnitude larger.

though the Bank's lending did impose *some* fiscal cost to its member governments, this cost fell steadily over time and the IBRD's growing financial strength drastically reduced the cost of ownership: easier borrowings and comfortable equity reduced the need for additional paid-in capital; higher reserves and the sterling track record on defaults diminished the risks to the callable part of subscribed capital.

The governance structures of the Bretton Woods institutions had tried to balance power held by larger shareholdings, with accountability in the form of larger financial contributions to the IBRD's capital. Over time, financial trends in the IBRD led to a weakening of this link to the extent that by the late 1990s, the marginal cost of influence was negligible. Delinking power from accountability is a sure recipe for inviting trouble, and so it proved in the case of the Bank.

The effects of the changing financial dynamic of IBRD were, however, eclipsed by those of IDA. The market-based autonomy that the IBRD gained for itself was slowly eroded by the public monies that were the mainstay of IDA. The seeds were contained in the replenishment procedures of IDA—its periodicity and burden-sharing procedures—which rendered it extremely susceptible to the goodwill of major shareholders. In any burden-sharing scheme, the most powerful member sets the tone. From the late 1960s onward as the United States began a long process of reducing its financial share, other donors began to link their contributions to that of the United States—which paradoxically increased the bargaining power of United States even as its contributions declined. The periodicity meant that every three (sometimes four) years, new demands could be made on the institution. The peculiarities of the U.S. budgetary process, wherein annual authorizations were an additional choke point, not only ensured that the exercise became perennial, but further enhanced U.S. influence. IDA became the tail wagging the Bank dog.

Through the 1960s and especially 1970s, the Bank managed to secure increases in IDA while maintaining a considerable degree of operational autonomy. This state of affairs began to change from the early 1980s onward when the United States began to exercise its muscle in a much more unilateral and preemptory manner. Any occasion when the Bank Group asked its shareholders for additional funds was now seized on by its nonborrowing shareholders as an opportunity to exercise leverage. Because capital increases for the IBRD, IFC, and Multilateral Investment Guarantee Agency (MIGA) were increasingly rare—just once each in the 1980s—IDA replenishments became the principal mechanism for exercising leverage. The Bank, handicapped by weak leadership and desperate to obtain additional resources for sub-Saharan Africa, both oversold the benefits of IDA and complied with each additional demand. African governments, desperate to obtain any money, signed conditionalities without much intention and even less capacity to see them through. Other governments soon began to imitate the United States, and donor interference in Bank decision making increased in the 1980s as IDA deputies increasingly began linking IDA replenishments to changes in Bank Group policies. As a result, the locus of major policy decisions de facto shifted from the IBRD's Executive Board—the body charged by its articles to make policy decisions—to the IDA deputies and by extension to the richer countries. This is also one reason why donor countries have refused to lengthen the replenishment cycle of IDA (from three to, say, six years)—it allows them to keep the Bank on a shorter leash.

The reliance on governmental monies resulted in a shift in power (most acutely in the United States) from the executive branch to the legislative branch and nongovernment actors. Given the reality that "the dynamics of the transnational advocacy process itself campaigns to focus on *available* pressure points—for example, in the case of U.S. environmental NGOs lobbying the U.S Congress to pressure the Bank," what is made available, whether by Congress or another legislature, is hardly random or necessarily designed to enhance the welfare of poor countries (Fox and Brown 1998a, 15, emphasis added). It is hardly a surprise that Congress was less likely to make itself available on issues that may have considerable impact on the welfare of LDCs, such as textile imports or a less onerous interpretation of intellectual property rights, but was more forthcoming if an issue added to conditions on or through the World Bank and staved off U.S. financial commitments.

A different tack was taken by some donors, particularly the Nordics and Japan, who were much more financially forthcoming relative to their economic wealth than the United States. By supplementing the institution's budgetary resources through trust funds, these countries sought to shape institutional priorities and governance by bypassing the Bank's budgetary process.[5]

THE PREEMINENCE OF THE UNITED STATES
IN WORLD BANK GOVERNANCE

Given the critical role of the United States in creating the Bank and its financial, political, and intellectual leadership in supporting the institution, the preeminence of the United States in the World Bank's governance was only to be expected.[6] More surprising, however, is the degree to which this preeminence has persisted despite the sharp decline in the voting power of the United States in the institution (from 35 percent in 1947 to 16.5 per-

5. By the end of fiscal year 1999, the World Bank was administering 2,790 trust fund accounts whose fiduciary assets totaled $2.24 billion; see World Bank (1999a, app. n. H).
6. For a historical analysis, see Gwin (1997).

cent in 1999) and the Bank's financial dependence on the United States, whether directly through capital contributions or indirectly through access to its financial markets.

There are three major reasons for the continued dominance of the United States in the World Bank's governance. First, the United States has been more willing to exercise power, driven in part by financial imperatives. With the end of the Cold War and the withering of U.S. bilateral aid programs (the ratio of U.S. foreign aid to World Bank lending declined from 1.15 in 1969–71 to 0.25 in 1997–98), the Bank's resources have become more important in the political calculus of the United States even though U.S. financial contributions to the Bank have declined. In the case of the IBRD, U.S. contributions to its capital amounted to $1.9 billion by 1998, just one-half of the $3.8 billion (figures are in constant 1995 U.S. dollars) more than forty years earlier. Current cash outlays on the IBRD are zero and unlikely to change in the near term. The 1997 IDA appropriations were $700 million. In comparison, the Bank group spent nearly $1 billion of its administrative budget in the greater Washington, D.C., area (substantially more, it may be added, than the federal government gave to the government of the District of Columbia).[7] In the case of MIGA, the newest member of the World Bank family, the paid-in portion of its late 1990s capital increase was financed by transfers from the IBRD's net income ($150 million), which came principally (approximately 80 percent) from loan charges. With the United States refusing to either dilute its shareholding or put new money into MIGA, a paradoxical situation has risen wherein poorer countries are paying for the richer countries to maintain their shareholding even though they maintain their dominance of decision making.

Second, there are few countervailing pressures from other shareholders. Unsurprisingly, LDCs, particularly low-income ones, have little influence. Their economic travails have left them hard-pressed, and LDC unity, which was always limited to begin with, has become even more fractured. Collective action has been rendered more difficult by diverging interests, driven by wide differences in economic performance among LDCs. Other major powers have by and large kept a low profile as well. Some have been only too happy that the United States was taking the lead—and the heat—for doing what they wanted anyway, whereas others were unwilling to jeopardize their wider bilateral relationships by challenging the United States openly. This was particularly true of Japan, whose financial contributions increased very substantially during the 1980s and 1990s. Japanese influence was further undermined by the ham-handed policies of its powerful Ministry of Finance,

---

7. This excludes capital expenditures, which amounted to more than one-half billion dollars in the 1990s in Washington D.C. For comparison, this figure exceeds what the institution has loaned for urban development to any other city in the world.

which insisted on unloading bureaucratic discards on the Bank to increase the low Japanese representation in the institution. Europeans, especially France, were more willing to challenge U.S. influence, but even they—amply demonstrated by the decision to create the European Bank for Reconstruction and Development (EBRD)—felt that their interests were better served by institutions more under their control. Or they acquiesced as long as they could ride their own hobbyhorses, such as Francophone Africa in the case of France, Russia in the case of Germany, or simply pressing the case for their nationals in senior management positions.

Third, the continued dominance of the United States is not just a result of its willingness to play hardball while other countries played possum but an inevitable outcome of what Joseph S. Nye (1990) has called the "soft power" of the United States. In the case of the World Bank, this has manifested itself through two key civil society actors: academia and the NGOs. One of the principal roles of the World Bank has been as an information intermediary. This function has entailed (among others) collecting, generating, and legitimizing data and an imprimatur role. Thus the Bank is seen as a "development Moody's," putting its seal of good housekeeping on LDC economies. As emerging markets have become more important in the global economy, institutions that have a virtual monopoly on seemingly credible data on these economies are privileged. The importance of this role has been considerably enhanced by epistemic and methodological shifts in the social sciences. There has been a relative privileging of economics within the social sciences. International institutions that recruited economists became more privileged, relative to their counterparts in other multilaterals such as the UN and other multilateral development banks (MDBs). In addition, in the social sciences in general, the greater use of numerical data is considered a sign of quality. The Bretton Woods institutions possess the holy trinity of social science research—data, financial resources, and human resources—and as a consequence offer probably the largest single environment for comparative work on LDCs.

These intangible factors are an important reason why U.S. influence has grown: the much higher percentage of Bank staff educated in the United States than in its early years and the shaping of key Bank policies by a wide array of U.S.-based civil society actors—academia, think tanks, NGOs, and the like—a natural corollary both of the institution's geographical location and the sheer intellectual strength of U.S. institutions. The latter not only supply the best and the brightest to these institutions, but also provide a legitimization role for the outputs of these institutions. The circular flow of data, students, and faculty shapes and reinforces particular viewpoints.

The increasing participation of NGOs in the World Bank's governance has also enhanced U.S. influence, particularly in policy formulation (Wade 2001a). Participatory institutions can often yield highly inequitable outcomes as a result of the inequality of the participation process in already un-equal settings, resulting from the unequal consciousness of needs and the unequal ability to articulate demands or transform these demands into de-cisions. With hundreds of thousands of NGOs globally to choose from, the agenda of those with the largest resources—financial and human—is likely to prevail. In this respect, again, the influence of Washington-based NGOs is dominant. To be sure, the agenda of the U.S. Treasury is often at odds with that of many Washington-based NGOs. But without their influence (working through the Jubilee 2000 movement), the heavily indebted poor countries (HIPC) debt forgiveness initiative for the poorest countries would not have progressed even to the limited degree it has. Nonetheless, despite the many differences between the executive and legislative branches and the Washington NGOs, they share a broad belief about how much the country contributes to the institution (even fifty years after the Bank's establishment, the *New York Times* refers to all World Bank lending as "aid") and, stemming from that, a sense of entitlement about shaping the Bank's trajectory.

The effects of these factors have been magnified by the microgeography arising from the Bank's location in Washington D.C. This renders the insti-tution much more visible to the legislative branch, whose indignation at the World Bank is quite out of proportion to either its members understanding of international institutions or the extent that taxpayer money is being used to support what many regard as an overpaid, out-of-control, bloated bu-reaucracy. John Maynard Keynes had a keen awareness of the combustible mix of political psychology and microgeography when he had pressed for the Bank's headquarters to be located in New York instead of Washington, D.C. Congress's pique at international institutions, together with its control of IDA appropriations, gives an entry point for NGOs. The physical prox-imity makes it easier for the U.S. policy community to engage and thereby influence the Bank.

These arguments on the role of the United States have been strongly con-tested. Joseph Eichenberger, director of the Office of Multilateral Develop-ment Banks at the U.S. Treasury, argued in 1999 that international financial institutions should not be autonomous: "they are publicly owned institutions and members should have the right to exercise oversight." Moreover U.S. taxpayers provide for a "large" amount of World Bank financing. Further-more, he challenged the assertion that IDA was a Trojan horse, arguing that "the U.S. exercises control through the IDA because it can." As a contribu-tor it has "the right to maintain oversight and the IDA is one method. . . . Moreover, borrower countries also have control within IDA. 180 members vote in the IDA, despite the fact that only 30 are payer countries. . . . Bor-rowers do in fact influence the IDA. Borrowers review every loan before the Executive Board." He went on to justify the aggressive U.S. role as necessi-tated further by the fact that the "The World Bank exercises no intellectual leadership. All significant changes which have taken place have been imposed from outside by the shareholders" (remarks at the Reinventing the World Bank conference, Northwestern University, 5 May 1999, on an earlier draft of this chapter).

The view that the Bank is a public institution and shareholders have the right to maintain oversight is uncontestable. But there is a distinction between oversight and control. And although U.S. taxpayer money is undoubtedly at stake, there are serious questions about the degree of influence exercised by the United States and its net financial contributions to the institution. Moreover, international institutions need a degree of autonomy if they are to serve the interests of their broad membership and not just the most powerful actors in the system. The argument that borrower countries have control over IDA because they vote on loans is beguiling but devoid of reality. IDA's influence on the institution is critically through its agenda-setting power resulting from the replenishment process, from which LDCs are completely excluded.

However, there is considerable merit to the argument that U.S. dominance is in part due to the abdication of responsibilities by the borrowing countries, for instance, in not taking any interest in administrative budget decisions and not subjecting loans to critical analysis. LDCs are reluctant to press for administrative budget reductions, fearing that management will penalize them by the squeezing administrative resources devoted to their program. And they do not criticize or vote against loans to other countries, fearing that what goes around will come around. Whether moving from open voting to secret voting in the board would result in shareholders' votes being more closely aligned to their true preferences is an open question.

CHANGING GOVERNANCE: CONSEQUENCES

The shifts in the contours of the Bank's governance have inevitably had consequences for the institution. The effects in three areas are particularly important: the increasing politicization of the institution, the effectiveness of the institution as a result of mission creep, and the priorities of the institution.

The more overt political role and actions of the World Bank and IMF in the 1990s stems from a variety of factors: the changing understanding of factors that affect development; the decrease in the inhibitions about state sovereignty, especially after the collapse of the Cold War; and growing strength and pressures from nonstate actors. But a critical factor has been increased pressures from large shareholders, in part because they are increasingly insulated from the possible downside financial risks if their actions precipitate arrears or default. The large increase in reserves of the World Bank and the virtual absence of defaults over fifty years have meant that the risks from potentially large contingent liabilities have been driven to virtually zero. The design of the Bretton Woods institutions attempted to balance the incidence of risk (and the resulting financial burden) with a differential distribution of power. In other words, power came at a price. But because the marginal cost of power has tended toward zero, the major shareholders appetite for driving the institutions to increasingly risky actions has grown.

This politicization has been manifest in the increasing use by the G-7 and the United States, in particular, of the World Bank to underwrite their interests. Substantial pressure has been put on the Bank (and the IMF) to do more for Russia, despite staff reservations about credit risks. These risks are spread among all members, but the political benefits are privatized, with the White House appropriating those resources as part of "what America is doing for Russia." The degree to which policy pundits in Washington reflexively believe that a thorny foreign policy problem can be dealt with by telling the Bank to do or not do certain things is troubling. This trend is reflected in the pressures on the allocation of the IBRD's billion-dollar-plus net income to support foreign policy agendas. Although the use of this income for lending to Bosnia or Gaza was been justified on the grounds that it benefited all the Bank's members, it simply serves to highlight the magnitude of efforts directed by the international community and the Bank to Bosnia and Gaza compared to Liberia and Rwanda, despite the much more acute human tragedy in the latter two countries (Kapur, 2002).

The current structure of the World Bank's governance—with its low financial and political risks to major shareholders—has resulted in the institution becoming far more invasive of country sovereignty, especially through governance-related conditionalities (GRCs). Although governance is undoubtedly a fundamental factor in development, this issue is ricocheting back on the World Bank's governance itself. In a world of unequal nations, GRCs cannot be applied equitably. The risk of unequal treatment of borrowers is increased by the vagueness that attaches to GRCs, which forces the international financial institutions to apply a greater degree of judgment and discretion. Moreover, applying GRCs is an uncertain art, and the combination of greater intrusiveness, risks, and discretion that are inherent in GRCs requires greater accountability both of the Bank and its principals.

To sanction the move into GRCs, the World Bank has been resorting to legal wriggles. Although the World Bank has always been vulnerable to the political pressures from its major shareholders, GRCs have opened the door more widely, soiling the technocratic smock that provides credibility to their prescriptions. In the last IDA replenishment, IDA 12, Deputies "stressed that governance is a broad-based concept intended to encompass *all* factors that impact on a country's ability to assure *sustained economic and social development and reduce poverty and noted that addressing those factors is compatible with IDA's mandate*" (International Development Association [IDA] 1998, par. 24, emphasis added). But Article V, Section 6, of IDA's *Articles of Agreement*

(World Bank 1960) provides that "the Association and its officers shall not interfere in the political affairs of any member; nor shall they be influenced in their decisions by the political character of the member or members concerned." The sweeping language used in IDA (1998) will make it difficult for the World Bank's management to protect the institution from politically motivated pressures. The soul of the GRC agenda is a belief in rules, yet the World Bank has been bending the rules governing itself while preaching the virtues of rules to others (Kapur 2001).

The protracted negotiations for the soft windows and the frequency of these negotiations has meant that consensus has been reached principally by trying to accommodate multiple and varied interests. The result has been a burgeoning agenda of the World Bank and a concomitant overload of objectives and conditionalities. The objectives, although laudatory in and of themselves, pay little attention to the World Bank's comparative advantage, as opposed to other multilateral institutions, in advancing these objectives. These now include fostering the private sector; environmental considerations; social dimensions (poverty, women in development, and indigenous peoples); governance, democratic development, and human rights, in turn including issues of accountability; transparency; rule of law; and participation.

Moreover, the widening agenda of the World Bank, with the new objectives added to and not substituted for previous objectives or institutional missions, means a further erosion of its effectiveness. Observers of government bureaucracies have long recognized that multiplicity of missions impairs bureaucratic incentives as well as eroding institutional autonomy (see Wilson 1989).[8] Furthermore, this also weakens the important function of the Bank as an "institution of restraint," one that restrains countries from behavior with short-term costs but long-term payoffs. The adherence to rules is considered the better policy for individual countries in the longer run, as well as the better policy for collective welfare. But the effectiveness of institutions of restraint is critically dependent on their adhering to a norm of self—restraint themselves.

Instead, by incessantly confusing what is good for development with what the Bank should be engaged in, borrowing countries are saddled with poverty projects with standards and implementation intensities that stack the deck against success. The result: high rates of project failure, foreign exchange debt in sectors where it is quite unnecessary, and an undermining of efforts at self-reliance in areas that are the most basic responsibilities of any government (for instance, primary education). Moreover, the asymmetrical bearing of risk means that the Bank is less unwilling to treat borrowers as guinea pigs by pushing new development doctrines as it strives to maintain an image of being on the cutting edge of development doctrine.

8. For a more formal analysis of these results, see Dewatripont, Jewitt, and Tirole (1999).

There is little doubt that numerous Bank projects have had problems and in some cases their effects have been devastating, both ecologically and in human terms. Pressure from civil society actors has been important in ensuring that in the case of specific investment projects, at least, project risks are better analyzed and their burden is distributed in a manner so as to ensure that those least able to bear risks do not bear the brunt of the burden. But as Albert Hirschman (1970) pointed out several decades ago, all projects have problems—some are resolved better than others. The idea that all Bank projects should be successful is logically flawed—if that were possible, there would be no reason for the institution. And even interventions by NGOs, including purely humanitarian ones driven by the best of intentions, involve trade-offs (e.g., between the pursuit of rescue and political order) and can also end up causing more harm than good (Pasic and Weiss 1997).

Relentless pressure on the Bank, however, obscures another reality: the Bank is a small actor whose global efforts for the most part have been dwarfed by much more powerful forces, the sheer scale of demographic pressures, the rising material aspirations of billions of people, the information revolution, external shocks both political and economic, and technological change. It has rarely accounted in the aggregate for more than 2 percent of investment in LDCs. The physical and human costs of poor national policies, poor investments, poor national leadership, and the meddling of the superpowers have vastly exceeded the worst efforts of the Bank. Its efforts directed at persuading borrowers, donors, and the private sector to eschew white elephant projects have little visibility. Indeed, for some NGOs pillorying the Bank and portraying themselves as valiant Davids battling a Goliath that is wreaking havoc on the world's environment and the world's poor are not irrelevant to their financial imperatives of fund raising. Ironically, such demonizing reinforces the idea of untrammeled agency on part of an international institution, thereby ensuring that attention is deflected from the institution's principal owners and borrowing country elites.

Given the reality of the governance of the World Bank, and even more of the international system, the inordinate focus by NGOs on the World Bank has served as a red herring that has drawn attention away from the forces and institutions that are having a much greater impact on the well-being of LDCs. The argument that international NGOs press all countries equally on matters affecting the well-being of the poor may seem contrary to my contention that the result of these pressures has been to amplify rather than dampen the pressures by rich countries on poor countries. However, the same force when applied to two objects will move the weaker object a much greater distance than the stronger object. The net result is a widening of the distance between the two objects. This has been evident both in the World Bank and, even more, in the international system. The result has been a strengthening of U.S. influence and power in both settings, as measured by the ratio of U.S. power to the financial burden it bears.

Although NGOs have been at the forefront in pressing the international community on writing off the debt of the poorest countries, the rich countries have moved painfully slowly on this issue. Meanwhile, the parallel pressure on the World Bank has had more results. The differential impact on the World Bank relative to the major shareholders of the Bank has meant that debt forgiveness has come more from the World Bank than from the rich countries. Because the World Bank's resources for debt forgiveness come from its net income, which in turn is generated by loans to lower-middle- and middle-income countries, the initial burden of HIPC fell on these countries rather than on the rich countries.

A similar skewness has resulted from arguments that the Bank is simply a money-pushing institution interested only in large grandiose projects. Not only does this argument have a limited factual basis, especially in the case of IBRD, but it has only served to reinforce a view that resources do not matter. An institution so seemingly preoccupied with money pushing could hardly have declined from being the fourth largest bank (in assets) in 1960 (before IDA was added) to the sixty-second largest (thirty-fourth if IDA is included) by 1997, even though the share of banks in global financial intermediation fell. It is even more curious that an institution seemingly so single-mindedly money-pushing should see its lending plateau in the 1990s (except for lending to bail out private creditors in Mexico and the Asian crisis countries), even though global flows jumped by leaps and bounds, and whose net lending is likely to be virtually zero over the next decade.

If a financial intermediary seemingly so obsessed with pushing money has seen its relative position decline so starkly, what does this say about the money pushing by the private sector? And if the Bank has supposedly done so much damage even though its lending is puny, the damage done by all others must be great indeed. It is curious how little we hear or know of that damage. The emphasis on the World Bank has not only meant more limited attention put on other international institutions and institutional mechanisms whose actions have greater impact on LDCs, but has also resulted in little pressure for regulation of international capital flows despite the fact that in reality they dwarf those from the World Bank. This is especially the case for non-IDA-only countries, which account for 85 percent of the population of LDCs.

The attacks on the Bank for its secretive nature are another example of the imbalances that have arisen in the resulting outcomes. Pressures for more openness emphasized the importance of greater external scrutiny and, with it, better quality control. In the late 1990s, the Bank put into place a new disclosure policy and opened public information centers. These changes also reflected broader intellectual currents that began emphasizing wider societal participation in decisions affecting them—with access to information seen as the key to moving society in this direction. Although laudable in principle, these decisions were made in a manner that distorted the outcomes. Bank staff and management discussed drafts of the disclosure policy with Washington-based NGOs before most executive directors saw the drafts—as became evident when some of the latter received their first drafts from the NGOs! Thus it was not surprising that, rather than first increasing efforts at information dissemination in the borrowing countries themselves, where informational problems are most acute, especially through the availability of project and program documents in local languages, the Bank opened expensive information centers in developed countries, beginning with Washington D.C., where information about the Bank was already most easily available.

Perhaps the most crucial issue area where shifts in governance have mattered relates to accountability. Pressures from NGOs stemming from failed Bank projects led to the setting up of an Inspection Panel in order to improving institutional accountability. The circumstances of its birth paid little heed to such concepts. Unilateral pressure applied by one body, the U.S. Congress, using the leverage of IDA, forced the issue onto the agenda. The vote to create the panel was close, sealed only after the United Kingdom reluctantly went along, trading U.S. support for its drive to secure the 1997 annual general meetings in Hong Kong. And after these changes occurred, the U.S. Congress did not release the money as promised, demonstrating that accountability may have become a one-way street.

As expected, the Inspection Panel examined specific investment loans while eschewing decisions or nondecisions undertaken at the behest of the G-7 and other actors, which may have contravened its articles. The Inspection Panel would certainly not investigate if (and why) the Bank contravened its articles' proscription against taking political considerations into account in its lending decisions when it did not lend to Vietnam or to Iran, even though staff acknowledged that these countries' policies, especially with regard to poverty alleviation, were better than those of many other countries the Bank continued to lend to. Nor would the panel investigate the reasons for the Bank's desisting from pressing for devaluation of the CFA franc and the enormous costs of that nondecision, nor, for that matter, what drove lending to the Democratic Republic of Congo (formerly Zaire) that left a nonaccruing debt exceeding $1.2 billion to IDA. The pressures by major shareholders to keep poorly performing senior managers on for reasons of parochial nationality and donor gyrations, which are intrinsically time inconsistent but incessantly reshape the Bank's priorities, are also outside the purview of accountability. During the negotiations of IDA 9 in the late

1980s, at the insistence of the United States, private sector development was put at the top of the Bank's priorities. By the mid-1990s, concerns about private sector development were muted, replaced now by social development as the donors' fashion *du jour.* The fact is that capacity and institution building, including market institutions, are inherently long-term processes, requiring a patience that is inherently at odds with the short-term operational horizons of ever-changing donor fads.

The dilemma of accountability in a field in which causal links between individual inputs and outcomes on the ground years later are exceedingly difficult to establish is hardly resolved by creating a new bureaucratic entity. Institutional accountability in the case of multilateral institutions is not just of staff and managers, but must include shareholders who time and again have used the Bank to further their political interests, whether as borrowers or as major powers. It must be emphasized that the Bank's policy prescriptions and operational stances are all approved—more or less unanimously—by the Bank's owners, exercising their prerogatives through the executive directors. Even more, as was the case with the instructions of the IDA deputies in the context of IDA replenishments, many were imposed on the institution by its major shareholders for a variety of domestic reasons. The record on this is unambiguous. Consequently, to whatever extent the Bank has failed, it is the wider Bank—its management, board, and, above all, major shareholders—that bear the brunt of the responsibility. With power must come responsibility, and there can be no doubt where the locus of power lies.

Cries of accountability also blithely ignore the accountability of the NGOs themselves. The uproar over the notorious Narmada project revealed what any observer of India is well aware of: governments in India are weak, prone to corruption, and quite imperfect in dealing with the core issues of social justice. But they are democratically elected and accountable in that imperfect manner that democracies often are. In theory, local NGOs have a certain social accountability that comes from an embeddedness in which rhetoric cannot be easily divorced from action. But to a considerable extent, their accountability, like that of many international NGOs, is upward to the funding agencies—not necessarily to the people they claim to serve.

Greater intrusiveness into the workings of the World Bank has not been accompanied by any significant increase in accountability, except in the form of a closer surveillance by donor governments and NGOs whose overriding concern is that the international financial institutions comply with the increasingly broad and detailed terms of reference set by them. There is little accountability to borrowers. Accountability, in general, has proven exceedingly difficult to implement in practice. It is naturally resisted by the institutions themselves, which view autonomy as necessary to the fulfillment of their role as international civil servants. It is hardly surprising that internal norms and internal leadership have been half-hearted at best with respect to accountability.

NGO pressure also has had mixed effects on the development discourse. Ever mindful of appearances, the Bank has sought to paper over the inevitable conflicts between competing objectives by a mindless win-win argot that substitutes saccharine for substance and avoids the reality of trade-offs (as exemplified by its much trumpeted Comprehensive Development Framework, CDF). This "vision of economies operating with undistorted commodity markets and freely flowing capital, with social policies that deliver social services in an equitable manner, officiated by a multiparty political system, innocent of corruption and pure of purpose," as Brian Van Arkadie has noted, is "an attractive Utopia, but not particularly realistic" (1996, 127). The development process took centuries in the now-rich countries. And although there is good reason to believe that the process can be hastened considerably, we have little understanding of what happens to institutions and social structures when the process of change accelerates.

CONCLUSION

The changing governance of the World Bank reflects the relative disempowerment of poor countries, although not necessarily of poor people, in the international system. Its consequences for development, however, remain ambiguous. On the one hand, attention to issues of transparency, accountability, and good governance seems to reduce the arbitrary and skewed power structures in many LDCs and thereby improve the prospects for development writ large. On the other hand, the Bank seems to be replacing one set of privileged actors by another and simply shifting the locus of the problems of transparency, accountability, and good governance. It is striking, for instance, that every magic bullet the donors have ever found to turn things around in Africa have concerned some recipient country failure rather than the donors' own failures.

There can be little doubt that governance structures—including types and forms of representation, voting and majority rules, and veto points—matter in what international organizations do and how they do what they do. But as the evidence in the case of the World Bank indicates, informal influences also matter in the shaping the contours of governance (Woods, 2000). This should not be surprising. The limited correspondence between formal structures of governance in international organizations, including forms and degrees of participation and democracy, and the content of their policies has long been evident in the different multilateral development banks (African Development Bank [AfDB], Asian Development Bank [ADB], EBRD, IBRD). Although they vary considerably (albeit not radically) in their structures of governance, their trajectories have been more or less similar.

It has become a common belief that the performance of international institutions, such as the World Bank, would dramatically improve if only they were more democratic. The idea, although seductive as a normative principle, is, however, likely to prove structurally impossible in practice. An unpleasant reality of international institutions is that, whatever form of governance and decision making prevails, they will not be democratic in the sense of democracy as a system of popular control over decision making (Dahl 1999).[9] Structurally international organizations will always face a democratic deficit. As Robert Dahl (1999) has argued, even in countries with deep-rooted democratic structures, it is notoriously difficult for citizens to exercise effective control over key decisions on foreign affairs; their influence on international institutions is likely to be much less. One country one vote (as in the UN) might seem more democratic than one dollar one vote (as in the Bretton Woods institutions), but both violate the notion of democratic equality inherent in one person one vote. Given this reality, accountability in the World Bank is more likely to be achieved if the institution's goals and the mechanisms to achieve them are modest in scope, rather than pressing for ambitious social engineering and hoping that mechanisms for transparency and accountability can be found to keep the institution honest.

9. Dahl's skepticism of the possibility of designing democratic international organizations is shared by James Tobin (1999).

CHAPTER FOUR

State Simplification and Institution Building in a World Bank–Financed Development Project

Jonathan R. Pincus

The World Bank's capacity to reform itself is most apparent in the composition of its lending program. Since the late 1940s, the focus of Bank operations has passed through a number of discernible phases, moving from an early concentration on discrete foreign-exchange-intensive infrastructure projects; through poverty alleviation projects such as integrated development schemes, structural, and sectoral adjustment; and on to the present-day concerns of knowledge, governance, and institutional development. These changes have typically come about as gradual shifts in emphasis and degree rather than as radical realignments of priorities and methods (Pincus 2001). As such, they reflect a process of institutional adaptation to changes in the Bank's own leadership, external economic and political factors, shifts in the prevailing economic development orthodoxy, and the accumulation of region and sector-specific experience in the Bank and client governments.

The past few years have seen another fundamental rethink of the role of development assistance—a process of stock-taking that has extended beyond the World Bank to include the large bilateral donors as well. This is perhaps to be expected in the wake of the economic and political upheavals of the past decade, most notably the collapse of the Soviet Union, the acceleration of private capital flows to developing countries, and the financial crisis in Asia. There were some Bank-specific factors as well, including the proximity of these events to the fiftieth anniversary of the Bretton Woods conference—a coincidence that excited a good deal of speculation about the future of the Bank and International Monetary Fund (IMF)—and the aggressive reformist stance adopted by James Wolfensohn upon assuming the presidency in 1995.

By early 1999, the Bank had issued an impressive array of research reports and policy statements on development aid, sectoral policies, development economics, and the Bank's role as a development agency (e.g., Wolfensohn 1999; Stiglitz 1998a, 1998b; World Bank 1997k, World Bank 1998d, World Bank 1999q). These documents give us a good sense of the current leadership's views and some indication of the possible implications of these ideas for lending operations. What has begun to emerge is a Bank keenly aware of and, in marked departure from past practice, prepared to discuss openly a range of fundamental issues relating to development assistance in general and the Bank in particular. Some of these issues—such as the fungibility of development funds, disenchantment with loan conditionality among donors and clients alike, and the importance of the local institutional capacity and supportive macropolicies—suggest a deemphasis on project lending or a lowering of ambitions with respect to the development impact of investment projects. The Bank's study of aid effectiveness, for example, is uncharacteristically blunt: the fact that funds are fungible means that projects are not necessarily important as vehicles of development finance. Instead, they are most useful as learning experiences, capacity-building exercises, and inducements to institutional change. "*The value of development projects,*" according to the Bank, "*is to strengthen institutions and policies so that services can be effectively delivered.* . . . [T]he most critical contribution of projects is not to increase funding for particular sectors, but to help improve service delivery by strengthening sectoral and local institutions" (World Bank 1998d, 3, emphasis in original).

Thus by the end of the 1990s, the Bank had, ironically, moved much closer to the arguments put forward by Albert Hirschman in his 1967 classic *Development Projects Observed.* Hirschman, one of the most celebrated dissenters from the Bank orthodoxy of his time (1984, 90), focused on the unintended economic and political consequences of investment projects while professing little faith in rates of return as a measure of an individual project's contribution to development. Anticipating the current emphasis on knowledge and institution building, Hirschman recognized early on that the main benefits to be gained from projects may in fact relate more to the creation of political space for innovation, skills development, and shifts in personal values among key groups of decision makers or beneficiaries than to the project's intended economic output.[1]

Yet a great distance still remains between the Wolfensohn Bank's rediscovery of the role of knowledge and institution-building and Hirschman's unintended consequences, trait-making, and uncertainties. A basic theme

1. "Our conclusion is that there are hardly any 'pure' side-effects. Important side-effects are likely to be mixed—that is, they will be essential or valuable inputs as well as intangible outputs. Attention must therefore be paid to them by the project analyst, not only for the purpose of evaluating their benefits, but mainly to make sure of them for the sake of the success and mere survival of the project itself" (Hirschman 1995, 168).

running through Hirschman's political economy is the idea that development is highly resistant to simplification and quantification.[2] An early and forceful critic of social engineering, he is consistently skeptical about the ability of governments and donor agencies to predict or measure the impact of their actions. Because each project is embedded in a unique political, economic, and institutional context, a single project design could result in a vast range of development outcomes. He therefore urges flexibility and modesty in project design and the evaluation of projects, which, he recognizes, requires an in-depth knowledge of local conditions and a keen eye for unexpected opportunities for innovation (Hirschman 1995, 185–88).

Despite the World Bank's new development rhetoric, current management has found it difficult to heed Hirschman's call for a greater sensitivity to the local political and institutional context in its lending operations and modesty in the planning, design, and evaluation of development projects. This is most blatantly apparent in calls for a "long term, holistic and strategic approach" in the form of a "comprehensive development framework" (Wolfensohn 1999, 30). Having taken on board the notion that development funds are fungible and that the most important benefits derived from development projects are in some sense external to the projects themselves, we would expect greater emphasis on experimentation, iterative planning, and qualitative assessment of development outcomes. The arrival of the comprehensive development framework, however, suggests that the inclination toward social engineering remains as strong as ever. Underlying the objective of achieving a comprehensive approach to development and development planning is the belief that somehow these largely intangible benefits can be programmed, produced, and measured much like any other project output.[3]

This chapter argues that these tendencies have deep roots in the ideology and structure of the World Bank. It shows that the Bank's approach to lending operations imposes a bias toward simplification and standardization and against local knowledge and contextual specificity in project design, implementation, supervision, and evaluation. This bias operates in part through institutional incentives favoring quantity over quality described in the now-famous *Wapenhans Report,* which drew attention to internal pressures on task managers to emphasize the volume of lending over

2. As he makes clear in the preface to the reissue of *Development Projects Observed,* Hirschman's "Hiding Hand" and "storytelling" are in part a conscious reaction to the rise of technocratic methods associated with Robert McNamara's U.S. Defense Department and social cost-benefit analysis (Hirschman 1995, viii–ix).

3. Imagine Hirschman's reaction to this statement from a 1998 Operations Evaluation Department portfolio review: "Projects are no longer the appropriate vehicles for development assistance unless they are connected to balanced country assistance strategies focused on structural reform and capacity development and owned by borrowers and other partners" (World Bank 1999b, 1).

project quality (Wapenhans 1992). Other, more subtle factors, however, are also at work. Prominent among these are the natural alliances that form between Bank task managers and line ministry officials in client states and their shared desire to simplify complex social, economic, and political conditions to facilitate project planning and implementation. In James Scott's useful terminology, both task managers and line ministries seek to make society "legible" for the purposes of centrally formulated policies and interventions (1998, 5).

While making this argument, I introduce case material from a particularly noteworthy World Bank project, the Indonesian Integrated Pest Management Training Project (IPMTP). This project is relevant to the main themes of the chapter for several reasons. First, integrated pest management (IPM) arose in part as a direct response to ecological and institutional problems associated with the crop-intensification efforts commonly referred to as the Green Revolution. Given that World Bank has identified the Green Revolution as the paradigmatic case of knowledge-intensive development, the Bank's experience with IPM has important implications for the Wolfensohn Bank's rhetorical emphasis on knowledge generation and dissemination (World Bank 1999q, 4). Evidence that the Bank itself is aware of the significance of IPM can be found in the high profile accorded to IPMTP in a number of prominent Bank documents, including the *World Bank Participation Sourcebook* (World Bank 1996l, 216), the 1998 *Annual Report* (World Bank 1998b, 80), and the 1999 *World Development Report* (World Bank 1999q, 108).[4] IPM is likely to remain a focus of attention as the Bank searches for ways to attach some operational relevance to its theorizing about knowledge, participation, and governance.

Second, the central importance of local knowledge or the logic of place to the effective implementation of IPM underscores some of the obstacles that the Bank must confront in its efforts to strengthen institutions for development. As we show, operational imperatives within the Bank act as a brake on the effective implementation of the institutional aspects of projects, where institutions are understood as functioning entities at the local level rather than in the bureaucratic sense. Thus the concept "institution building" was hotly contested during the course of IPMTP implementation, with the Bank allying itself with the central government apparatus against project beneficiaries and—paradoxically—the project design.[5]

---

4. This is despite the project's small size ($32 million over five years) relative to Indonesia's overall lending portfolio.

5. My own involvement in IPM projects in Indonesia provided a unique opportunity to collect relevant case material and was a great help in formulating the views set out in this chapter. In 1991, I worked with a UN Food and Agriculture Organization (FAO) team to conduct an impact evaluation of the U.S. Agency for International Development (USAID)-funded IPM training project that preceded the World Bank project. I also took part in the midterm review of IPMTP in 1995.

The next section of the chapter considers the Bank's new rhetoric on the importance of knowledge generation and institution building and introduces Scott's concepts of state simplification and legibility. We then turn to the case of the Indonesian IPMTP, paying close attention to the contested terrain of institutions and institution building at the national and local levels. The final section presents some conclusions and discusses the implications of IPMTP for the future of Bank-financed development projects.

KNOWLEDGE, INSTITUTIONS, AND STATE SIMPLIFICATION

Knowledge and institutions have moved to center stage in the World Bank's development rhetoric. The 1999 *World Development Report: Knowledge for Development* opens with the proposition that emphasizing the role of knowledge creation and dissemination in economic development implies recognition of the "critical importance" of institutions (World Bank 1999q, 2). Drawing heavily on the work of Joseph Stiglitz, then chief economist, on the economics of information, the report argues that success in promoting development depends crucially on closing the knowledge gap between rich and poor countries and that this in turn requires poor countries to adopt policies and build institutions that are conducive to the efficient spread of knowledge (World Bank 1999q, 3; Stiglitz 1998a).

The main shortcoming of the knowledge bank approach is that in order to render knowledge conceptually tractable within the confines of Stiglitz's information theoretics, it must be treated as a neutral quantifiable commodity (Standing 2000, 751). From this perspective, knowledge is a garden-variety public good that is undersupplied by the market, giving rise to the need for government intervention to close knowledge gaps. The question of whose knowledge and what legitimately constitutes knowledge is left unaddressed because this would necessarily raise political issues relating to the power relationships underlying the social construction of knowledge and the existing obstacles to open access to information. For example, the idea that governments should promote regulatory institutions that encourage transparency and fairness in financial markets is uncontroversial, but this is arguably less a problem of building new institutions or teaching technicians how to increase the flow of information than redressing power imbalances that are deeply embedded in the financial system (Fine 2001, 8). Yet explicit recognition of the political nature of knowledge and information cannot be easily reconciled with the Bank's public commitment to noninterference in the internal political affairs of member countries.

This poses a problem for the Bank as a knowledge bank in that adherence to this sort of economic reductionism is at odds with the institution's need for an operationally relevant approach to knowledge and learning. It is not immediately apparent that the Bank will be able to identify knowledge-oriented projects and programs that address real development problems given the confines of its technocratic orientation and comparative advantage as a development bank. Improving the quality of public institutions is one possibility, but the Bank's track record in this area is not encouraging (Berg 2000, 495). Investment in schools is another, but funds are fungible, so Bank involvement may not in fact lead to more investment in the education sector. Closing the information technology gap is an appealing idea, but the private sector is perfectly suited to this task.

From this perspective, the paradigmatic case of the Green Revolution is of great importance to the knowledge bank idea (World Bank 1999q, 4). Agricultural intensification is a concrete example of a set of useful government interventions in support of knowledge generation and dissemination relevant to productivity and poverty reduction. Governments and international agencies can provide support for agricultural research and extension services to generate and spread new technologies, governments can strengthen legal protection for intellectual property rights to encourage private sector involvement, microcredit can help farmers buy new seeds, and public education can prepare small farmers to accept technologies and cope with risk.

The Bank's interpretation of the Green Revolution as a process of closing knowledge gaps is instructive. The great advantage of this view, at least from the perspective of Bank operations, is that it portrays the problems of rural poverty and technological backwardness in a broadly apolitical, nonthreatening way that should appeal to donor and client governments alike. Distributional issues are reduced to asymmetric information; conflict becomes a principal-agent problem. Like the Arrow-Debreu school that they claim to oppose, the proponents of the economics of information deal with power relationships—not by placing them in their specific social and historical context but by abstracting from real situations following the precepts of methodological individualism. Knowledge and information are public goods, so the more we have of them the better. Asking who is to possess the knowledge and what it is to be used for is irrelevant. To use the standard public goods metaphor, it is akin to asking who is to use the lighthouse and what they are to ship. Moreover, the fact that the economic impact of knowledge and information is so difficult to measure is positively useful from the operational perspective. It is far easier to justify a proposed project on the basis of assumed public benefits (citing the usual caveats concerning the methodological problems involved in measuring their real impact) than to show quantitative evidence of increased output or productivity. The rapid growth of the agricultural extension sector in the Bank has been partly attributed to loose standards of appraisal that typically characterize these sorts of training projects (see World Bank 1997a, 64–68).

Yet knowledge, information, and technology—and, more important, the institutions designed to generate, disseminate, and apply knowledge—are not neutral. There are many different kinds of knowledge and many ways of creating it and using it once it has been obtained. In the context of Asia's Green Revolution, knowledge was for the most part not simply created and evenly disseminated in the way that light is shared from a lighthouse. Instead, huge investments were made in pursuit of a certain kind of knowledge, namely standardized rice technologies designed for use in fertile irrigated lowlands. Once these technologies were realized, they were then used as the centerpiece of a series of vast national experiments in social engineering. The objective of these experiments was the administrative reordering of entire production systems along more rational, scientific lines. The main components of the new systems were the promotion of genetic uniformity in the main food grains; the development of industries to produce the required supplies of seeds, fertilizers, and pesticides; massive investment in irrigation and drainage to create the ecological conditions suited to the new seeds; the development of infrastructure and institutions required to distribute inputs and market outputs; the delivery of credit to farmers to facilitate the use of the new inputs; and the creation of research and extension systems to promote adoption by small farmers (Anderson, Levy, and Morrison 1991).

These experiments were hugely successful measured in terms of the achievement of their main objectives of increasing the rate of growth of agricultural output, employment creation, and poverty reduction (Lipton and Longhurst 1989). One of the keys to success was the willingness of these intensification programs to depart from a radically simplified understanding of farmers' production problems. This interpretation was in part predetermined by the nature of the preferred solution—the engineering of superior plants under controlled laboratory conditions. As is often the case, the point is best made by imagining the road not taken. Despite large gaps already existing between rice yields on experiment stations and in farmers fields in the early 1960s, nowhere in southeast Asia did rice intensification focus on making up this shortfall (Anderson, Levy and Morrison 1991, 82). Part of the reason for this was (and still is) that farmers work in such a wide range of agroecological conditions and face such variety of production problems that no simple solution exists that could be applied in all or even many situations. Adopting a strategy of increased production through closing the yield gap in specific locations would mean that progress would necessarily be slow, modest, and piecemeal. Although this was (and remains) a viable strategy, it failed to capture the imaginations of governments, international agencies, and agricultural researchers swept up by the dream of a single scientific solution to the food problem.

In *Seeing like a State,* James Scott makes the important point that, in acting on "high modernist ambitions" such as these, states must render the highly complex situations found in the real social or natural world tractable or "legible." Like cadastral maps, these "state simplifications" summarize those aspects of reality that are of interest to central decision makers while screening out information deemed unnecessary to the purpose of transforming society or nature (1998, 87). But a simplified reality is a partial reality, and one that is likely to omit details of crucial local significance with negative implications for the success of the overall project. Standardized solutions, such as Green Revolution production packages, often must be adapted to local conditions before they are of much use in real situations. Yet state planners view local adaptation as a form of resistance that must be overcome if they are to realize their ambitions for social change. Thus even the most ostensibly apolitical technical scheme contains an important political dimension:

> [T]he unspoken logic behind most of the state projects of agricultural modernization was one of consolidating the power of central institutions and diminishing the autonomy of cultivators and their communities vis-à-vis those institutions. Every new material practice altered in some way the existing distribution of power, wealth, and status; and the agricultural specialists' claims to be neutral technicians with no institutional stake in the outcome can hardly be accepted at face value. (286)

As we see later, the failure to adapt these standardized packages to local agro-ecosystems nearly spelled disaster for Indonesia's Green Revolution. Agricultural intensification in Indonesia, as in other countries in the region, achieved its greatest successes when farmers proved adept at adjusting these packages to suit their particular circumstances despite local officials' best attempts to enforce uniformity in input use and production methods.

All policy making—whether carried out by central states, development agencies or nongovernment organizations (NGOs)—entails some degree of simplification. The greatest achievements of social democracy, such as universal education and health care, have depended to a large extent on governments' ability to render social reality legible for the purposes of large-scale social change. Scott's contribution is to illuminate the power dynamics underlying policy makers attempts to carry out programs based on social, economic, and technical generalizations in situations in which local conditions vary substantially from their core assumptions. He argues that the great disasters in social engineering of this century—Soviet collectivization, compulsory villagization in Tanzania, China's Great Leap Forward—have occurred when an aggressive, high-modernist ideology has taken root in authoritarian states. In these cases, the state possessed sufficient powers of coercion to enforce compliance and communities and individuals lacked the political capacity to resist. "In sum," writes Scott, "the legibility of a society provides the capacity for large-scale social engineering, high-modernist ideology provides the desire, the authoritarian state provides the determination to act on that desire, and an incapacitated civil society provides the leveled social terrain on which to build" (Scott 1998, 5).

Scott's analysis of state simplification reveals the ideology implicitly underlying technocratic approaches to knowledge such as those put forward by the Bank. The depoliticization of knowledge amounts to an attempt to sidestep the crucial question of what counts as legitimate knowledge and who is to decide (Standing 2000, 751). Is the agricultural planner, possessing higher degrees in agronomy or agricultural economics, willing to recognize the practical knowledge possessed by farmers? What sacrifices would this entail in terms of personal or institutional power, prestige, or access to resources? Does the agriculture ministry have the institutional capacity to implement plans based on anything more complicated than the most skeletal, stylized facts of the agricultural system? Do farmers possess the political capacity to resist the state's attempts to impose its version of knowledge if it is incompatible with their own? Viewed from this perspective, the idea that knowledge is a value-neutral public good serves the interests of institutions and individuals that possess sufficient power to enforce their version of what constitutes legitimate knowledge. Unsurprisingly, these are often the bureaucrats, engineers, and social scientists on whom institutions such as the World Bank rely to implement their projects and programs.

The Bank therefore has strong reasons to cling to its technocratic approach to knowledge and institutions. Although the Wolfensohn Bank has shown an increasing tendency to take on political issues such as governance, decentralization, and strengthening civil society, this is only possible as long as it adheres to the sanitized language of welfare economics and refrains from overt discussion of politics in concrete situations (see World Bank 2000f, chap. 5, for a clear statement of the Bank's approach to these issues). The Bank must remain on guard against accusations of meddling in domestic political affairs, not only because its *Articles of Agreement* require it to do so, but also because its authority as a development bank—and hence its attractiveness to donor countries—depends largely on its claim to technical, objective expertise. Moreover, the Bank must also avoid situations in which it inadvertently undermines the central institutions of client states on which it depends to execute its lending program. Thus, although the Bank's has moved closer to Hirschman's appreciation for the institutional and learning effects of development projects, it has yet to heed his advice that these effects are best understood in the context of the concrete conditions surrounding each project.[6] Initiatives such as Wolfensohn's comprehensive de-

6. "Upon inspection," Hirschman writes, "each project turns out to represent a unique constellation of experiences and consequences, of direct and indirect effects. This uniqueness in turn results from the varied interplay between the structural characteristics of the projects, on the one hand, and the social and political environment on the other" (1995, 186).

velopment framework are strongly suggestive of what Hirschman terms "the technician's dictatorial ambition" of attempting to program and measure the full set of direct and indirect effects of development projects (Hirschman 1995, 180). The Bank's impulse to social engineering remains as strong as ever, although now couched in the language of participation and partnership. Yet, as we see in the case material that follows, the tension between state simplification and participation is easier to resolve on paper than in the actual implementation of development projects.

THE INDONESIAN INTEGRATED PEST MANAGEMENT TRAINING PROJECT

Indonesia's Green Revolution in rice was the single most impressive achievement of the New Order government of President Suharto. The near tripling of paddy production between 1970 and 1990 was realized primarily on the basis of an unprecedented acceleration in the growth of land productivity, particularly in the densely populated rice bowls of Java, Bali, South Sulawesi, and North Sumatra. New technologies and the means to deploy them were extended to millions of small farmers over a relatively brief period of time. This was, to use Scott's terminology, a high modernist endeavor *par excellence:* science, harnessed to the power of the state, was used to raise the living standards of large segments of the population.

Rice intensification required the mobilization of the administrative apparatus on an immense scale. Irrigation works covering more than 2 million hectares were rehabilitated, with new projects extending over another 1 million hectares. A system of seed production centers was established to deliver the new seeds to farmers, together with a network of research stations to test them as they became available. The agricultural extension system expanded from 1,750 field workers in 1970 to 36,500 in 1990. Roads and storage facilities were put in place together with elaborate systems to produce and subsidize fertilizers and pesticides, purchase output, distribute credit, and conduct market operations to defend floor and ceiling prices and to regulate foreign trade (Van der Eng 1996; Fox 1993).

Rice intensification represented the best and the worst of the state's high-modernist ambitions. State simplification was very much in evidence in the form of standardized village institutions, such as cooperatives, farmer groups, and village security councils, which were dropped from above into a wide range of rural settings. These suffered predictably high rates of attrition, in fact if not on the record. The World Bank–supported extension system, as in other countries in the region, relied heavily on fixed technological packages consisting of high-yield seed varieties and uniform dosages of fertilizers and pesticides. Farmers could unpack these by adapting them to conditions in their own fields, but many were also coerced into using inputs they did not want by extensionists and village officials seeking to meet the rigid regional and national targets for adoption (Timmer 1993, 158).

Standardization meant a loss of ecological diversity. Although Indonesia possesses something like 8,000 traditional rice cultivars, by 1974 53 percent of irrigated rice was under four high-yield varieties (HYVs) (Fox 1993, 216). Greater genetic uniformity, high doses of nitrogen fertilizer, close planting, and higher cropping intensities resulted in increased pressure from pests and diseases. The accepted science of the day in turn called for the use of broad-spectrum insecticides and fungicides to keep these threats to the rice crop at bay.

But the system was unstable. By the 1970s, a previously minor insect pest, the rice brown planthopper (BPH), was causing substantial crop loss across southeast Asia's intensive rice-producing regions. The release of BPH-resistant varieties by the International Rice Research Institute (IRRI) and national breeding programs offered some relief, but the pests adapted quickly. For a time it appeared that the plant breeders and insects were locked into a Darwinian struggle to the death in Asia's rice fields. Food security in countries such Indonesia depended heavily on the ability of scientists to produce ever-more-resistant rice varieties to help keep farmers one step ahead of the BPH. By the end of the decade the scientists were losing. In 1979 alone, 750,000 hectares were affected by BPH, amounting to 8.5 percent of the country's rice area (Useem, Setti, and Pincus 1992, 450).

In early 1980s, however, new research at IRRI revealed that BPH was a pesticide-induced pest (Kenmore et al., 1984). Insecticides destroyed the natural enemies of BPH, for example spiders and beetles, which normally kept BPH under control. The absence of natural enemies created opportunities for the pests to multiply and reach densities high enough to cause serious economic damage. A decrease in insecticide use in rice fields would therefore reduce the likelihood of BPH outbreaks. This finding offered a way out of the breeder-BPH race and appeared at an opportune time for Indonesia. Although IR-36, the most successful of the BPH-resistant rice varieties, had held up admirably, several popular national varieties were faring less well against the pests. An acceleration of BPH outbreaks in 1984—coming at time of declining oil revenues and hence tighter foreign exchange constraints—heightened concerns within the government that large-scale crop losses would spell disaster for Indonesia's fragile economy.

Following intensive lobbying by national and international scientists, President Suharto issued a decree in 1986 banning fifty-seven broad-spectrum insecticides from use in paddy fields and called for the adoption of IPM as the nation's pest-control strategy. IPM is an approach to pest management that promises to treat the causes rather than symptoms of pest pressure. Rather than mask the problem of ecosystem imbalance with pesticides, farmers would develop an awareness of the ecological principles of population dynamics and the complex interrelationships between plants, water, soils, weather, fertilization, and pests. Based on this understanding, farmers could then tailor their practices to the conditions in individual rice fields.

But shifting the system away from pesticide dependence—and the redistribution of power and profits that this entailed—was too thorny a political and institutional problem to be resolved by one decree. To begin with, the presidential decision promised more than it could deliver. For example, the fifty-seven insecticides banned by the president were only prohibited from use on rice, which meant that they were still allowed for use on other crops such as vegetables and would therefore remain in local markets. The decree also increased the number of pest and disease observers (PHPs), central Ministry of Agriculture (MOA) staff whose job it was to monitor farmers' fields and report the data to the local authorities and the ministry in Jakarta. These data on pest populations were often the trigger needed by central or local agriculture officials to declare an outbreak and release free or heavily subsidized pesticides into the affected region. Close financial and political relationships between the chemical companies and ministry officials created incentives for the latter to find pest problems and release pesticides to control them.

Another threat to the nascent IPM policy was the pesticide subsidy. At the time of the presidential decree, the government shouldered 85 percent of the farm-gate pesticide price, a program that cost the government over \$100 million per year. MOA officials and chemical companies argued that reducing the subsidy would result in unprecedented crops losses and would therefore imperil the nation's food security. However, technocrats in the economics ministries, anxious to find ways to reduce government expenditures, criticized the subsidy as unnecessarily costly. In the face of intense opposition from the MOA, the Finance Ministry reduced the subsidy in stages to 75, 55, and 40 percent of the farm-gate price before eliminating it in 1989. Total pesticide production fell from 56.6 to 23.7 thousand tons per annum from 1986 to 1989 (Linser 1991). Not coincidentally, the reported incidence of BPH outbreaks declined dramatically as pesticide use retreated from the high levels of the early part of the decade.

The ideological and financial commitment of the MOA to a chemical-based strategy of pest management, however, remained a serious threat to the country's nascent IPM policy.[7] For the architects of the government's rice intensification program, pesticides provided a lever of control that they felt they could not do without. Aside from their financial interest in pes-

---

7. This was amply demonstrated in 1987–88 when the MOA was given responsibility for IPM training using proceeds from the second phase of the National Agricultural Extension Project (NAEP) funded by the World Bank. Using standard training and visit extension methods favored by the Bank, the MOA exhausted a total of \$4.1 million over a seven-month period with no observed impact in the field (Government of Indonesia and United Nations Food and Agriculture Organization 1991).

ticide dependence, agricultural planners trained in industrial agriculture remained unconvinced by the argument that micromanagement of population dynamics represented a viable substitute for the control over nature afforded by the power to determine when and where to drop pesticides. Pesticides provided some security against the unpredictability of agricultural production and reinforced the power of the ministry over recalcitrant and technically backward farmers. IPM was seen as an untested and risky production strategy that would effectively subvert the existing order by strengthening the bargaining power of tradition-bound cultivators over the progressive, scientifically minded specialists responsible for safeguarding the nation's food supply.

Phase I: The Rise of a Competing Paradigm

The proponents of IPM in Indonesia understood from the beginning that they had set in motion a contest between local and central control and between contextual practical knowledge and rule-based decision making. The cycle of chemical dependence could only be broken if farmers could unpack the technologies promoted by the extension system. Unpacking the technology meant dispensing with administrative control over the production system (i.e., the "proper" fertilizer dosage and the "correct" seed variety). Cultivation practices needed to be tailored to each field in each season, requiring experimentation with the full range of alternatives, whether or not the alternatives were currently part of the most recent intensification campaign.

But the institutional odds were stacked heavily against IPM. The fortunes of the rice intensification programs improved as Indonesia recovered from the BPH disasters of the 1970s. The symbolically important target of rice self-sufficiency was reached in 1984, reinforcing the MOA's mandate to push ahead with its agricultural research and extension efforts. Proponents of the IPM program did gain a key ally in Minister of Development Johannes B. Sumarlin, who favored the establishment of a national IPM program within the Development Planning Ministry to sidestep the sensitive issue of the MOA's financial interests in pesticide production and distribution.

Using the proceeds of a U.S. Agency for International Development (USAID) policy grant, Sumarlin contracted with the UN Food and Agriculture Organization (FAO) in 1989 to set up a program housed in the national planning agency BAPPENAS to develop and pilot IPM training curricula. The resulting method was based on the concept farmer field schools, or groups of twenty-five or so farmers who met with an IPM trainer one morning per week for the duration of the growing season. Fields schools were organized around two study fields: the first was cultivated based on standard practice in the locality; the second was according to IPM principles. In practice this usually meant a comparison of *Supra-Insus* (a MOA technology package) and the collective weekly decisions of field school farmers. Each week the field school observed both fields, collecting samples of plants and insects and recording data on soil, water, and weather conditions; plant health; and pest damage and any other relevant information. The farmers then broke up into small groups to produce agroecosystem drawings based on the data collected in the field. The drawings and samples were then discussed with the larger group, and a decision was taken on an appropriate set of actions (or no action) for each plot. The role of the trainer was to facilitate the discussion and encourage farmers to answer their own questions through experimentation. The intent was not to substitute an IPM package, which in any case would have been a contradiction in terms. The idea was to convey the notion that there is no "right" answer that applies everywhere and at all times and to help build farmers' self-confidence and ability to question the centralized commands emanating from the extension system.

The FAO team of national and international experts immediately began training MOA PHPs in ten training centers across the country. The choice of PHPs as the main IPM trainers served two purposes. First, the PHPs were the logical choice from the perspective of previous technical training, and thus the decision made administrative sense. In addition, the political intent of the IPM project was to redirect the energies of these core MOA staff away from pest surveillance—and the use of surveillance data as a trigger for the release of pesticides—and toward farmer training in IPM methods. Thus from the early days of the project, control over the pest observers emerged as a focal point of conflict between the MOA and the IPM program housed in BAPPENAS.

If the BAPPENAS IPM program had stopped there, the MOA would not have had occasion to raise much fuss. Even the concept of farmer field schools, based on the idea that the opinion of farmer groups carried as much weight as that of trainers or extension agents, was ideologically acceptable in a country with strong local traditions of consultation (*musyarawah*) and consensus building (*mufakat*). After all, a skilled trainer with a strong technical background could be counted on to steer the discussions around to favor the intensification package if need be. Moreover, there was no immediate reason to assume that the FAO project would ever reach a scale that could be considered threatening to the MOA's nationwide *Bimas* (mass guidance) program.

The stakes were raised, however, when the FAO program, extending well beyond the confines of its original mandate, reached over 200,000 farmers with season-long farmer field schools during its first two years of existence. Thus a rather sizeable farmer-training program had managed to grow up alongside Indonesia's official agricultural extension system. Although originally set up as a training-of-trainers project, the FAO group recast their efforts as a national IPM program with the expressed intention of reaching a majority of Indonesia's rice farmers. Of perhaps more importance to the future shape of the program, farmers who had already taken part in IPM farmer field schools began in a spontaneous, unplanned manner to set up field schools for other farmers. Run at their own expense, or perhaps with the help of the village governments, these farmer-to-farmer field schools revealed a level of enthusiasm about IPM training that took even seasoned field staff by surprise. Soon farmer trainers were talking about IPM villages and joining ranks to form local IPM organizations. Field staff were caught up in the excitement as their role shifted from enforcing national directives to bringing useful skills to farmers in the mutually supportive environment of the field school (Useem, Setti and Pincus 1992, 468).

By now the momentum for change was too great for the MOA to resist openly, although trench warfare did continue between the MOA's Directorate of Crop Protection (DITLIN) and BAPPENAS over the (as of yet unofficial) national IPM program. Most worrying for DITLIN was the fate of the 2,000 plus PHPs, now graduates of the IPM training-of-trainers program. Within this group was a core of over three hundred IPM field leaders (or senior trainers) who had developed a fierce loyalty to the IPM program. Although officially under DITLIN and responsible for running the directorate's pest monitoring and forecasting system, they had in effect been hijacked by the FAO program and converted into proponents of a competing extension paradigm.

Phase II: Enter the Bank

In 1992, USAID funding for policy support was retooled, forcing an end to direct funding of the FAO program. BAPPENAS invited the World Bank to consider a follow-up project to build on the successes of the original venture. During the project-design phase, the Bank provided BAPPENAS with a bridging loan of $5.3 million derived from undisbursed funds from the Third National Agricultural Extension Project (Loan 2748-IND). Both the government and the Bank had high hopes for the follow-up project. BAPPENAS was enjoying its unaccustomed role as project manager, and the prospect of a World Bank project appeared to some mid-level officials as an ideal way to finance their career-advancement strategies. The Bank, in the wake of the United Nations Conference on Environment and Development (UNCED), was badly in need of viable environment-friendly projects. Moreover, the poor performance of successive Bank-funded training-and-visit extension projects heightened interest among agricultural-sector task managers for alternative project ideas.

Despite this coincidence of interests, the early stages of collaboration did not augur well for the new IPM project. As previously noted, the elimination of the subsidy had led to a sharp drop in pesticide consumption, and as a result the immediate threat of severe pest outbreaks had receded. With the return to normality, the attention of the economic ministers inevitably turned from crop protection to other matters. This, in combination with changes at the top of BAPPENAS, left the project bereft of top-level political protection. The shift from grant to loan financing also strengthened BAPPENAS relative to the FAO team, which found it increasingly difficult to obtain information relating to project finances.

The question of the institutionalization of the project was the subject of the most heated exchanges between the World Bank, government of Indonesia (GOI) and FAO during the process of project preparation and later during the implementation phase. These conflicts reflected the specific interests of the three parties, but also revealed tensions within the Bank's own approach to development effectiveness and institutional development. This was apparent in official Bank documents of the day and, I argue, remains unresolved in the new initiatives put forward by the Wolfensohn Bank. The Operations Evaluation Department's (OED) 1992 review of evaluation results, for example, was sharply critical of the absence of meaningful farmer participation in agricultural projects (World Bank 1994b, 111).[8] Foreshadowing more recent restatements of its rural development policy, OED called for greater flexibility and more experimentation in design as a means of countering the tendency toward rigidity and hierarchical control in World Bank projects (see, for example, World Bank 1997a). Yet the same document sought an explanation for the slow progress in the field of institutional development in the formulation overly complex projects and lack of institutional ownership among borrowing governments (World Bank 1994b, 138). This conflict between participation, on the one hand, and institutional ownership and clear lines of command, on the other, emerged as a major point of contention in the implementation of IPMTP and signaled the Bank's ambivalence in the face of these competing priorities.

In the case of IPMTP, institutionalization covered what were in fact two separate issues: the administrative home of the project and the organization of the field management system, including the role of farmers and farmer groups in project management. Conflict over these aspects of project design and implementation emerged as Bank task managers grew increasingly wary of efforts to promote forms of organization and activities that strengthened the participatory aspects of the project, but that could also potentially undermine the central authorities on which it depended for project implementation.

The question of the project's institutional home arose early in the process of project preparation. The Bank, although cognizant of the close relation-

8. This criticism was echoed in an internal review of India's training-and-visit agricultural extension program (Macklin 1992, 25) and a later sectoral review (World Bank 1997b).

ship between crop-protection officials and the chemical companies, argued that the sustainability of the IPM program required that the new investment project eventually move from BAPPENAS to its natural home in the MOA's DITLIN. The FAO team countered that the MOA's crop protection and extension policies reflected a strong bias toward centralized decision making that made it an inappropriate choice as the main implementing agency. In the end, the project design—as codified in the Bank's *Staff Appraisal Report* (World Bank 1993e)—left the project in BAPPENAS, but called for greater MOA participation in the working group that was to manage the project on a day-to-day basis.

These debates were quickly overtaken by events. Following the installation of the new cabinet in 1993, it soon became apparent that key players in BAPPENAS who had provided the project with some measure of protection had lost influence. Lacking clear direction from the top, lower-level officials seized control of the project and set about using project funds for their own purposes. According to the first World Bank supervision mission, the project had "departed radically from the design as described in the SAR [Staff Appraisal Report] and as agreed upon by the Bank and the Government during negotiations" (World Bank 1993a, 4). Unit costs soared above those estimated in the project design, but few farmers were receiving training. Meanwhile, BAPPENAS had launched a series of initiatives—for example, training programs in upland vegetables and in East Timor—that were unrelated to project objectives. Here the Bank was willing to invoke the project design to effect a bureaucratic transfer of the project; yet, as we see later, the Bank was equally prepared to dispense with the project design when this suited its own operational needs.

After a lengthy period of bureaucratic skirmishing, the project was transferred to an ad hoc management team under the MOA's secretary general, the second-highest ranking official in the ministry. The intention was to escape the problems that had emerged in BAPPENAS without surrendering control over the project to the MOA's DITLIN (Hammig 1998, 12).[9] However, successive Bank supervision missions took issue with this structure, arguing that the project would be more efficient and sustainable if it could be accommodated within the existing government hierarchy. Immediate operational issues, particularly the problem of securing counterpart funding, were given priority over the project's *raison d'être* of reforming the govern-

9. This was a risky move because BAPPENAS was in a position to retaliate for the loss of the project by depriving it of government cofinancing. This did in fact emerge as a major obstacle to project implementation by the time of the midterm review in October 1995. Although allocations increased in subsequent years, the government was forced to cancel $6 million of the original loan, largely as a result of low levels of rupiah financing. Curiously, the Bank's final evaluation report applauds the government for "the high priority in its funding in spite of severe budget constraints" (World Bank 2000b, 8). In fact, funding levels increased after the onset of the financial crisis and were lowest during the period 1993–97.

ment's approach to both agricultural extension and crop protection. According to the *Midterm Review,*

> Without a "home" in a line Department, the process of planning and budgeting is constrained by the lack of direct ties to a budgetary unit from which the project DIP [*Daftar Isian Proyek* or government budget allocation for development projects] is allocated. Furthermore, under this structure, too many programmatic decisions must be made by Working Groups. This is not a sound management practice, since committees are better suited to promotion of inter-departmental cooperation than to implementation. The mission recommends that the MOA reviews the current project structure and design a more efficient management system for the implementation of IPM activities during the remaining project period, bearing in mind the incongruity between some current crop protection practices and the IPM model. (World Bank 1995b, 15)

Sustainability, from the Bank's perspective, required that DITLIN be assigned full responsibility for project implementation despite DITLIN's clearly expressed reservations concerning the goals and methods of the project.[10] This, unfortunately, did not resolve the Bank's operational problems. Although DITLIN took charge of the project immediately after the midterm review, subsequent supervision missions continued to criticize the project's "weak and ineffective" central management (World Bank 1997b, 8). Astoundingly, the Bank was still holding out for a "possible resolution of the continuing conflict between IPM practice and pest surveillance" in the fifth year of project implementation, shortly before the project was due to close (World Bank 1998a, 9).

The problem facing the project at the field level was to put in place a management system that could deliver centrally controlled resources to the field without compromising flexibility and local control over training activities. This required setting up a chain of financial accountability and field-based planning that was independent of the existing provincial- and district-level agricultural service agencies.[11] Fearing that these agencies would use the project to push existing extension and intensification programs rather than IPM, the project design called for the establishment of district program of-

10. An indication of DITLIN's opposition to the project was its refusal to change the job descriptions of the PHPs under its control to officially include IPM within their core responsibilities.

11. Agricultural service offices (*Dinas Pertanian*) had been devolved to provincial governments and were no longer under the direct control of the MOA. The MOA operated through regional offices and retained responsibility for technical support to provincial and district *Dinas.*

fices staffed by IPM field leaders. Field leaders—still officially (PHPS) under DITLIN—were the technical and managerial core of the USAID-funded project. Highly motivated and already possessing four years of experience as IPM trainers, they were well placed to take a leading role in the planning and implementation of field activities under the World Bank project. Their main role was to promote the formation of active farmer groups, who would take a progressively larger role in the planning, implementation, and evaluation of project activities.

Yet this reliance on field leaders and farmer groups presupposed a view of sustainability that was directly opposed to the Bank's emphasis on institutionalization within existing government agencies. The main objective of the project from this perspective was not to use the project to promote reform within government institutions but rather to create a sizeable constituency of IPM farmers and farmer groups outside of the government hierarchy that would both resist pesticide-based crop-protection strategies and promote locally relevant technological change. Field leaders would act as community organizers, channeling central funds into locally planned activities and encouraging farmer groups to initiate farmer-to-farmer training, farm-based research, and farmer networking (Hammig 1998, 15). After the completion of the project, the organizational role of the field leaders would revert to the farmer groups rather than to the local agricultural service agency.

This was an approach to sustainability that neither the government nor the World Bank could swallow. Although the main features of the field management system were codified in the loan agreement—and thus legally binding—the Bank was unwilling to take decisive action to enforce the project design.[12] Within two years, the field management system had been surrendered to the provincial agricultural service agencies, which proved unable to deliver sufficient amounts of funds to the field in a timely manner. Field leaders were never authorized to hold working project funds, effectively removing them from the disbursement system. The late arrival of funds and shortages of essential training materials had a negative impact on training quality, and the marginalization of the field leaders effectively insulated central decision makers from the demands of farmer groups.

Yet the Bank remained reluctant to confront the government on this is-

---

12. The experience of IPMTP resonates with the discussion of noncompliance in *The Wapenhans Report:* "In an era of heightened concern over the importance of prudent governance, it is unacceptable that instruments of transparency and accountability are neglected. The Bank, in response to non-compliance, can suspend the right of the Borrower to make withdrawals, or can (under certain circumstances) cancel the undisbursed balance of the loan; but these remedies are rarely exercised. Usually, staff and managers respond to non-compliance by ignoring it, waiving it, or occasionally taking informal steps to deal with it—such as requesting the borrower not to submit withdrawal applications or holding up a successor loan" (World Bank 1992, 20).

sue. Rather than press for the field-based management system called for in the original project design, successive Bank supervision missions instead indulged what can only be described as an obsessive-compulsive urge to count the number of farmers trained and to compare these (largely fictitious) numbers to the totals set out in the staff appraisal report.[13] This suited the operational needs of the Bank, which required simple, quantified measures of project achievements at the national level for the purposes of internal reporting and disbursement of funds. As Scott notes, the administrators who gather and employ these aggregated statistics are fully aware that the numbers conceal as much as they reveal (1998, 81). Yet in screening out local variations in the quality and content of training activities, the statistics on the number of farmers trained served the important purpose rendering the project "legible" for planners and accountants in the Bank and the MOA.

But the emphasis on quantity over quality had more pernicious effects. Both the Bank and MOA relied increasingly on strategies that sought to adapt the project to the needs of the government's administrative system rather than to use the project to effect change at the central and local levels. Activities that would affect the project's rate of return—such as farmer field schools—were given priority over equally important, although less easily quantified, activities such as farmer research, networking, and planning meetings (World Bank 1998a, 14). The needs of the existing disbursement system were paramount. The experience of Neils Röling, an independent consultant on the midterm review mission, is instructive:

> The Mission had to constantly struggle against the tendency to adapt IPM implementation to the needs of the Government system. For example, at one point, we seriously considered the proposal not to have IPM field schools in the dry season because the Indonesian administrative system does not allow funds to be drawn down to the field between March 31st and half June. This absurd situation must be the product of a system that is not accountable to its clients. Administration and management should serve implementation, not the other way round. (Röling 1995, 5)

The Bank, however, drew a different lesson from the experience. The mistake, according to an internal report, was to establish project structures that were not integrated from the start into the existing bureaucratic structure:

13. According to a technical audit conducted by an independent consultant, "The data provided by national, provincial and district program offices refer to the number of field school units conducted and records are not kept of the number of farmers actually completing training. . . . In general, data collection is perceived as having an administrative rather than project management function, an attitude that works against the interests of the project" (Braun 1997, 17).

Setting up separate, parallel structures to manage projects is always tempting and seldom leads to post-project sustainability. The separate national and regional offices of the project and of the FAO TA [technical assistance] team established during the pilot phase continued through the life of IPMTP. The national, provincial and district governments are now faced with the challenge of integrating the district and sub-district project units, the support and guidance provided by the PIU [project implementation unit] and the FAO-TA team, into their regular operations to ensure sustainability of project achievements. (World Bank 2000f, 12)

This, again, reflects a view of sustainability as bureaucratic persistence[14] rather than the large-scale adoption of practices and values promoted by the project. A basic contradiction existed between the government and World Bank's shared notion of institution building as reinforcing the existing hierarchy and the project's focus on institutionalization at the farmer level.

STATE SIMPLIFICATION AND OPERATIONAL IMPERATIVES

IPM was in many ways an attempt to reintroduce complexity and politics into a system that had been aggressively simplified and depoliticized. The complexity came in the form of diverse farmer management strategies tailored to the agroecological conditions in their individual ricefields. It also came in the varied levels of organization and vigor of farmer groups and in their capacity to shape or at least moderate the impact of crop protection and intensification programs put forward by local and national agricultural agencies. Viewed from this perspective, the project's technical aspects could not be separated from the political goal of creating the space within the established hierarchy for experimentation and heterogeneity. The project sought to generate and make practical use of knowledge, but of a kind of knowledge that could not be easily divorced from the political context in which it was created, legitimized, and conveyed.

This posed a dilemma for the Bank. On the one hand, IPMTP presented the institution with an opportunity to associate itself with a high-profile knowledge-intensive project designed to increase agricultural productivity on the basis of locally based, participatory methods. The project's undeniably green credentials were another important selling point. That the intention of the project was to rein in the bureaucratic apparatus of the Green Revolution—institutions largely underwritten by Bank financing—signaled a fundamental change in the Bank's approach to rural development. On the other hand, the project threatened to force the Bank to confront the polit-

14. I am indebted to Russell Dilts for this evocative term.

ical realities lurking behind its rhetorical edifice of participation, partnership, and support for civil society.

This dilemma expressed itself most clearly in the competing notions of institution building underlying project implementation. Although on paper the project design assumed a mutually supportive relationship between farmer groups and the bureaucracy, an unspoken tension existed from the outset, pitting the command-and-control philosophy of the MOA and agricultural service agencies against local demands for greater autonomy and political voice. For the MOA and its local representatives, institutionalization could only mean accommodating the project within the existing bureaucratic apparatus as a complement to ongoing programs. For IPM field leaders and farmer groups, however, institution building would take place at the farmer level and would take the form of organizations and networks of farmers largely independent of the government hierarchy.

The Bank was therefore left in the uncomfortable position of deciding who its main clients really were: the government, which had signed the loan agreement, or the farmers, who were to be the project's main beneficiaries. It is here that the inadequacy of vague references to partnership and consensus building is most apparent. Although the interests of the state and the classes, organizations, ethnic groups, and others that constitute civil society sometimes coincide, this is by no means a normal or even common occurrence. Take, for example, Wolfensohn's attempt to circumvent the issue in the document setting out his comprehensive development framework:

> Countries must be in the driver's seat and set the course. They must determine goals and the phasing, timing and sequencing of programs. Where there is not adequate capacity in the government to do this, we must support and help them to establish, own, and implement the strategy. And we must work to achieve the strategy with our colleagues in the government, in the international development community, the civil society, and the private sector. In some countries the long and short-term goals will be set by a process of public debate and consensus building led by the government with all sections of society. In other countries, the establishment of goals will continue to be set more centrally. (Wolfensohn 1999, 9)

The implication is that whether national goals are set through political competition or more centrally is of secondary importance. However the strategy has been formulated, the Bank will help the state to implement it. Countries have their own political structures, and it is not up to the Bank to tell them whether these are appropriate or not. This is consistent with the Bank's *Articles of Agreement*, its technocratic worldview, and its historical mission of lending to client states. Yet it is not as easily reconciled with the institution's rhetorical emphasis on public participation, governance, and strengthening civil society. The problem is that the attempt to cleanse the country's development strategy of it political content is itself political: like knowledge, development loses its meaning when removed from a specific political context.

Returning to IPMTP, it is therefore not surprising that, given the choice, the Bank found it necessary to identify itself with its clients in the Indonesian state and their conception of institutionalization. Institutional development thus came to be defined as slotting the central project apparatus into the appropriate agency within the existing bureaucratic structure. Faced with the dilemma of enforcing compliance with the project design or accommodating clients within the MOA, the Bank opted for the latter. Control of the project was delivered to the individuals and agencies that had the most to lose from its success.

For the task managers charged with responsibility for supervising the project, the decision was not a difficult one. Operational imperatives were at work that limited the range of realistic choices and obliged them to rely heavily on their counterparts in the central line ministries (Pincus 2001). For example, the need of operations staff to reach predetermined lending targets results in "pressure to lend," in other words, institutional incentives that favor the formulation and approval of new projects over the monitoring and supervision of ongoing projects (Wapenhans 1992). Pressure to lend encourages Bank operations staff to identify their interests with those of their clients in the recipient government. Task managers, who typically operate in one sector, develop working relationships with government officials in the relevant ministries. These officials, who implement projects under the supervision of the task manager, are also responsible—or are closely connected to the people responsible—for the approval of the next proposed Bank project for the sector. Given that the task manager wants the project and the government needs the loan, it does not take long for an understanding to develop in which problems associated with existing projects are overlooked in exchange for a smooth path for new projects in the pipeline.

Pressure to lend helps explain the lengths to which operations staff will go to oblige their counterparts in client states. For example, the Morse Commission investigating the Narmada dam controversy was stunned to find that "the Bank is more concerned to accommodate the pressures emanating from its borrowers than to guarantee implementation of its policies" (quoted in Rich 1994, 253). In the case of IPMTP, the Bank similarly acceded to the government's strategy of reducing the project to a centralized funding mechanism for a uniform set of training activities. Operational imperatives dictated that the development objectives of the Bank's real client—the central state—took precedence over the competing interpretations of the project's goals.

The Bank also had internal operational reasons to consent to this de facto reformulation of the project. From the time of the project's midterm review, the task managers responsible for IMPTP had grown increasingly anxious about the lack of reliable documentation of project outputs. Of particular concern were the projected economic rate of return of 32 percent published in the *Staff Appraisal Report* and the project's need to demonstrate that it could achieve this result (World Bank 1995b, 7; 1996b, 2; 1997b, 2).[15] The fear was that failure to match this benchmark would reduce the likelihood that internal Bank evaluations would award the project a mark of satisfactory. In Scott's (1998) terms, the project had to be made legible to the Bank's own reporting system, and legibility required extreme simplification of field reality. Ironically, although the Bank had condoned the government's systematic noncompliance with the legal covenants of the loan agreement, it would not tolerate underperformance relative to the estimated (and largely mythical) economic rate of return. The technicians had achieved their dictatorial ambitions, but at the cost of a unique opportunity for the Bank to give operational meaning to its rhetorical fixation on knowledge, participation, and institution building.

CONCLUSION

The Indonesian IPM Training Project was a rare development project in that it was designed with the explicit intent of reversing a tendency toward state simplification of complex ecological and social reality. In retrospect, the vehicle of a World Bank–funded government-implemented project was particularly ill-suited to the task of promoting the development of local autonomous organizations and local knowledge. Despite a rhetorical shift emphasizing institutional change as an important output of development projects, the Bank in the case of IPMTP was not prepared to take the political steps necessary to pursue a notion of institutional change that in effect represented a challenge to the status quo.

Although some of the difficulties encountered by IPMTP in Indonesia were project-specific, the basic problem of reconciling the Bank's rhetorical emphasis on knowledge, participation, and institution building with the real impact of its lending operations is more widespread. The Bank's approach to these issues is impoverished by its technocratic orientation and unwillingness to come to grips with the political dimensions of the development

15. To meet these requirements, the Bank commissioned two separate impact studies conducted by external agencies in addition to the existing monitoring and evaluation system, a management information system, and an independent technical audit (World Bank 1998d, 9; Braun 1997).

process. However, as we have seen, the attempt to cleanse development of politics is itself political: the Bank, failing to deal explicitly with the political implications of knowledge and institution building, in the end implicitly supports the simplifying, centralizing tendencies of its client states.

This tendency is particularly dangerous in light of the Bank's renewed emphasis on the importance of institution building. Having rediscovered the fungibility problem, the Bank is once again placing great stress on the secondary or external benefits associated with development projects. Projects, according to this logic, are not necessarily important in their own right but contribute to development in so far as they promote institutional strengthening and the spread of knowledge in specific sectors and places. As discussed at the beginning of this chapter, this is in some senses a return to themes put forward by Albert Hirschman in the 1970s. Lacking Hirschman's political acumen (although not his propensity for self-subversion), the current Bank leadership undermines its own efforts in this sphere by adhering to a narrowly technocratic approach to both knowledge and institutions.

CHAPTER FIVE

Criminal Debt

Jeffrey A. Winters

In the past, donors knew who were the corrupt leaders but they went
ahead and gave them loans.

KWESI BOTCHWEY
former finance minister, Ghana

We know exactly where our money is going. . . . We do not tolerate
corruption in our programs. On this principle there is no compromise.

JEAN-MICHEL SEVERINO
World Bank vice president

Since its founding, the World Bank has participated mostly passively in the
corruption of roughly $100 billion of its loan funds intended for develop-
ment.[1] This poses three major challenges for the institution. The first is legitimacy. It is difficult for the Bank to claim a leadership role in development
when its loans and projects have been tainted for decades by gross corruption. The willingness of rich governments to support the Bank financially is
also undermined. The second challenge is response. The Bank cannot begin to retard the rate at which funds are stolen without a thorough understanding of why and how the money was lost. The Bank needs a realistic
assessment of its capabilities and limits if it is to ensure that its funds are used
for their intended purpose. The third and final challenge is responsibility.
At present, indebted populations across the developing world are contrac-
tually bound to repay their World Bank loans, including the many billions
in criminal debt stolen with the Bank's knowledge by corrupt government
officials and their cronies. But legal principles are being enforced selectively
and narrowly. The World Bank cites contractual obligations as it presses borrowing populations hard on debt repayment. Meanwhile, the multilateral

---

1. Botchwey, the speaker of the first epigraph (Masebu 1999, 1), is a member of the Global
Coalition for Africa, a nongovernmental organization (NGO) based in Washington, D.C.,
and he heads the coalition's unit on the African debt. The total African debt owed to bilateral and multilateral lenders at the end of 1999 was approximately $300 billion.

development banks (MDBs), which are explicitly obligated under their international charters to safeguard their loans against theft, are not being held financially accountable for failing to uphold their own obligations. The Bank's knowledge that its funds have been systematically stolen over a period of decades, combined with its failure to take effective measures to reduce these losses, violates the Bank's charter and makes it legally responsible for a share of the corrupted funds. Thus far, indebted populations have borne all the financial burden for the hemorrhaging of development funds. A fair and legal arrangement would obligate the World Bank to share in the fiscal burden for these losses. It is impossible to reinvent the Bank without confronting its role in permitting these funds to be stolen over such a long period and the legal implications of its having done so.

This chapter focuses on these last two challenges of response and responsibility. The World Bank began in the late 1990s to acknowledge publicly that corruption of development assistance was a serious problem and, more grudgingly, that its own loan funds were involved. However, the Bank has misdiagnosed why and how corruption occurs. Partly as a result, the responses the Bank has adopted to combat corruption are unlikely to be effective. As for responsibility, the case of Indonesia, which is neither unusual in the developing world nor the most egregious example, shows that Bank officials were aware from the earliest years of the Suharto regime in the 1960s that massive government corruption was a problem. They also knew that Bank loans were as vulnerable to theft as any other resources in the system. Yet the Bank did nothing of significance in Indonesia for three decades to safeguard the money it loaned. The Suharto regime, which was overthrown in 1998, borrowed almost $30 billion from the World Bank. According to the best estimates available, approximately one-third of this, or $10 billion, was systematically stolen with the Bank's full knowledge and thus is criminal debt. The Bank is bound under international law to share the burden of this criminal debt, not only for Indonesia, but for all client states where similar or worse patterns of corruption are found. Although precise figures are not available, a conservative estimate of total criminal debt for the World Bank globally is roughly $100 billion since the institution began lending.[2] The total combined criminal debt for all MDBs could double this figure. Whatever the exact figure, it is ponderously large. If forced to bear even one-third or one-half of its criminal debt burden, the World Bank would be damaged financially and its richest shareholders would certainly have to draw on the guarantee funds that back the institution's sterling credit rating. As appalling as it may be for some, particularly in the Bank, to

2. This estimate is based on the Bank's total lending and the conclusion that Indonesia is reasonably representative of corrupt practices globally. In fact, the figure of one-third is, if anything, an underestimate for Indonesia. Bank officials and staff quoted in this chapter make it clear that for many Bank clients the levels of theft were vastly higher.

consider such a prospect, it is important to recall that this same criminal debt burden is already being wholly borne with devastating results elsewhere by the world's poorest populations.

THE PROBLEM OF CORRUPTION

There are many learned studies of corruption that examine and define it from a variety of perspectives. Most definitions focus on behavior. The World Bank's most comprehensive statement on corruption, the 1997 Framework, defines it simply as "the abuse of public office for private gain" (World Bank 1997f, 8). This is a useful starting point if we intend to view corruption as an economic development problem that can be addressed mainly through Bank projects and loans designed to improve governance. The 1997 Framework states that "corruption tends to flourish when institutions are weak and government policies generate economic rents" (12). This observation is true enough, and it does provide clear project targets that the Bank can focus on to reduce corrupt practices. But such a view begs prior questions that tend to get short treatment in Bank analyses of and solutions to the problem: Why are institutions weak and why are government policies generating economic rents? The way the Bank frames the issue is shaped by two factors: by an explicit political constraint built into the institution's *Articles of Agreement* that forces it to deal only with economic matters[3] and by an institutional compulsion to respond in ways that tend to generate additional lending and require the provision of expensive technical expertise.

The perspective on corruption offered here does not start with behavior, institutions, or government policies and does not necessarily require new lending, new projects, or the transfer of technical expertise. Rather, the emphasis is on power and leverage. Power relations lie at the heart of corruption. Beyond the role of individual conscience, which is a realm better left to moralists, it is the absence of effective detection, constraints, and punishment that makes corruption possible and probable. These are absent because power is concentrated in ways that block effective checks and balances in politics. Corruption ranges in scale from petty to grand, in scope from personal to systemic, and in impact from negligible to ruinous. But it is rarely caused by a lack of education or training (everyone knows what corruption is) and can rarely be addressed significantly by simply writing bet-

---

3. Article IV, Section 10, reads: "Political Activity Prohibited: The Bank and its officers shall not interfere in the political affairs of any member; nor shall they be influenced in their decisions by the political character of the member or members concerned. Only economic considerations shall be relevant to their decisions, and these considerations shall be weighed impartially in order to achieve the purposes stated in Article I" (World Bank 1993b). Of course, economic affairs are inherently political, and the Bank and everyone else knows this. Bank conditionality in loans, structural adjustment lending, and other forms of Bank pressure all interfere in the political affairs of members. The only question is on which political issues the Bank chooses to twist clients' arms, not whether it twists them.

ter laws, reorganizing institutions, or upgrading personnel through integrity workshops.

On the scale that matters for discussions of the Bank's role, corruption occurs in societies because power is held and maintained in such a way that individuals or groups who steal or misallocate public resources understand they can act with near-impunity.[4] Most countries where corruption is endemic have reasonably good laws on the books. The problem is implementation and enforcement. This leads to an immediate question: What should be the primary focus of the Bank's response to the challenge of corruption? To answer, it is important first to distinguish clearly among efforts directed at reducing corruption at a narrow microlevel, in projects and programs financed by the Bank; at a middle level, within and across whole societies; and at a macrolevel, in the relations and transactions among countries globally.

Given the domestic power relations underlying systemic corruption in many borrowing countries, and tempering that consideration with a realistic assessment of the Bank's leverage and limitations, the most efficacious Bank strategy to combat corruption would be to adopt a "sandwich" approach—this means its anticorruption efforts should be focused overwhelmingly at the narrow microlevel (Bank project supervision) and the macrolevel (international coordination). These are the levels at which the Bank has the greatest advantages. It is precisely in the nexus between the Bank and its borrowers that the Bank has both the leverage and the legal justification to act forcefully and consistently against corrupt practices. As a multilateral body, it also can play an effective coordinating and legitimating role to strengthen international institutions, norms, and sanctions linked to corruption.

The Bank is at its weakest, most ineffective, and most vulnerable at the middle level—in the battle against systemic corruption across whole governments. Here the central issue is the pattern of power concentration in society. The Bank will have its weakest impact at this level while encountering the greatest disruptions in its relations with borrower countries, the Bank's Board of Directors, and the international community. Moreover, it is the proper task of groups and actors in each society where corruption is rampant to challenge the power relations that make the abuses possible. The Bank is ill-equipped to put checks and balances in place, except in its own projects and activities and in the international environment. Regrettably, it is precisely at this middle level of the corruption problem that the Bank has decided to focus its efforts. "The main thrust of the Bank's support for coun-

4. Although the causes of corruption are almost entirely domestic to societies, the focus here is not on the institutions and practices of borrowers but rather on the role and practices of the World Bank. Although corruption within states is mentioned repeatedly in this chapter, the point is not to analyze crony capitalism but rather the Bank's engagement with the internal power relations that allow corruption to flourish.

tries' anticorruption efforts," declares the Bank's 1997 Framework, "will be in helping to design and implement government programs" (World Bank 1997f, 26). But there is also an immediate admission that this main thrust will be muted and diluted by the Bank's political constraints:

> Thus corruption can be addressed by Bank staff as an economic concern within the framework already approved by the Board for governance issues. This framework provides scope for the Bank to help countries by advising on economic policy reform and strengthening institutional capacity. However, the Bank's mandate does not extend to the political aspects of controlling corruption. And though the engagement of civil society is crucial for the long-run control of corruption, there are obvious limits on the extent to which the Bank, as a lender to governments, can directly support civil society's efforts to control corruption. So while the Bank's mandate provides scope for the institution to help countries control corruption, it shapes the way the Bank may respond. (25)

The benefits for the Bank of working at the micro- and macrolevels and avoiding the mezzolevel are several. First, because the Bank can control through internal decisions how its loans are used, it can respond rapidly and credibly to the chorus of critics charging that Bank funds are being stolen on a massive scale (which damages the reputation of the Bank and exposes the institution to legal challenges). Second, the Bank would, quite properly, no longer be responsible for any lack of progress in reducing corruption at the broader societal level. The Bank's own studies recognize that systemic corruption is complex and cannot be addressed quickly. The Bank can and should support good governance, with reducing corruption understood as a component of that goal, but it is a mistake to make reducing corruption across the country the centerpiece of the Bank's response to kleptocracy. And third, by using tighter fiscal supervision built into its own projects as a best practices model, the Bank can more credibly position itself as a leader in the international effort to combat corruption in bilateral and multilateral lending.

It should be noted that there is a serious flaw in the Bank's reasoning regarding its rights and justifications for using a reduction in or even a cutting off of loans as an instrument in its narrow-beamed efforts to attack corruption in its own projects. Moreover, this reasoning places unnecessarily severe constraints on the Bank's ability to use loan curtailment and cessation as part of what it terms its lending strategy for a country. The 1997 Framework states, "[I]f the level of corruption is high so as to have an adverse impact on the effectiveness of Bank assistance, according to factual and objective analysis, and the government is not taking serious measures to combat it, the Bank can take this as a factor in its lending strategy toward the country" (World Bank 1997f, 24). The Bank is reluctant to be much more direct than this about the problem in its pronouncements to kleptocrats. Beyond this, the most obvious problem with this statement is that the Bank goes too far in justifying all its actions in economic terms and ignores the fact that its fiduciary mandate in the Bank's *Articles of Agreement* (discussed next) is not predicated on the overall development performance of the country. Particularly because the Bank faces the threat of embarrassing legal challenges that could cost it many billions of dollars in debt write-offs, it is perverse to suggest that it can only base its response to endemic corruption on strong indications that development is being adversely affected. The Bank should declare that it is bound by international law and treaties to take effective action against corrupt practices.

The *Articles of Agreement* are unambiguous on the point that the Bank may not meddle in domestic political affairs. But the articles are equally unambiguous that, as a matter of basic operation, the Bank will not tolerate the corruption of its funds. Thus these injunctions are parallel and of equal legal standing. It is reasonable to infer that the founders of the Bank did not consider the theft of Bank funds to be an internal political affair but rather a fiduciary matter between the Bank and its clients. On this reading, the corruption of Bank funds alone is reason enough, under the charter, for the Bank to adjust its lending strategy progressively downward to zero, if necessary. It is unnecessary and counterproductive for the Bank to dilute the strength of the mandate in the charter by making any response contingent on broader economic effects associated with corrupt practices nationally. The Bank could make its strongest contribution to reducing corruption by declaring without apologies and sensitivities that its *Articles of Agreement* vest the Bank with unambiguous rights and responsibilities to safeguard the integrity of its loan funds. Moreover, it should deny any charges that the reduction or cutting off of lending based on sustained patterns of corruption is in any sense political. And finally, parliaments and legislatures in creditor countries around the world would be well within the spirit and letter of the Bank's charter were they to back the institution's rigorous enforcement of the mandate contained in the *Articles of Agreement*. Indeed, they should base their continued support for the Bank in part on how seriously the fiduciary responsibilities are carried out and, if they do not, be willing to bear the material and reputational costs if aggrieved populations sue the Bank and its directors in the World Court for willfully and illegally contributing to their criminal debt burden.[5]

5. Three years after the 1997 Framework was unveiled, the Bank produced two additional major documents. One was a study of the progress the Bank had made in the three years since it began taking corruption more seriously (World Bank 2000d) and the other was a guide for staff specifically focused on preventing fraud and corruption in Bank projects (Aguilar, Gill,

CRIMINAL DEBT

Most countries have public debt that must be repaid to creditors by their citizens. Criminal debt refers to the share of total borrowed funds that has been stolen by government officials, their families, and associates. Even though the benefits from these resources were enjoyed privately, the fiscal burden of repaying criminal debt is borne publicly. Governments can borrow in a variety of ways and from a variety of creditors. Although all borrowed funds taken by corrupt actors may appear to be indistinguishable from the perspective of those doing the stealing, the legal and political status of corrupted debt varies depending on who the creditor is and the channels through which the resources are supplied. Governments can incur debt directly by issuing bonds, where the purchasers of the bonds (the creditors) can be foreign or domestic, individuals or institutions. Some countries also incur sovereign debt by borrowing abroad from commercial and official (multilateral and bilateral) sources.

The World Bank is one such source of foreign official capital flowing through a multilateral channel. To a greater degree than most creditors, the World Bank and other MDBs carefully tie the resources they lend, specifying often in baroque detail the purposes for which funds are being supplied. A commercial bank might also pay considerable attention to how a borrower intends to use loan funds. But of greater concern to private creditors is simply the ability of the government to repay its obligations. For institutions such as the World Bank, a development agency chartered under the United Nations, the ability of client countries to repay their debts is important but not decisive. The Bank justifies its continued existence, and certainly its large staff of development economists, on the grounds that it engages deeply in the policy choices and project priorities of its clients. As the Bank repeatedly points out in its public relations materials, the Bank does not just lend, it combats poverty. Another key difference is that unlike private lenders, the World Bank is bound by law to follow its money and ensure that borrowers do not redirect credit for unintended purposes. Thus criminal debt in cases involving the World Bank is not just a ledger entry of stolen resources citizens must repay, but also a legal obligation for the Bank itself if it fails to prevent the chronic theft of loan funds.[6] This is true even if the Bank is consistently paid back on time, in full, and with interest.

---

and Pino 2000). The guide's bold opening sentence gives the impression that a shift might have occurred in favor of legal over economic justifications for combating corruption: "World Bank staff have the crucial fiduciary duty to ensure that loan funds are used for their intended purposes" (Aguilar, Gill, and Pino 2000, v). Unfortunately, in the remainder of the document's four parts and eight exhibits spanning more than fifty pages, this legal-fiduciary angle is mentioned again only once in passing.

6. Criminal Debt is distinct from odious debt. "Odious debt" in international law is defined as loans accumulated by an unrepresentative and oppressive government that were used to repress a country's citizens. It does not matter if the loans were used according to prevailing

The legal culpability and fiscal liability of different creditors—private or official, individual or institutional—vary because the actors involved and the power relations among them within the chain of debt supply change in crucial ways depending on the source of debt. The level of grand, or systemic, corruption in a society is related directly to the nature of a country's internal power relations. Military dictatorships, civilian authoritarian regimes, and warlord states present citizens with minimal opportunities for limiting the share of total public debt that ends up as criminal debt. If a dictator borrows domestically by selling bonds for highway improvements and most of the funds end up in accounts in the Cayman Islands or as a palazzo in Venice, this is an outcome that reflects power relations within the society. The responsibility for the theft and the fiscal liability for the resulting criminal debt burden is wholly between the citizens and their leaders. With a change in power relations and a change in regime, there may be a day of reckoning for the officials and military officers who accumulated the purely domestic component of the country's total criminal debt. The determining factor is domestic politics and power relations.

But only part of all criminal debt originates wholly from within the national context. Another part originates from international sources. For this portion, both the power relations involved and the burden of legal and fiscal responsibility are different. And it is here that the World Bank and its operations are relevant. Just as there is a power relationship between a government and its people, there is also one between the World Bank and its client governments (and, by extension, the indebted citizens). Debt accumulated and stolen domestically is a purely domestic concern. But what of debt accumulated through an institution such as the World Bank and systematically stolen by client governments and their cronies? The share of criminal debt that originates from sources such as the World Bank merits separate treatment because the Bank not only has the leverage to prevent (or at least greatly diminish) the accumulation of foreign criminal debt from its own lending, but it also has a strong legal mandate in its charter to do so.

LEGAL RESPONSIBILITIES OF THE WORLD BANK

The *Articles of Agreement* are the founding charter of the World Bank, setting forth the Bank's purpose, membership, operations, rights, limitations, and responsibilities. It is a binding constitution subject to all the rules and norms

---

law for their intended purposes or were stolen by officials. It is grounded on the principle that an illegitimate government cannot legitimately accumulate debts on behalf of an oppressed population. The concept is intended as a warning to creditors against considering risk narrowly in terms of likely ability to repay. The principle of odious debt means there is also the risk of wholesale legitimate repudiation. Criminal debt is much narrower than odious debt and, were the repudiation of criminal debt to be threatened, it would be because the population burdened with repayment never received or benefited from the borrowing. See Ndikumana and Boyce (1998, 195–217); Adams (1991).

of international law. For the purposes of the present discussion of corruption and accountability, the most relevant part of the charter is Article III, Section 5, paragraph c, which states: "The Bank shall make arrangements to ensure that the proceeds of any loan are used only for the purposes for which the loan was granted, with due attention to considerations of economy and efficiency and without regard to political or other non-economic influences or considerations" (World Bank 1993b, 4). This is an unambiguous statement against allowing Bank funds to be corrupted. It places a clear burden and responsibility on the Bank to make arrangements that ensure that its funds are not stolen or misallocated, and it admonishes the Bank to carry out this function in a manner that is economical, efficient, and unbiased politically.

The legal implications of this article are profound. The Bank's charter is silent on the fiscal burden the Bank must bear if it fails to fulfill its responsibilities and allows a share of its lending to become a significant part of a population's criminal debt burden. But it is obvious that the World Bank is a recognized legal entity under international law and faces legal procedures that range from internal grievance hearings, through international mediation, to jurisdiction of the International Court of Justice (the World Court).[7] No suit to demand relief of criminal debt linked to Bank loans has ever been brought by a client government that has succeeded a kleptocratic dictatorship, nor have any class action suits been brought by aggrieved citizens or nongovernmental organizations (NGOs). This remains an untested area of international law.

The legal position of the MDBs, including the World Bank, regarding challenges to loan repayment has been most extensively examined by John W. Head, whose work builds on the writings of Aron Broches, general counsel of the World Bank in the 1950s and 1960s (Head 1996, 214–34; Broches 1959, 1995). Head writes that any controversy between the World Bank and borrowers shall be submitted to arbitration by an arbitral tribunal. A three-person arbitral tribunal is set up to hear the dispute in accordance with procedures it establishes. The tribunal then renders a decision that is enforceable in national courts. Head writes that "the instituting party is to notify the responding party of the claim being made, the relief being sought,

---

7. The World Bank does open the door for the International Court of Justice and the UN to play a role in disputes involving the Bank and its clients (World Bank 1985, art. X, sec. 10.03, par. c). In September, 1993, the Bank created its Inspection Panel (discussed at greater length by Jonathan Fox, chap. 6 in this volume), which was designed to provide an independent forum for people directly and adversely affected by a Bank-financed project. Aggrieved parties can use the panel to request that the Bank act in accordance with its own policies and procedures for a specific project. The scope of the panel is severely limited by the condition that no requests can be made after the closing date of a project or once 95 percent of a project loan has been disbursed. In short, the Inspection Panel is useless as a forum for redress of criminal debt that has already accumulated.

and the name of the arbitrator it has appointed. Within 30 days after such notification, the responding party is to name the arbitrator it has appointed" (Head 1996, 220 n. 50). The two sides are then supposed to agree on a third arbitrator (called an umpire). If they have not agreed on this third person within sixty days of the initial notification by the instituting party, the umpire will be appointed by the president of the International Court of Justice or the secretary general of the United Nations. These procedures have never been tested with regard to Bank violations of Article III, Section 5, paragraph c of the *Articles of Agreement*.

The Bank's responsibility depends on how seriously it implemented the mandate in the articles to ensure, in a cost-effective manner, that its funds not be diverted or stolen. What arrangements were made and how strongly were they enforced? And can the Bank demonstrate concrete results through, for instance, a declining pattern of corruption in the projects it funds? Here it is relevant to look not only at the procedures the Bank has on paper, but also what is done in practice in the field and the results these practices have yielded.[8] What does the Bank do to guard its funds generally, and what was done specifically in the Indonesian case?

PROJECT SUPERVISION ON PAPER

The Bank produces a tremendous volume of booklets and procedures associated with its operations (and even more in its research and public relations divisions). One key booklet, entitled *The Project Cycle,* sets forth the six stages of a Bank project, from identification through negotiation and board approval, and finishing with evaluation once the project is completed. The penultimate stage is implementation and supervision, which the booklet describes as the "least glamorous part of project work," though it admits that it is "the most important" (Baum 1982, 7).

Troubling issues arise even at the level of the description of the implementation and supervision stage, and even more so in actual practice. "Once a loan for a particular project is signed," the document says, "attention in the borrowing country [and at the Bank itself] shifts to new projects that are coming along." It adds that "this attitude is understandable." Turning to the question of the Bank's mandate to follow its money, the document is surprisingly cavalier in downplaying the supervisory role of the Bank:

8. Part of the explanation—although hardly a legal excuse—for why the Bank has not lived up to this mandate rests with the geopolitical motives of major powers such as the United States. A remarkably candid 1996 U.S. Government Accounting Office study observes that "much of the impetus behind U.S. participation in the Bank during the Cold War era was derived from the perceived utility of the Bank in containing communist expansionism in the developing world. One Bank official commented, for example, that because of U.S. concern about communist insurgency in the area, the Bank remained active in several sub-Saharan African countries long after the corrupt nature of these governments became evident" (General Accounting Office [GAO] 1996, chap. 2).

The Bank is required by its Articles of Agreement to make arrangements to "ensure that the proceeds of any loan are used only for the
purposes for which the loan was granted." While this "watchdog"
function has been and remains important, the main purpose of supervision is to help ensure that projects achieve their development
objectives and, in particular, to work with the borrowers in identifying and dealing with problems that arise during implementation.
(Baum 1982, 8)

In a document reproduced by the tens of thousands and circulated to every
development ministry in every client country of the Bank around the world,
only lip service is paid to project supervision in general and to fiscal accountability of loans in particular. At the level of the signals the Bank sends
on paper, such "while this" clauses give the unmistakable impression that the
Bank's commitment to following the money is half-hearted at best.

A fair response from the Bank would be that the project cycle document
was last revised in 1982 and the Bank's position on supervision, and particularly its culture and seriousness about corruption, has changed dramatically since then. But as recently as April 1999, it was apparent that the
position had not changed much. "We look more than anything else at what
the project achieves," explained Katharine Marshall, a senior official with
the Bank, "not really the money. We look, for instance, at whether schools
get built, not how the money was spent to build them." Julian Schweitzer, another senior official at the Bank, went even further, making direct reference
to the estimate that one-third of the Bank's funds loaned to Indonesia was
stolen and became criminal debt. "If you take the amount of 30 percent
loss," Schweitzer explained, "it means 70 cents [on the dollar] got used for
development after all. That's a lot better than some places with only 10 cents
on the dollar" (Katharine Marshall and Julian Schweitzer, interview, World
Bank Headquarters, Washington, D.C., 10 April 1999).[9] He was referring to
certain Bank clients in Africa where nearly all of the loan funds are misallocated, diverted, unaccounted for, or simply stolen.

The Bank's first systematic attempt at addressing corruption was the 1997
Framework mentioned at the beginning of the chapter, which admits that
the Bank "should address corruption more explicitly than in the past,"
adding that the Bank was "often reluctant to confront corruption openly because of the issue's political sensitivity and *the lack of demand from borrowers for
assistance in this area*" (World Bank 1997f, 5–6 emphasis added). The document further notes that in the Bank's "vast store of country reports" and its
many thousands of economic and sector reports accumulated over decades

9. Marshall and Schweitzer were specifically designated to discuss the Bank's current views
and practices with the author.

of studying, analyzing, and working deeply within blatant kleptocracies, the subject of corruption is almost never addressed directly but "can be inferred (even if the term is seldom used)" (17–18). Were the Bank to find itself in court attempting to defend its record of due diligence with regard to Article III and its fiduciary responsibilities, the documentary evidence would, by the Bank's own admission, be rather thin. The unwillingness even to utter the word "corruption" between 1944 and 1996—opting instead for obfuscating terms such as "rent-seeking" (which means "eager to rent something" to everyone except economists)—demonstrates a profound reluctance on the part of the Bank to take action against corruption, not only at the level of concrete action but even at the level of discourse.

The 1997 Framework on corruption is a rich document. Its main purpose is to provide an economic justification for the Bank's heightened attention to pandemic corruption (it is a governance matter and "a major barrier to sustainable and equitable development"), and to rationalize a new lending and project-oriented response to the problem. Thus the Bank intends to "design and implement anticorruption strategies," "reform economic policies and strengthen institutions," "support national anticorruption efforts," and help corrupt borrowers get the "basics of public policy and management right" (2–6). All of this requires billions in new lending, projects, expertise, training, and workshops for everyone from elementary school principals to judges to bureaucrats.[10] As already noted, this document paved the way for the Bank to focus most of its attention at the middle level, inside governments and across whole countries—that is, inside the sandwich.

In the course of developing the 1997 Framework and the rationalization for all of this new Bank activity, the authors offered an important insight that ends up being glossed over because it badly undermines the drive to focus the Bank's effort at the societal level rather than at the much more manageable and effective microlevel of project supervision and implementation or macrolevel of international coordination. The document sets the stage for this insight by arguing that corruption is a divergence from formal rules: "A defining characteristic of the environment in which corruption occurs is a divergence between the formal and the informal rules governing behavior in the public sector. The Bank is unaware of any country that does not have rules against corruption, although not all countries have all the rules that may be necessary." In a passage that refers to the Indonesian case in the

---

10. In October 2001 the International Bank for Reconstruction and Development (IBRD) website contained a section entitled "Ten Things the Bank Does." Number seven showcased the institution's response to corruption. "Since 1996, the Bank has launched more than 600 anticorruption programs and governance initiatives in almost 100 client countries. Initiatives range from training judges to organizing workshops and teaching investigative reporting to journalists." It also mentions tough new guidelines in procurement (International Bank for Reconstruction and Development [IBRD] 2001).

footnote, the document continues, "Where corruption is systemic, the formal rules remain in place, but they are superseded by informal rules" "Seen in this light," the document continues, "strengthening institutions to control corruption is about shifting the emphasis back to the formal rules." The rub, of course, is in this innocent notion "shifting the emphasis." Edging closer to the crux of the matter, the document says that the Bank must start "by understanding why the informal rules are at odds with the formal rules and then by tackling the causes of the divergence" (13).

The obvious problem here is that whether the Bank is shifting an emphasis or tackling a cause, in most instances the divergence the document refers to is none other than a manifestation of the power of individuals and groups in society to routinely ignore the rules and regulations in the legal books. In short, corruption leaves behind the pristine realm of economics and reassumes its place in the supposedly untouchable realm of power and politics. The document offers a fleeting recognition of this point that ends up getting glossed over in the rest of the text: "In some countries the primary reason for divergence may be political," the authors admit, "a manifestation of the way power is exercised and retained. *This limits what the Bank can do to help outside the framework of its projects*" (13–14, emphasis added). In fact, this is true not just in some countries, but in nearly all the severely corrupt countries the Bank has as clients. And in this single passage, the authors of the 1997 Framework deliver the death blow to all the other plans and strategies they discuss for the Bank's grand response to systemic corruption. The greatest danger for the Bank's future and credibility in this area is that if most of its efforts are not focused on dramatically reducing corruption in the narrow realm of the Bank's own projects, damaging reports of serious corruption in Bank projects will continue to surface.

PROJECT SUPERVISION IN PRACTICE

The 1997 Framework and subsequent documents on corruption (World Bank 2000d; Aguilar, Gill, and Pino 2000) state that preventing fraud and corruption in Bank-financed projects is one of four levels at which the Bank is now combating corruption. Although this element is crowded out by the much larger discussion of the Banks plans for new projects and lending to fight corruption, it is worth discussing actual project supervision for two reasons: to assess whether changes proposed in the 1997 Framework or announced subsequently by the Bank will be effective and to gauge the vulnerability of the Bank to legal action for gross negligence and direct violations of the legal mandates in its *Articles of Agreement* in its past and current operations. It is not terribly difficult to demonstrate that the fiduciary mandates in the Bank's charter were seriously neglected in the Bank's voluminous paper trail—both in its reports and in its procedure booklets. But a much more important indicator of Bank guilt or innocence on the charge of collusion in allowing criminal debt to accumulate in its own operations is in the routine supervision practices on the ground and in the field. Thus, the first question is, was there a gap between policy and practice in safeguarding loaned funds? And second, even if the procedures on paper were carried out to the letter in practice, were the safeguards adequate and did they reasonably meet the standards of the mandate in the articles? In the parlance of development specialists, who speak of a results orientation, can the Bank point to concrete results over time in the form of evidence of a low or declining rate of theft of the resources it loaned?

This review of project supervision practices draws on the author's extensive field research on the Indonesian case and numerous confidential interviews with Bank officials in Jakarta and Washington beginning in 1990 and ending in 2001. The most recent interviews were with Bank staff who worked on more than one hundred projects in several African countries. The interviews and field visits are supplemented by documentation and reports, some of which were leaked by Bank staff members who were eager to accelerate the pace of reforms and were frustrated by what they described as a dominant culture of indifference to corruption. Pushing the pace of reforms has included revealing internal information that is potentially quite damaging to the Bank's reputation and undermines its denials of culpability for the accumulation of criminal debt (and by extension its fiscal liability to absorb a portion of the losses).

This section makes liberal use of quotations from Bank staff with extensive experience in Bank operations, project supervision and implementation, and internal efforts to challenge the culture of indifference on corruption inside the Bank. It should be noted that these internal sources see a mixed picture in the Bank since the late 1990s. On the one hand, the problem of corruption is receiving more attention now than at any time in the Bank's history, but, on the other hand, supervision budgets are smaller for projects and new schemes have been hatched to facilitate disbursing money faster to client countries and with less accountability. The intense pressure to disburse loans conflicts not only with project quality, but also with any efforts to ensure that funds get used for their intended purpose. This section concludes with findings by the U.S. government General Accounting Office in April 2000 showing that the Bank's efforts to combat corruption have yet to yield significant results. These findings contradict the Bank's own more upbeat assessment of the progress it is making (World Bank 2000d).

The supervision of projects consists of many components. For fiscal purposes, the most widely used instrument for the Bank is audits. "We insist that all projects are audited by accredited agencies in the countries concerned," a senior Bank official pointed out when pressed on whether the Bank was fulfilling its fiduciary mandate set forth in Article III (Katharine Marshall, interview, World Bank Headquarters, Washington, D.C., 10 April 1999). The fact that the Bank requires audits by accredited agencies certainly signals that the institution is both serious about and effective in meeting the fiduciary mandate of its charter. But what counts is not procedures on the books or hoops jumped through. What matters is what actually happens on the ground and whether those activities constitute effective arrangements to ensure that Bank funds get used for their intended purpose.

The people in the Bank who know the most about this are its task managers, the individuals who oversee more closely than anyone else the design, implementation, supervision, and evaluation of Bank projects. Although Bank officials regularly state that effective systems of financial management and documentation are in place and functioning, current and former task managers who watch as billions of dollars disappear tell a very different story. On how well project expenditures are documented, a seasoned task manager explained the situation this way:

> They're documented in a very weak way. There's so much of it where we just don't know. We're trying to make progress [in following the money], and it's happening now. It never happened before, with some rare exceptions. It is happening, but it's a long way from achieving critical mass [as a standard Bank mode of operation] in terms of being able to step back and say "we've got a reasonably tight program here, we're on top of it."

(Unless otherwise noted, the quotations used in this section are from confidential interviews conducted in Washington, D.C. in April 1999.) In response to senior management's assurances that reliable audits are conducted, this individual disagreed:

> They've always had that [local accredited audits]. But the big pressure for the longest time, and it still exists to a large degree, is [that] the audit has to be done on time. But the quality of the audit? Whether they do anything about it afterwards? That for a long time was irrelevant. The only thing that came up on the radar screen [in the project management process or cycle] was "the audit hasn't been submitted, the audit's overdue." That would come up. In many cases, you get an audit in—and this was the past, and I'm sure they've cut down the time lag on it—in many cases the audit would come in a year and a half, sometimes two years, after the fiscal year in question. It's too damn late—because whatever was wrong, forget it.

The real opportunity for an auditor to call attention to serious irregularities in a project is not through the standard boilerplate numeric report, but through what the Bank calls a management letter. A task manager with extensive project experience explained:

> Even assuming the audit points to serious errors, in many cases they
> don't submit "management letters," which are basically, apart from
> the number crunching, letters that gives the auditor's opinion on
> the fiscal management of the project. Either you don't get them [the
> letters], or if you do get them you don't pay attention. The auditors
> themselves—and I've talked to a number of them—they admit freely
> that all they do is look at the books. If the books balance, they say
> "we've looked at it according to international auditing standards,
> and we find that the records are in order." But the records them-
> selves could be fraudulent. Auditors will tell you it's not their job.

Apart from these routine and arguably ineffectual audits, there is a stronger
weapon in the task manager's supervision arsenal known as a postprocurement audit.

> [T]hat's when you bring in what we call a post-procurement audit,
> and you actually go out and check [the validity of invoices]. Typi-
> cally, "you bought three hundred air conditioners? Where are they?"
> You look at a couple. "There's three in this building? Let me see
> them." Check the price. This is a class A air conditioner and you
> were billed for a class B air conditioner at twice the price—you
> know, whatever it is, you go out and check. So the [routine] audits
> don't tell you a thing. In fact, I can tell you from my own personal
> experience that in many cases, really good book keeping where the
> records are impeccable, you found flagrant fraud being committed.
> The books are beautiful. The weird thing is why the corrupt borrow-
> ers don't make a better effort to produce a really good set of books,
> because that wows everyone. "You want something?" Bing, you can
> access it. "Oh this contract? Here are the records on it. Here's the
> contract." You got the whole thing. And I've gone in, it's all there,
> but it's all fraud.[11]

11. The respondent continued, "I've argued for years that having a system is fine. Having an
accounting system and having safeguards and audits—it's all fine in principle. But if you don't
have people who are running the system who are trustworthy, you're in bad shape." He said
that spot-checking is needed all the way through a project. "When I used to go out in the field
on a project, and very few task managers would do this, I would spend a day with the accountant on the project. And I would just randomly say 'let me see this, this and that [in-
voice],' and then I would take those transactions and go from A to Z with them. Go out and
see whether in fact this vendor exists. And I've had cases where they didn't exist. You have an
invoice, a name of a company, and they supplied office machines. You go look, there's some
office machines sitting there, and you can't count all of them. They've never been used.

Thus it is fair to ask, has the Bank reasonably satisfied its Article III mandate if it claims that it conducted routine annual assessments of project books by accredited auditors? According to a task manager who worked on more than one hundred projects in Africa, such claims fall short.

> You've got to go beyond what's on paper. It's only paper. We've had cases when we go out in the field. You go to the [project] accounting office and you ask for documents. "Oh we don't have them. They're over at the ministry. They're somewhere else. We'll have them for you next week." I swear to God, some guy sits up all night writing up invoices. You can see, it's the same handwriting. Fifty different suppliers and it's all the same handwriting. And sometimes they're so saturated with writing that they put the same thing down on five different invoices without knowing it or picking it up. And it goes through the system. And then our guys [back at Bank headquarters] look at it and don't even pick it up.

The accredited auditors conduct narrow assessments that are almost pro forma and that do not detect fraud that ranges from the subtle to the blatant. The task manager concluded: "And so, money gone. In the accounting sense, everything is fine." In direct response to the assurances from senior management that responsible audits were being conducted on projects, this individual added, "But you have to keep in mind, if they said they're doing post-procurement audits, fine. If they're doing a spot audit of the books, it's next to useless. . . . The whole thing is a farce. If somebody tells me a project has been audited, I say, 'So what? Let me see the audit.'"[12]

They're just sitting there. So you have this sense they were just bought for the sake of buying them. You go out and you check at a store that sells office machines—the same make and model number. You price it and you find it's half the price of what we're billed for. You go to the address [of the vendor] and they don't exist. You ask around the neighborhood and they never did exist. So here I've got a fraudulent invoice for equipment that isn't really being used at twice the market price. I mean if that isn't fraud, I don't know what is. And so you come back with that information, and you find that it's a pattern, you know you've got a serious problem on your hands. The auditors don't pick that stuff up."

12. The source added, "They never really audited the lending operations. They audited the Bank's own internal budget. We had the Operations Evaluation Department auditing the projects, but not necessarily from a financial point of view, just from a goals point of view. It was indeed required every year to have a local audit done. But if the audits don't uncover the problems sufficiently, or if they skirt the problems, and if they don't submit a management letter, which would detail in written form the problems, then you've only got a paper exercise that doesn't bring about any changes." One task manager I interviewed pointed out that there are also serious conflicts of interest within the international auditing profession that cast doubts on the reliability of audits of the books for Bank projects. He explained, "I had a case where an independent auditor performed audits on a project. They had probably ten times more business on that [same] project—setting up a management information system, setting up accounts, and so on. I asked [a professional accountant at a major firm] if there's

One argument worthy of careful consideration is that tighter supervision is expensive and that reaching a high degree of certainty that Bank funds are not being stolen could be even more costly to the Bank and its clients than the resources currently being lost. "You're always balancing efficiency against stopping leakage," a senior Bank official pointed out (Julian Schweitzer, interview, World Bank Headquarters, Washington, D.C., 10 April 1999). Article III explicitly requires that, in carrying out its fiduciary responsibilities on projects, the Bank give serious consideration to matters of economy and efficiency. Is it really feasible to conduct postprocurement audits more aggressively, to price air conditioners, or to absorb and follow up on management letters from auditors that raise troubling patterns of corruption? The 1997 Framework explains:

> The extent to which the Bank can check statements of expenditure is constrained by several factors. At headquarters it is often difficult to match items claimed for reimbursement with line items in the project accounts and to determine whether the items are eligible for Bank financing. Moreover, Bank staff conducting supervision missions carry out only limited on-site reviews of documentation due to claims on their time for resolving other project management and implementation problems. (World Bank 1997f, 24)

The number of transactions involved is not small.

> The stocks of IBRD [International Bank for Research and Development] and IDA [International Development Association] projects currently disbursing are $88.4 billion and $42.5 billion, respectively, against an annual flow of new loan approvals of $14.5 billion and $6.9 billion, respectively, in FY96. This stock of projects collectively generates about 40,000 individual procurement contracts annually, of which 10,000 (60 percent of value) are conducted under international competitive bidding rules, and 20,000 (30 percent of value) are conducted under local bidding rules. About 10,000 contracts un-

---

a conflict of interest if I'm an accountant-auditor, and I've set up the books, and I've assisted the client in financial management, and now I come in and audit that same client. [He] said, 'Yeah it is, but it happens all the time.' He said it's something that the industry has never tried to address. The accounting industry, like the banking industry, is not going to jeopardize their relationships with their clients. If you're Price Waterhouse Coopers Librand, are you going to go in and audit the books of your client and say that things are in atrocious shape with all kinds of fraud and embezzlement? All you can do is say the books are in order. It's very difficult to get somebody who can do it in an unbiased way. And even when those firms are not directly involved with a particular project or company, they often have the government or a ministry as a client. For them it's a business decision. He told me that it is a conflict, but we don't look at it as a conflict."

dergo prior review by Bank staff (60 percent of value). The remainder are subject to what is termed "post-audit" selective checking after the event to verify that procurement followed the procedures specified in loan documents. (24 n. 27)[13]

It is not clear whether in claiming the remaining 30,000 contracts are subject to postaudit selective checking that the Bank means that the audits are actually carried out or that the contracts are simply eligible for such oversight. A source who worked for years as a task manager argues that postaudits are, in fact, rarely carried out.

> In a post-procurement check, you take a transaction from A to Z. How can we, a banking institution, claiming to be the financial partners in an operation, and having the right of supervising the project in the physical sense, how can we go out there in a two-week supervision mission and not spend a day with the accountant? I can assure you, it does not happen. It is only the rare occasion that it does. (confidential interview, Washington, D.C., April 1999)

On the trade-off between cost and effectiveness, the former task manager agreed that we need to be realistic. "There's no question that any institution is going to have inefficiency and money stolen," he said. "The point is, do you just sit back and say 'oh it's all right,' or do you make the best effort to contain it?" As a practical matter, he argued that the key was to target the worst cases to set a tone: "You take the most egregious cases and you deal with it." He continued, "I always like to point out, you've got speed limit signs on the highway, and these represent all the safeguards on paper that Bank people talk about putting in place. But if you don't have a cop behind a billboard every so often, and if they don't see someone pulled over every so often, then people don't obey the speed laws." He drew an additional parallel to the Internal Revenue Service (IRS) in the United States. Tax payment is the United States is similar to local Bank project management in that both involve self-reporting. The IRS enforces honest reporting by in-depth and aggressive audits of only 1–3 percent of all corporate and individual tax payers. There are cash penalties for errors and jail penalties for fraud. Although the actual risk of being audited is low, many tax payers fear they will be caught if they cheat. It is not that a large number of audits is conducted, but

---

13. Thus 30,000 out of 40,000 procurement contracts, representing three-fourths of total purchases and 40 percent of total value, are not carried out under international competitive bidding rules. It is overwhelmingly in this realm that some 30 percent of the value gets stolen inside Indonesia. Note that a single project could have hundreds and even thousands of procurement contracts within it in any given year. Although 40,000 sounds like a staggering number, the number of active projects is much smaller.

that tax payers know there is a real chance their fraud will be detected and that there will be real and even serious consequences for committing fraud. It is this concern with being caught or paying a price that is most lacking in the Bank's approach.

Many task managers at the Bank complain that in many instances corruption is so pervasive in Bank projects that after decades of developmental effort in which corruption is tolerated, there are very few positive results that can be shown from the lending and projects. One task manager with more than a decade of experience on projects across a variety of sectors and in numerous countries rejected the claim by the senior Bank official (quoted previously) that although a 30 percent loss to corruption is a problem, there is still a significant and positive impact from the other 70 percent:

> That's the old argument, isn't it? They've been saying that for years.
> . . . There are a couple fallacies there, and it is much too cavalier an
> attitude. That's because, in fact, my experience has been—and it's
> the experience of a lot of other people there [on the operations side
> of the Bank]—if they're busy stealing 30 percent, they're not paying
> any real attention to the other 70, even assuming 30 percent is all
> they're taking. What you're really doing is really ruining the whole
> effectiveness of the investment itself. I try to tell people . . . it's like
> giving the money to buy a car but they're stealing the money that
> would buy the gasoline. So what good is the car? It is a fact, I can
> demonstrate it, and I'll stand by it. I'll prove it anytime.

He offered the following example:

> You cut corners and nobody cares. If you let out a contract for
> $2 million, and you get the few civil servants at the top sharing
> $600,000 or 30 percent, do they care if the contractor puts in con-
> crete that is just sand and water? Do they care if the contractor
> doesn't put reinforcing steel in the structures? They don't care. So
> when Bank people say we're at least getting 70 cents of good devel-
> opment on the dollar, no you don't. Because the contractor either
> has to make back the money that he's kicked back, or he just figures,
> "hey, it's open season, I do what I want and no one is going to chal-
> lenge me." And so you have this feeding frenzy, and the end result is
> you get very little development.[14]

14. He also rejected arguments that small-scale corruption does not seriously undermine projects. "If you see that happening [on a small scale]," he said, "you can almost bet that with every bit of procurement there's some hanky panky going on one way or another. It adds up and it's a constant blood-letting, every day, money's going out, $500 here, $1,000 there, $3,000 there. It's a constant blood-letting. How can the project function?"

Putting aside who is fiscally responsible to repay the lost 30 percent, he questioned what genuine value a country or the poor really get from projects conducted in ways in which such levels of theft are tolerated: "If you get only one dollar out of ten that goes to the poor, is that really worth it? And have you done anything to strengthen the economy for the long term? No. You've only nourished a corrupt government that has no intention of providing services. To me, those arguments are hollow."

He pointed to a startling pattern in the African projects that the Bank has funded for decades and in which he participated directly as a task manager. "All you have to do in the case of Africa is travel the length of the continent and see how many derelict projects, buildings rotting, infrastructure rotting because we financed it. . . . I can't remember one project in Nigeria, out of all the ones I worked on, that you could look back and say, 'Well, hey, we did a good job'—we, us and the Nigerians." As of the mid-1990s, he explained, the Bank had done approximately 2,200 projects in sub-Saharan Africa, nearly all of them being seriously undermined by the lack of Bank supervision.

> Ask anybody to tell you how many they can think of that really succeeded out of 2,200 projects. Even when you take out the calamities, the drought that has destroyed or hindered progress, or you take out the civil wars. Even when you take all those other factors out, you've still got an awful lot of things that have been done that have gotten nowhere. The money is spent and the debt is incurred. Is the infrastructure there? No. Is it being maintained? No. It's just an endless parade of failure.

He was cautiously optimistic about signs of progress:

> It is happening but it has yet to change the culture of the Bank to a considerable extent. I do see beginnings of it. People are using the word "fraud" in meetings. It's cropping up in memos on the operations side. I'm not talking about the PR side of the anti-corruption battle, where we have our EDI [Economic Development Institute] going out and conducting workshops, where they're training journalists how to expose corruption, or what to look for and how to deal with it in the press. These are all very positive things.

But he added that too often the Bank adjusts to criticisms and problems more with public relations campaigns than with substance.

> The thing that troubles me a lot is the Bank's way of dealing with issues—and I think this is still a major part of the Bank's culture—is

reorganize, shuffle around, change the names, do anything but actually deal with the issues. There's all this appearance—and appearances are everything—that we're doing something when in fact you see in a number of instances where not only are we not doing anything, but we're going backwards. I'm sure a lot of people would challenge me on that, but I don't think that their challenges would stand up.

At root, according to one task manager, the obstacles to dealing effectively with corruption today are the same ones identified in *The Wapenhans Report* in the early 1990s. The most important problem is the "culture of approvals," a tremendous pressure manifested within the Bank (although rooted also in political-economic pressures from lending states that want the business and sales generated by Bank projects). President Wolfensohn has elevated the status of improving project quality and challenging corruption within the Bank. But, explained the operations specialist, there is still a basic inconsistency even in Wolfensohn's approach:

> Although Wolfensohn came on board and there was more emphasis on supervision, there is still this schizophrenia. If you talk to task managers today, they have less budget for supervision now than they did five years ago. It's saying one thing and doing something else. We've got all these anti-corruption activities, and that's positive and long overdue. But at the same time there is still high pressure to lend, and we have things like this [the new draft certification proposal for disbursements] coming up that are going to make it easier to steal, and [provide] less budget for supervision. We're going in two contradictory directions.[15]

Wolfensohn's impact at the Bank has been mixed. There is no doubt that corruption has a higher public profile than at any time in the Bank's history. Many task managers in operations, who struggled in vain for decades to try to inject a higher awareness of corruption and its impact, now feel the tide is turning. But the incessant pressure to lend coming from the executive directors pulls in the opposite direction. According to one well-positioned task manager:

15. The idea behind the new disbursement plan is that a country's domestic project management capability will be evaluated, upgraded, and then certified by the Bank as fiscally qualified and thus responsible. The task manager found this approach alarming. "And they say now we will lend to you. Not only that, but because you have a system in place that we've approved, we'll give you the money in tranches. If you report back every quarter, or whatever, we'll just keep releasing the money. In my opinion, and a number of other people at the Bank—certainly people at the operational level—it's just inviting more problems because even with the controls we have in place now, this spot-checking and so on, we can't begin to do justice to proper fiscal management."

I think Wolfensohn has opened the door now. You hear so many stories about him. My sense when I walk down the halls is that one in five may be positive about Wolfensohn, but the other four are not. One way or another he's turned their world upside down, some of them more than others. He is unfortunately sending some mixed signals, and frankly that's the biggest complaint I hear. When I talk to people in the hall, they say "anti-corruption, right, but then he's pushing us for lending." I think the biggest complaint I hear about him is that he's sending these contradictory signals. It's a fair and true complaint. But I also think that if I were in his shoes, knowing the Bank as I do, I'm amazed that he's done what he's done. You're talking about an entrenched bureaucracy that has not only been accountable to no one in the past, but has had so much wealth to play with that nobody could touch them, no one was able to touch them, no one wanted to touch them. And here this upstart comes in and starts screaming and jumping up and down, and swearing and everything else. And this is just a total shock. He has turned their world upside down. But at the same time, how do you change a huge bureaucracy with the kind of history the Bank has, and the power that it has? I'm surprised he's been able to do what he's done. I have a feeling if it were entirely up to him, that we wouldn't be getting these mixed signals quite so much. But he's got to play ball with some people some of the time. This is not a one man show, as much as he tries to make it so.

The answer, this individual agrees, is to reduce lending until the quality of administration and supervision in projects, both on the Bank's part and on the borrower's side, is improved to a degree that the resources are not squandered. He concluded: "We're a long way from turning the corner on the Bank's culture. There will not be real progress until there's a genuine slowing down of the lending program. Historically, but certainly over the last 20 years, you could demonstrate with ease that the Bank has lent more money than the borrowers could absorb."

There is no disputing that since the mid-1990s the World Bank has been talking more about the problem of corruption. But what has been achieved in practice? The United States Congress became so alarmed by the Bank's failure to ensure its loan funds were not stolen that it requested an investigation by the GAO. The GAO published its findings in a devastating report in April 2000 entitled *Management Controls Stronger, but Challenges in Fighting Corruption Remain.* That the Bank's previous arrangements to safeguard loans were weak was not even a matter open for dispute by the GAO team. The objective of the investigation was to determine the effectiveness of new efforts on the part of the Bank since 1995. Although noting some progress, the GAO found that "challenges remain and further action will be required before the Bank can provide reasonable assurance that project funds are spent according to the Bank's guidelines" (General Accounting Office [GAO] 2000, 5). The GAO also concluded that "the Bank and some borrowers do not always comply with Bank procedures on project auditing and Bank supervision of borrowers' procurement and financial management practices" (6). The investigators reported that "Bank studies on the quality of Bank supervision do not fully address key performance problems reported by external and internal auditors" (6). Finally, the GAO found that the Bank "does not publicly report progress in implementing management control improvements" (6–7).

The GAO found that Bank officials and staff were aware that their loan supervision was poor. The investigators wrote:

> Although the Bank has long had an internal audit function and a system of management controls, the Bank recognized that its internal oversight mechanisms were weak, according to several officials we spoke to. These officials indicated that the Bank lacked a central focal point for reporting and reviewing allegations of wrongdoing and sufficient expertise to investigate allegations of wrongdoing. In addition, while the Bank expected its staff to exhibit strong ethical behavior, the Bank did not have a strong ethics awareness program. The Bank's external auditor reported in 1998 that the Bank's internal audit department—a key management oversight unit—had a fairly restricted scope of audit coverage and played a limited role within the Bank. For example, about 78 percent of the 206 internal audit reports conducted from fiscal years 1995 through 1997 were focused on administrative compliance issues, such as country mission office procedures, rather than on determining whether project funds were being used as intended. (GAO 2000, 11)

The findings could hardly be more damaging. Even after the Bank's new aggressive stance on corruption, only one in five internal audit reports after 1995 dealt seriously with Article III mandates that the Bank ensure its funds are used properly. Commenting on new procedures at the Bank to reduce how much is stolen, a source at the GAO explained, "they can tell you how much they have spent but cannot tell you if it is being spent as intended" (GAO official, confidential communication April 2000, Washington, D.C.). This finding supports testimony from Bank task managers that anticorruption arrangements before 1995 were utterly ineffective.

When the GAO report was submitted, Senator Mitch McConnell, who had requested the investigation, released a letter criticizing the past practices of the Bank and its slow progress in correcting the most serious problems that lead to criminal debt. Among the problems with the Bank's efforts at reform, Senator McConnell writes that "new initiatives introduced [by the Bank] in 1998 to improve financial and procurement procedures only apply to 14% of the Bank's 1,500 projects. In recent audits, 17 of 25 borrowers showed a lack of understanding or noncompliance with procurement rules. GAO's review of 12 randomly selected projects identified 5 projects where the borrowing countries implementing agencies had little or no experience managing projects." He added that "[the] GAO determined that solving [corruption] problems is made more difficult because audits are often late and of poor quality, and the Bank does not evaluate the quality of audits" (McConnell 2000).

Senator McConnell also raised the problem of corruption in Indonesia, particularly his "concern about flagrant abuses which compromised the World Bank's program in Indonesia." According to the senator, "The Bank's Country Director [Dennis de Tray] ignored internal reports detailing program kickbacks, skimming and fraud because he was unwilling to upset the Suharto family and their cronies whom he believed were responsible for Indonesia's economic boom" (McConnell 2000).

THE INDONESIAN CASE

Indonesia has the potential to be a test case for discovering if legal challenges are a viable channel through which to win relief from the high levels of criminal debt accumulated through Bank projects and to influence the Bank to more quickly bring its project supervision in line with the mandates set forth in Article III. The regime responsible for stealing public funds was pushed out in 1998 and was replaced in 1999 by a democratically elected government. The Indonesians can also show that Bank funds were systematically stolen and that the Bank or the governments controlling the Bank were aware of the rampant corruption pervading the Indonesian state. Indonesians are well positioned to plead at the International Court of Justice that they are burdened by a staggering level of criminal debt that accumulated in part because the Bank violated Article III and negligently loaned billions to the Suharto regime despite detailed knowledge not just of corruption throughout the system, but also of corruption within their own project portfolio.

The World Bank has tried to evade responsibility for and knowledge of corruption in their project in Indonesia. But their defense is weak. In an excellent history of the Bank, based on access to tens of thousands of internal documents and files, Devesh Kapur and colleagues write that with regard to an early awareness of corruption in the Suharto government, "the Bank clearly had this issue in view from the beginning of its (1968) renewed relationship with the country. But the relevant documents convey little sense that the phenomenon had to or could be fully eradicated. Indeed, [Robert] McNamara himself did not warm to the issue until late in his tenure, at which time he became quite vociferous." The authors continue:

In his final presidential visit [in 1979] he gave almost the same message verbatim to assembled ministers then to Vice President Malik, and finally to President Suharto, face to face. McNamara explained that "it was also necessary to maintain the emphasis on reducing corruption. Outside Indonesia, this was much talked about and the world had the impression, rightly or wrongly, that it was greater in Indonesia than in any but perhaps one other country. . . . It was like a cancer eating away at the society." (Kapur, Lewis, and Webb 1997, 492)[16]

There is no hint that this lecture from McNamara resulted in any tightening of Bank supervision of projects in Indonesia. Indeed, although his plan was not adopted, the Bank's resident director proposed moving away from projects and providing Indonesia with large sectoral loans that would leave control over disbursement entirely to a government that the Bank's own top management viewed as among the most corrupt on the planet. Perhaps recognizing that McNamara was unlikely to shift the Bank's posture toward Indonesia, President Suharto "is recorded as making no trace of a response to the demarche on corruption" (Kapur, Lewis, and Webb 1997, 492). Suharto certainly recognized that his country had a uniquely close relationship with the Bank and McNamara—"Indonesia was the presidentially designated jewel in the Bank's operational crown" (493). At a minimum, it is apparent that there was an early appreciation in the World Bank of the ruinous levels of corruption being perpetrated in Indonesia under Suharto's military-backed rule.

It was not until the late 1990s that the corruption issue erupted into full public view in Indonesia. At the end of July 1997, the World Bank's country director, Dennis de Tray, and the vice president for East Asia and the Pacific region, Jean-Michel Severino, issued an angry press release denying that roughly a third of the Bank's loans to Indonesia routinely leaked into the hands of corrupt officials in the Indonesian government. They were responding to a press conference in Jakarta reporting that the conventional wisdom inside the Bank, both in Indonesia and among Indonesia hands in Washington, was that such levels of corruption were common.[17] The Bank's angry press release characterized the statements made in the Jakarta press conference as dishonest, saying they had "misrepresented" the Bank's work on behalf of Indonesia's poor. Severino said that the Bank had checked the accusations and had "found nothing to support such an estimate" of corruption of Bank funds. The estimates had, however, been based on inter-

16. The authors are quoting from a memorandum of the then director of the Resident Staff, Indonesia, Jean Baneth.
17. I was the primary speaker at the press conference and was directly involved in the debates that ensued.

views with Bank officials, both in Jakarta and the United States spanning the period 1990–97. The Bank's denial, carried on newswires around the globe, said the accusations were "demonstrably untrue" and that the Bank's staff "know exactly" where all the loan money goes. It added, "We do not tolerate corruption in our programs. On this principle there is no compromise" (World Bank 1997g).

Even as these false and misleading statements were being distributed, Bank staff in Jakarta were drafting a secret document that would not be leaked until nearly a year later. Entitled *Summary of RSI Staff Views Regarding the Problem of "Leakage" from World Bank Project Budgets* and dated August 1997, the document presents what it terms an "operational overview" of the corruption problem in Bank projects in Indonesia.[18] The document opens with this "unequivocal statement of fact": "Documentation of procurement, implementation, disbursement and audits for Bank-financed projects are generally complete and conform to all Bank requirements; we have moved aggressively to resolve each and every irregularity for which we have documents (as well as many cases of preventive action and informal corrections of problems)." This declaration is followed immediately by a direct admission that in Indonesia the Bank had not made effective arrangements that ensured that the funds it loaned were used for their intended purpose: "In aggregate we estimate that at least 20–30% of GOI [government of Indonesia] development budget funds are diverted through informal payments to GOI staff and politicians, and *there is no basis to claim a smaller 'leakage' for Bank projects as our controls have little practical effect on the methods generally used*" (World Bank 1997m, emphasis added).

Among other things, the document makes the following points:

1. That some officials were expected to pay bribes in order to be placed in "wet" (lucrative) positions in the bureaucracy linked to development projects.
2. That leakage pressures increased during the two years leading up to the 1997 national elections and that Suharto's political party machine, GOLKAR, was the culprit behind the additional squeeze on the system.
3. That audits by government officials at the ministerial and provincial levels are designed mainly to find issues or "mistakes" in project implementation, that can then be fixed or ignored for a fee ranging up to 10 percent of the project value.
4. That corruption across Indonesian government ministries is not

18. In January 1999, another Bank document on Indonesia was leaked. This one cited corruption as one of a set of "serious structural problems which were well known to the Bank" (World Bank 1999f, 1).

uniform, in the experience of Bank staff, and ranges from relatively low (less than 15 percent, although on very large loans) in the Ministry of Health and the Ministry of Mines and Energy; to moderate (15–25 percent) in eight ministries, including agriculture, education, public works, and religious affairs; to high (over 25 percent) in an additional four ministries, including forestry and home affairs.[19]

Over the course of the New Order, the Bank loaned Indonesia almost $30 billion. The best estimate of theft rates in Indonesian projects is one-third of the loan value. Thus Indonesia's criminal debt linked to World Bank sources is roughly $10 billion. During the military dictatorship of Suharto, Indonesian citizens were extremely limited in their abilities to expose and stop corruption by government officials and Suharto cronies. The same cannot be said for the Bank. If it had been committed to fulfilling its fiduciary mandate in Article III, it could have raised the corruption problem as a matter that by law the Bank was mandated to address. It could have taken a variety of measures, including intensifying the supervision of its projects, thereby reducing the levels of corruption in its own operations, even if it could not stop the rampant corruption across the government. It could have threatened gradually to reduce its lending to Indonesia over a period of years if the leakage of Bank project funds was not progressively curtailed. And as a last resort, it could have halted lending completely on the grounds that continued lending under circumstances of persistently high levels of theft was incompatible with the Bank's *Articles of Agreement*. The Bank did none of these things.

In a 1998 article published in Indonesia's main English-language daily, the *Jakarta Post*, the Bank's resident director attempted to deny any Bank responsibility for Indonesia's criminal debt burden by shifting all the responsibility to the Indonesian side (de Tray 1998). He invokes the Bank's notion of "ownership" of projects—a concept designed to get governments to embrace Bank projects more thoroughly in the partnership between the Bank and borrowers.

The development projects and reform programs the Bank finances do not belong to us: they are owned by the government. It is the government that is responsible for ensuring that the money it borrows is spent for the purposes intended and that it is protected from leakage through bribery and corruption. This is not to say that we take

19. This report, also known as the Dice memorandum, was followed in October 1998 by a World Bank mission report written by Jane Loos confirming the pervasiveness of corruption in Indonesia. See Bruce Rich (chap. 2 in this volume) for a discussion of the Loos report (World Bank 1999f, chap. 2).

no action ourselves in this regard. We have always audited, reviewed and monitored our projects to try to safeguard them. We have the strongest and strictest procedures of any development institution. We are continuously seeking ways of strengthening our controls.

The idea that a client state should own Bank projects makes good sense as a development technique to augment a government's commitment to the projects. However, this notion of ownership never appears in the *Articles of Agreement,* and it certainly cannot nullify the Article III legal mandate.

The evidence is clear that the Bank knew Indonesia was seriously corrupt as far back as the late 1960s. Moreover, the Bank's resident staff members in Jakarta argued in their confidential 1997 assessment that although Bank procedures were followed, the procedures were ineffective in stemming the accumulation of criminal debt from Bank operations. Furthermore, the new resident director for the Bank in Jakarta, Mark Baird, admitted publicly in a seminar that indeed the losses due to corruption had been huge. But when pressed on the question of the Bank's failures to ensure funds were used for their intended purpose, and thus the institution's legal obligation to share in the criminal debt burden, Baird responded: "According to the interpretation of the Bank's internal lawyers, the violations of Article III entitle us to call in all our loans immediately to Indonesia as due in full" (Mark Baird, resident director of the World Bank for Indonesia, comments at the Indonesia Next conference, May 2001, Grand Hyatt Hotel, Jakarta, Indonesia).

The World Bank's lawyers are entitled to their interpretation of the *Articles of Agreement,* and legal advocates for Indonesia's indebted citizens are entitled to their opposing view. It is a matter for a tribunal or the World Court to settle. Under a new democratic government, a clear legal basis exists for Indonesians to sue for relief of part or all of the $10 billion in criminal debt that accrued until 1998. For three decades, the Bank continued to supply new loans despite full knowledge that a significant share of the funds was being stolen. Indonesia's citizens continue to bear the burden of repaying these funds, plus interest, despite the funds' never being used for development purposes.

CONCLUSIONS

When elections were held and the new Indonesian government was installed in October 1999, it was immediately apparent that Indonesia's relations with the International Monetary Fund (IMF) and World Bank would have to be mended. Both institutions had suspended their fund transfers to Indonesia because of the Bank Bali scandal (IMF money) and because of Indonesia's brutal withdrawal from East Timor in summer 1999. The economic situation in Indonesia remained dire, and there was an almost 6 percent shortfall in the national budget. The gap would have to be filled through the Consultative Group on Indonesia (CGI), chaired by the World Bank. The structural power of a capital controller such as the Bank in such circumstances is enormous. Not surprisingly, not one word was uttered by the Wahid government or by the Megawati government that followed about the lost $10 billion. Indeed, Indonesia's top economic ministers have gone out of their way to reassure the Bank and the IMF that Indonesia will only ask for debt rescheduling, not write-offs.[20]

It is unlikely that the World Bank and its rich shareholder governments will confront their complicity in amassing a huge and criminal debt burden on poor Indonesians without popular political action aimed at the Bank and, ironically, the new Indonesian government itself. Demonstrations, lobbying, and protests would open up the political leverage Indonesian officials need to press the Bank for debt reductions. There are signs that pressure is beginning, although it is still at too low a level to have an impact. In January 2000, one thousand demonstrators gathered outside the World Bank mission in Jakarta demanding relief for stolen debt. When World Bank President Wolfensohn visited Indonesia in February 2000, he was met with angry protests and had his minivan pelted with rotten eggs. Any meaningful reinvention of the World Bank must include confronting the problem of stolen funds. This is not just a matter of institutional tinkering at the Bank, but also one of sharing the costs of debts still borne today from illegal practices in the past. The best way to ensure that the Bank will respond effectively to the corruption challenge is by forcing it to bear some of the financial costs of not doing so. This begins by enforcing Article III.

20. When Indonesia's chief economic minister inquired in a private meeting in Tokyo in early 2000 about writing off some of Indonesia's criminal debt, Bank officials reportedly said, "we cannot even begin to consider such a course of action" (confidential interview, Jakarta, 6 Feb. 2001).

CHAPTER SIX

The World Bank Inspection Panel and the Limits of Accountability

Jonathan A. Fox

In 1993, the World Bank's Board of Directors responded to international environmental and human rights critics by creating the Inspection Panel, a precedent-setting mechanism for public accountability.[1] Local-global civil society advocacy networks found allies in donor governments and their message resonated with internal World Bank concerns about the need to improve the effectiveness of its investments. Through the Inspection Panel, citizens of developing countries can now register direct grievances about the effects of World Bank noncompliance with its own social and environmental reform policies. In its first six years, the panel has generated a track record of diverse experiences that provide important lessons about transnational public interest coalitions and their impact on global institutions. Although the panel has no enforcement powers, its use of public transparency to encourage accountability has provoked waves of nationalist backlash that threaten to weaken its already limited autonomy.

Among the multilateral development banks (MDBs), the Inspection Panel is by far the most developed accountability mechanism allowing citizen access. Convened by the Bank's Board of Directors rather than by its management, the panel has been a remarkably autonomous body, permitting people affected by Bank projects the opportunity to gain some degree of diplomatic standing, potential transnational public interest allies, media access, and even the possibility of some tangible concessions. In spite of its limits, the Inspection Panel is one of the World Bank's most tangible institutionwide policy changes in response to almost two decades of environmental and human rights criticism.

The Inspection Panel's mandate is to investigate charges that official Bank policies were not followed in the design and implementation of projects. To be eligible, claimants must be people who are directly affected or a local representative acting explicitly on their behalf. The panel is composed

---

1. This chapter is a revised and updated version of Fox (2000b).

of three international development notables who are not Bank employees and reject any possible Bank employment in the future. Claimants must meet at least three conditions. First, aggrieved parties must show that they have been or are likely to be adversely affected by a Bank-financed project. Second, they must show that this threat or harm is related to the Bank's failure to follow its own policies. It is not enough to show that national governments, which implement Bank-funded projects, caused damage. Third, claimants must show that the problem was previously brought to the attention of Bank authorities and they did not respond adequately. Panel procedures recognize the possibility of reprisals against claimants and therefore allow claimants to remain anonymous. The identity of claimants must, however, be revealed to the panel (although not to the Bank), which means that the claimants must have some reason to trust the panel. In practice, advocacy nongovernmental organizations (NGOs) in the north and south have played this facilitating role of building the necessary confidence in the panel. More generally, northern NGO advocacy groups played key roles in the early period, but in the late 1990s most claims have come directly from the south, without intermediation and with little northern technical assistance.

The panel offers an important empirical test of the widely noted influence of nongovernmental actors in international relations, as well as the limits of that leverage. Here is an institution that all parties agree was created in response to sustained advocacy campaigns by coalitions of grassroots groups and NGOs in the south with advocacy NGOs in the north.[2] By creating the panel, the World Bank Board of Directors recognized the legitimacy of the normative principle that international organizations should be publicly accountable—defined as being in compliance with their own promises of social and environmental reform (commitments that were, in turn, responses to previous waves of protest).

Keck and Sikkink (1998) evaluate the impact of transnational networks in terms of stages: agenda-setting, encouraging discursive policy commitments from states and other actors, causing international or national procedural change, affecting policy, and influencing actual behavioral change in target actors. These stages are evident in the panel experience. The creation of the panel and the cases brought before it demonstrate the capacity of transnational advocacy networks to make World Bank accountability a legitimate international issue (agenda-setting). The panel experience also demonstrates the power of transnational advocacy networks to get the World Bank to recognize that its compliance with its own social and environmen-

2. On transnational advocacy networks, see Brecher, Costello, and Smith (2000); Cohen and Rai (2000); Florini (2000); Fox (2000a); Fox and Brown (1998b); Keck and Sikkink (1998); Princen and Finger (1994); Risse, Ropp, and Sikkink (1999); Smith, Chatfield, and Pagnucco (1997).

tal policies has often been inadequate (accountability politics). The panel's creation is also evidence of the capacity of transnational networks to promote new institutional access points for civil society (procedural change). But have there been changes in actual institutional behavior as a result of the panel? Do the World Bank and its nation-state partners actually comply more consistently with their own social and environmental reform mandates as a result of the panel? The evidence presented here shows that concrete results from the panel have been limited and its impact is ambiguous. Although partial responses were won in a number of cases, the findings here suggest that the impacts of transnational advocacy networks through the panel have often been indirect and to some degree based on the counterfactual logic that reform compliance would have been even worse in its absence. The key finding of this chapter is that although the Inspection Panel represents a remarkable example of multilateral-institutional innovation in response to transnational advocacy pressures, nation-states retain powerful levers to block accountability pressures much of the time.

The Inspection Panel is a particularly useful case for examining the process through which norms are nominally accepted by institutions before they are consistently respected by institutions in practice. The question here is, once institutions such as nation-states or the World Bank accept and make policies to respect more enlightened norms, how do international and national forces interact to determine the degree to which they actually comply with these policy commitments in practice? Thomas Risse, Stephen C. Ropp, and Kathryn Sikkink's (1999) approach suggests continued the predominance of international factors at this stage. More extensive comparative case analysis may indicate, however, that at this "final" stage of making institutional behavior consistent with human rights norms, domestic political factors often become primary. The panel's first six years suggest that the process of interaction between international and national factors that transforms normative, discursive, and policy changes into more tangible changes in institutional behavior has serious limits. Indeed, the panel has had a contradictory impact on Bank-state-society relations. It appears to subvert nation-state sovereignty in favor of broader notions of rights. But in practice the panel has also emboldened some nation-states to lead a backlash that seeks to block the implementation of transnational accountability reforms. For those concerned with reinventing the World Bank, this case study provides crucial information about the opportunities for and obstacles to reforming the Bank through incrementalism rather than, for example, reinvention through a second Bretton Woods summit. It also demonstrates that much of the power struggle over the Bank and its operations is not only horizontal, between shareholder governments (rich states against poor states), but also vertical, as south-north transnational coalitions press for change from below.

The Inspection Panel case, as well as the broader experience with social and environmental reform at the World Bank, suggests that transnational advocacy network-led changes often get stuck between their agenda-setting discursive and policy impact and their influence on the actual behavior of powerful institutions (Fox and Brown 1998b).[3] The panel experience suggests that the mix of transnational and national factors that can produce agenda-setting and policy victories at the international level may be different from the constellation of forces that has the capacity to make institutional behavior consistent in practice. The relative causal weights of international and national factors in this final institutionalizing phase may well shift toward the national arena.

REVIEWING THE INSPECTION PANEL

When the panel receives a claim, it sends a copy to the Bank management, asks them to respond within twenty-one days, and notifies the board. When management responds, the panel weighs the evidence from both sides to determine whether to recommend an investigation of the alleged policy violations. The panel can make a site visit as part of its preliminary review. The panel then makes a recommendation to the board, which decides whether to permit an investigation of the claim. After the board decision, management's response and the panel recommendations are made public. If an investigation proceeds, then the panel sends its final report and findings to both the board and management. Bank management then has six weeks to prepare recommendations on what actions the Bank should take in response the panel's findings. The board makes a final decision about whether to take action, and then both the panel report and management's recommendations are made public. Until procedures were revised in 1999, all proposed investigations required the active approval of the board, which mainly either tried to sidestep or thwarted them. After the 1999 board review of the panel, the rules prevented the board from objecting to proposed panel investigations.

The panel's mandate regarding accountability links three core concepts: noncompliance with Bank policies, material harm (or the threat of it), and causation (establishing the link between noncompliance and harm). The panel's point of departure is that the Bank has already established a wide range of social and environmental policy reforms that attempt not merely to "first do no harm," but also to actively promote poverty alleviation and sustainable development. Since the panel's creation, a core subset of these policies has come to be called safeguard policies within the Bank. Since the

3. An assessment of the impact of the North American Free Trade Agreement (NAFTA) advocacy campaigns comes to a similar conclusion (Fox 2000a).

panel was created, and partly as an effort to sidestep accountability, some of the policies have been "reformatted" (a process to be discussed later). Nevertheless, these reform policies are the benchmark standards that permit the otherwise vague concept accountability to be operationalized in practice. Table 6.1 summarizes these benchmark policies and their various stages of revision. In addition, the World Bank has also issued many other important sustainable development policy mandates since the mid-1980s involving gender, poverty reduction, NGO collaboration, community participation, water resources, and energy efficiency and conservation. Many of these additional policies are remarkably detailed and enlightened, but they are not written as minimum mandatory benchmark standards. This is in contrast to the safeguard policies, such as the requirement to carry out environmental impact assessments or action plans to minimize and compensate large-scale involuntary resettlement. The Inspection Panel was not designed to encourage higher levels of compliance with essentially good practice recommendations, and therefore these additional reform policies do not fall within the scope of its direct impact.

The Inspection Panel is extraordinary because any affected citizen in a borrowing country can seek recourse directly, without having to go through his or her national government. In this sense, the panel's very existence challenges key assumptions of national sovereignty, even though its mandate is limited to examining Bank policy failures rather than those of borrowing governments. At the same time, although the panel constitutes a transnational arena for managing conflict, it does not fully bypass nation-states because they remain represented on the Bank's Board of Executive Directors, which retains authority over whether the panel can investigate. Both donor and borrowing governments are represented on the Bank's board, and the panel experience has shown that the board is not always a pliable instrument of a handful of donor governments, as is widely assumed. This impression was reinforced by the fact that panel itself was created through the influence of northern donor governments on the World Bank. The United States led this process, inducing a consensus in spite of its minority voting power (17 percent of the shares in a one-dollar-one-vote system).

In the case of the creation of the Inspection Panel, the exercise of U.S. influence in favor of accountability reform was made possible by an unusual confluence of events. After all, U.S. policy influence at the World Bank usually focuses on a narrower set of interests, such as private banks concerned with the repayment of their international debts or exporters of U.S. capital goods to developing countries. Not only did the Democrats control both the presidency and Congress during a brief 1992–94 window, but an internationalist reformer, Congressman Barney Frank, controlled a key House banking subcommittee. For more than a decade, environmentalists and hu-

Table 6.1
World Bank Safeguard and Conversion Process[a]

Policy	Key Features	Conversion Status[b]
OP/BP/GP 4.01 Environmental Assessment	Potential environmental consequences of projects identified early in project cycle EAs and mitigation plans required for projects with significant environmental impacts or involuntary resettlement EAs should include analysis of alternative designs and sites, or consideration of "no option" Requires public participation and information disclosure before board approval	Approved January 1999
OP 4.04 Natural Habitats	Prohibits financing of projects involving "significant conversion of natural habitats unless there are no feasible alternatives" Requires environmental cost-benefit analysis Requires EA with mitigation measures	Approved October 15,1995
OP 4.36 Forestry	Prohibits financing for commercial logging operations or acquisition of equipment for use in primary moist tropical forests	Conversion incomplete
OP 4.09 Pest Management	Supports environmentally sound pest management, including intergrated pest management, but does not prohibit the use of highly hazardous pesticides Pest management is the borrower's responsibility in the context of a project's EA	Conversion complete
OD 4.30 Involuntary Resettlement	Implemented in projects that displace people Requires public participation in resettlement planning as part of EA for project Intended to restore or improve income-earning capacity of displace populations	Conversion incomplete
OD 4.20 Indigeneous Peoples	Purpose is to ensure indigenous peoples benefit from Bank-financed development and to avoid or mitigate adverse affects on indigenous peoples Applies to projects that might adversely affect indigenous peoples or when they are targeted beneficiaries Requires participation of indigenous peoples in creation of "indigenous peoples development plans"	Has not been converted; the Bank is consulting with indigenous peoples and NGOs prior to changing the policy

OPN 11.03 Cultural Property	Purpose is to assist in the preservation of cultural property, such as sites having archeological, paleontological, historical, religious, and unique cultural values Generally seeks to assist in their preservation and avoid their elimination Discourages financing of projects that will damage cultural property	To be issued as OP/BP/GP 4.11
OP/BP 4.37 Safety of Dams	Applies to large dams (15 meters or more in height) Requires review by independent experts throughout project cycle Requires preparation of EA and detailed plans for construction and operation, and periodic inspection by the Bank	Conversion complete
OP/BP/GP 7.50 Projects on International Waterways	Covers riparian waterways that form a boundary between two or more states, as well as any bay, gulf, strait, or channel bordered by two or more states Applies to dams, irrigation, flood control, navigation, water, sewage, and industrial projects Requires notification, agreement between states, detailed maps, and feasibility surveys	Conversion complete
OP/BP 7.60 Projects in Disputed Areas	Applies to projects in which there are territorial disputes present Allows Bank to proceed if governments agree to go forward without prejudice to claims Requires early identification of territorial disputes and descriptions in all Bank documentation	Approved November 1994

*From NGO Bank Information Center, "Toolkits for Activists." Available from http://www.bicusa.org/toolkits/policyTK/policy1.htm#recent; INTERNET. The full texts of the policies are available from World Bank, http://wbln0018.worldbank.org/institutional/manuals/opmanual.nsf; INTERNET. BP, Bank Procedures; EA, Environmental Assessment; GP, Good Practices; NGOs, nongovernmental organizations; OD, Operational Directives; OP, Operational Policies.

*All policies not yet converted are still in force in their old format. The Bank Information Center Website explains, "Operational Directives (OD) are the only Bank policy statements that are approved by the Board of Executive Directors and are mandatory for all Bank staff. They are the policy statements formally used by the Inspection Panel to determine violations of policy when claims from affected citizens are presented. These Operational Directives are being converted into a three-tiered format comprised of Operational Policies, Bank Procedures and Good Practices (OP/BP/GP). Operational Policies and Bank Procedures are mandatory—Bank management and staff must implement them in the Bank's operations. Good Practices on the other hand, do not constitute mandatory actions, but are guidelines that operational staff can use. The conversion process has unfortunately weakened the Bank's environment and social policy framework, by weakening language and by moving formerly mandatory requirements into the 'good practice' statement."

man rights activists (bolstered by Republican foreign aid critics) had been using U.S. Congressional oversight over foreign aid appropriations as a critical lever to push the U.S. government to call for World Bank reform (Bramble and Porter 1992; Bowles and Kormos 1995; Fox and Brown 1998a; Rich 1994; Sanford 1988; Kurian 1995). Until the early 1990s, however, these efforts had little effect on the World Bank.

By 1993, the credibility of the World Bank's promises to reform itself was at a dramatically low point. A media-savvy, broad-based south-north campaign against India's Narmada dam had obliged the Bank to create an independent commission that found systematic violations of Bank social and environmental policies, thus vindicating the critics. At the same time, the Bank had also just inadvertently released a major internal report that documented a pervasive culture of loan approval that undermined the quality of its investments (Wapenhans 1992). The Narmada campaign brought together the key levers posited by Keck and Sikkink (1998): information politics, symbolic politics, accountability politics, and leverage politics *par excellance*. Threats to withold foreign aid during the annual U.S. Congressional budget debate provided the institutional pressure point. The large U.S. environmental organizations, with their electorally influential constituencies and strong mass media access, provided the political leverage. Although these membership organizations were primarily domestic in orientation, their small international staffs were active partners of transnational coalitions and their joint letters of protest and concern could claim to speak for literally millions of constituents.

At the peak of the Narmada campaign, U.S. Congressional reformers, under pressure from transnational advocacy coalitions, threatened to cut appropriations for the World Bank's soft-loan window unless the Bank agreed to create a major accountability window and a new, more open information disclosure policy (Udall 1998; Fisher 1995; Sen 1999a, 1999b; Morse and Berger 1992). In short, transnational campaigns put the issue on the agenda, but the Inspection Panel's creation was made possible by leverage politics based on conjunctural, primarily domestic, state-society coalitions within the United States.

In addition to the articulation between transnational and national policy arenas, one of this chapter's principal findings is that the nation-states represented on Bank's board have retained a high degree of power over the panel's capacity to comply with its accountability mandate. Specifically, the Bank's board has provided a major avenue for the larger borrowing governments, which are represented directly, to challenge not only the panel's findings, but its jurisdiction as well. So far, the evidence suggests that transnational civil society pressure led some nation-states to create the panel, but that other nation-states, plus Bank management, have managed to prevent it from having a significant impact much of the time.

BROAD PATTERNS IN PANEL CLAIMS

When reviewing the Inspection Panel's first six years, several puzzles emerge. First, why did the panel receive claims from only fifteen different NGOs and/or grassroots campaigns?[4] The question is puzzling because the World Bank approves hundreds of new projects each year and only some of them have been influenced by its new sustainable development discourse. Even for the relatively few aware of the Bank's reforms and the panel, it turns out that using the panel effectively is easier said than done.

Table 6.2 shows that panel claims during 1994–99 have tended to focus on large infrastructure projects. Most charges of violations have focused on the policies involving involuntary resettlement, environmental assessment, and indigenous peoples. Of the fifteen civil society campaigns, eight involved primarily infrastructure projects: five hydroelectric dams (Arun, Bío-bío, Yacyretá, Itaparica, and Lesotho Highlands), a huge bridge (Jamuna), a power plant (Singrauli), and urban drainage (Lagos). Three more involved significant infrastructure components (Planafloro included roads in the Amazon, China Western Poverty Reduction included a dam and irrigation, and Ecuador Mining produced related maps). Forced resettlement in the name of conservation was also involved in another claim (India Eco-Development). Only the later claims focused primarily on qualitatively different issues, charging that the projects would worsen poverty (Brazil Land Reform and Poverty Alleviation Pilot and Argentina Structural Adjustment).

This pattern is consistent with the characteristics of the most controversial Bank projects, including India's Narmada dam, which provoked the creation of the panel in the first place. Compared to their share of the portfolio, large-scale infrastructure projects have generally provoked a disproportionate share of protests against the World Bank. Compared to less overt kinds of social costs, forced evictions tend to bring affected people together to resist common threats, as well as unite national and international environmental and human rights allies. Long-standing local and international controversies over how to deal with involuntary resettlement have led the Bank to develop one of its explicit and contentious benchmark standards. Internal as well as external studies show that achieving full compliance with this policy has proven to be quite difficult, in spite of its lightning-rod effect (Khagram 2000; World Bank 1994d, 1998l; Fox 1998; Thorne 1998; Picciotto, Van Wicklin, and Rice 2000).

The environmental and social costs of Bank lending for noninfrastructure categories may be less direct, but they are not necessarily less significant. One of the Bank's largest categories of lending involves national-level

4. Seventeen of the twenty claims filed by the end of 1999 came from civil society actors, but the Brazil Land Reform and the Lesotho Highlands water project each filed two claims, so fifteen distinct campaigns were involved. The remaining three claims came from domestic private sector interests and will not be addressed here.

Table 6.2
Inspection Panel Claims Filed, 1994–1999[a]

Country	Bank Project	Date Panel Claim Filed
Nepal	Arun III Hydroelectric Project	October 1994
Ethiopia	*IDA-financed credits to Ethiopia*	*April 1995*
Tanzania	*Tanzania Power VI Project*	*May 1995*
Brazil	Rondônia Natural Resources Management ("Planafloro")	June 1995
Chile	Bio-Bio Hydroelectric Project	November 1995
Argentina and Paraguay	Yacyretá Hydroelectric Project	September 1996
Bangladesh	Jamuna Bridge Project	August 1996
Bangladesh	*Jute Sector Adjustment Credit*	*August 1996*
Brazil	Itaparica Resettlement and Irrigation Project	March 1997
India	NTPC Power Generation Project ("Singrauli")	April 1997
India	Eco-Development	April 1998
Lesotho and South Africa	Lesotho Highlands Water Project	May 1998
Nigeria	Lagos Drainage and Sanitation Project	June 1998
Brazil	Land Reform and Poverty Alleviation Pilot	December 1998
Lesotho and South Africa	Lesotho Highlands Water/Diamond Mines	May 1999
China	Western Poverty Reduction Project	June 1999
Argentina	Special Structural Adjustment Loan	July 1999
Brazil	Land Reform and Poverty Alleviation (2nd filing)	August 1999
Kenya	Lake Victoria Environmental Management Project	October 1999
Ecuador	Mining Development and Enviromental Control—Technical Assistance	December 1999

[a]Italics indicates Private-sector-led cases IDA, International Development Association; NTPC, National Thermal Power Corporation.

loans that disburse quickly in exchange for economic policy reforms, usually known as structural and sectoral adjustment loans. This category of "non-project" lending reached had 53 percent of total Bank lending by 1999 (World Bank 1999h, 3).[5] As one World Bank social analyst put it, "all World Bank safeguard policies are meaningless when it comes to adjustment" (interview, World Bank, 5 April 1999). A comprehensive internal Bank review of structural and sectoral adjustment loans confirmed that they still systematically ignore social and environmental concerns (in spite of more than a decade of public debate over their impact) (World Bank 1999l).[6] In short, the majority of Bank lending eludes the mandate of the safeguard policies, and thus far the Inspection Panel has received only one claim that targets a macropolicy loan.

Making the direct connection between macroeconomic reforms and violation of the Bank's social and environmental policies has proved to be challenging, but the Argentina Structural Adjustment project claim set an important precedent. An Argentinian human rights NGO, the Center for Legal and Social Studies (CELS), found that the Argentinian government had cut the budget for a highly targeted, large-scale social program to support poor people's urban gardens (Pro-Huerta) in the context of a World Bank structural adjustment loan. CELS submitted a sophisticated complaint, arguing not only that this violated the Bank's antipoverty policy, but also that the budget cut violated the government's formal loan commitment to mitigate the effects of structural adjustment reforms on the poor (World Bank Inspection Panel 1999). The program budget was quickly restored, obviating the need for an inspection. This claim clearly produced a major, tangible impact.

Geographically, of the seventeen civil society claims filed during the panel's first six years, more than one-third of the cases involved Brazil (four) and India (three), if we include Nepal's Arun dam, which was designed to provide power to India. Locally based international environmental and human rights protests against Bank-funded infrastructure projects have long been especially prominent in Brazil and India, perhaps related to the den-

5. This internal discussion paper explains, "This was the first time in the Bank's history that adjustment lending exceeded investment lending. . . . For IBRD [International Bank for Reconstruction and Development], the share was 63%; this compares with 47% in FY98, and 21% on average during FY92–97. The IDA [International Development Association] adjustment share remained significantly below 25%" (World Bank 1999h, 3).
6. This confidential study explicitly recognized that "there appears to be a disconnect between Bank policy and practice" regarding the environmental impacts of these loans (World Bank 1999l, 2). In terms of their social impact, the study found that "because targeting vulnerable groups with improved public expenditure is not specified, the impact of reforms on the poorest remains unclear at best, and doubtful at worst" (8). This finding suggests that long-standing public interest campaigns to influence the Bank's approach to macroeconomic reforms have had much less impact than more focused environmental and human rights campaigns.

sity of their civil societies. Brazil was the scene of the media and popular imagery that framed the international protest campaigns in the 1980s as Bank-funded roads accelerated the burning of the western Amazon rainforest. Meanwhile, India witnessed the broad-based militant campaign against the Narmada dams. Both states are led by nationalist political classes for whom such infrastructure projects are powerful symbols of national development (Sen 1999a, 1999b). It is not surprising, therefore, that these nation-states' financial authorities led the 1999 backlash to weaken the Inspection Panel's mandate. In the subsequent two years, however, the panel has received claims from a more diverse array of countries.

The tangible impacts of panel claims have been very uneven. As is evident in table 6.3 only four of the civil society claims won clear-cut major victories for claimants. The panel found some claims ineligible because they were not convinced that Bank policy violations contributed to the alleged problems (Lesotho Highlands and Brazil Land Reform). In other cases the panel's proposal for an inspection was rejected by the board (Itaparica and India Eco-Development), based on governmental promises that the issues would be addressed. Until the panel's procedures were revised in 1999, the Bank's board was very reluctant to permit full-scale inspections.

One of the claims with the clearest evidence of major impact was the panel's very first. The planned Arun III dam was cancelled before construction began, reversing seven years of project planning. This case was a powerful example of the mutually reinforcing convergence of sustained transnational advocacy pressure and dissent internal to the World Bank. The external critique built on the transnational networks generated by the Narmada campaign; the internal critique came from senior operational officials (Udall 1998; Fox and Brown 1998b).

In the first two Brazilian cases, Planafloro and Itaparica, government promises of improved implementation were sufficient to convince the majority of the board to reject formal inspections. In both cases, the main campaign goal was not to block the project but rather to encourage compliance with the Bank's social and environmental goals. In the Planafloro case, Aurelio Vianna, then coordinator of the Brazilian Network on Multilateral Financial Institutions, reported that even though the Bank board did not approve a formal investigation, the claim resulted in "a deep change in the project. Civil society managed to create a large space in Planafloro, a $23 million fund for civil society projects. . . . On the other hand, the problems continue with government's relationship with the project, and between the local civil society organizations and the state and federal governments" (personal email communication, Brasilia, 11 May 1998, translation by the author). Official responses also included the extension of legal protection to large tracts of forest for indigenous peoples and rubber-tappers, as proposed by the project. The author's earlier assessment considered this to be a case

Table 6.3

Official Responses to Inspection Panel Claims Filed 1994–1999[a]

Inspection Panel Claims	Bank Management Response	Panel Recommends Investigation?	Board Approves Investigation?	Partial Concessions to Affected	Major Concessions
Arun III Hydro	Denied violations	Yes	Yes		Project withdrawn
IDA Ethiopia	*N/A*	*Found ineligible*	*N/A*		
Tanzania Power	*N/A*	*Found ineligible*	*N/A*		
Planafloro	Partial acceptance	Yes	No		Project restructured, power-sharing with grassroots groups, forest lands demarcated
Biobío Hydroelectric	N/A	Found ineligible	Independent study done	No	
Yacyretá Hydro	Denied violations	Yes	Partial (limited review)	Reservoir level temporarily capped, information centers opened	
Jamuna Bridge	Admitted claimants were affected	No; found that management responded		Compensation promised, but implementation weak	
Jute Sector	*Agreed with claimants and withdrew project*	*No*			Bank halted funding
Itaparica	Denied violations	Yes	No (roll-call vote)	Promised by government, then cut	
NTPC Singrauli	Partial acceptance	Yes	Yes (limited to desk review)	Local monitoring, created, limited compensation	
India Eco-Development	Denied violations	Yes	No	Changes proposed, but not implemented	
Lesotho Highlands	Denied violations	Found ineligible		No	

(continued)

Table 6.3
Continued

Inspection Panel Claims	Bank Management Response	Panel Recommends Investigation?	Board Approves Investigation?	Partial Concessions to Affected	Major Concessions
Lagos Drainage and Sanitation	Denied violations	No; questioned charges, accepted promises of compliance		Small increase in coverage of compensation advocates claim many affected people excluded	
Brazil Land Reform	Denied violations	Found ineligible		Promise to ease land-purchase terms, expropriable lands to be excluded	
Lesotho Highlands/Diamond	Denied violations	Found ineligible		No	
China Western Poverty Reduction	Asserted substantial or full compliance with all policies except for information disclosure	Yes	Yes (unanimous)		Board rejected project plan, loan proposal withdrawn
Structural Adjustment/Pro-Huerta	Denied violations	Found eligible but government response rendered claim moot			Government restored funding to social program
Brazil Land Reform (2nd)	Denied violations	Found ineligible			
Lake Victoria Environmental Management	Denied violations	Yes	Yes	Panel finds violations; board asks Bank management to improve its recommendations	
Ecuador Mining	Denied violations	Yes	Yes	Panel finds violations; Bank management and board response pending	

*Italics indicates private sector claims. IDA, International Development Association; N/A, not applicable; NTPC, National Thermal Power Corporation. Thanks very much to Dana Clark and Kay Treakle for input.

of significant partial concessions, but later field research found that the one-third of the restructured project budget put into civil society hands had led to a significant shift in the balance of power within the province (Rodrigues 2000). Although the restructured project left most of the funding in conventional developmentalist hands, the longer-term evolving power shift appears to be sufficiently significant to warrant recharacterizing the impact of the panel claim as a major concession (Aparico and Garrison 1999; Millikan 1998, 2001; Feeney 1998; Hunter 1997b).

The Chilean dam case involved the World Bank's private sector branch, the International Finance Corporation (IFC), which is officially exempt from the panel's mandate. The board did not want to expand the panel's mandate to the IFC and therefore refused to allow an inspection, but the claim led the Bank's president to commission an ad hoc independent review (Hair et al. 1997).[7] That review was quite critical, but the "IFC arranged for the Dresdner Bank to take up their equity position" (Goodland 2001, 5), thereby sidestepping World Bank policy commitments. The Chilean power company paid its debt in advance and successfully evaded World Bank scrutiny. Local communities as well as national and international environmental NGOs continued to protest, but have achieved negligible gains for those affected.[8]

In the case of the claim against India's Singrauli power plant, the board agreed to a desk review (a report not based on direct field research). Bank management responded by proposing an Action Plan that included a novel innovation in the form of an Independent Monitoring Panel composed of three Indian experts to provide a forum for grievances. This panel's recommendations were reportedly resisted by the government power company, however, and local activists reportedly felt that it lacked the support needed from the World Bank. Indeed, the representatives of the Singrauli claimants reported that "instead of improvement, the borrower became more hardened in its attitude toward those who testified or who wanted to reach out to the Panel" (Clark 1999, 17–18). This claim is an example of the risk of backlash against transnational civil society initiatives—the local human rights situation worsened and the claimants did not win tangible gains (Dana Clark, Center for International and Environmental Law, personal email communication, 8 May 1998. See also Udall 1997; Human Rights Watch 1998; Jones and Jendrzejezyk 1998).

In the Bangladesh Jamuna Bridge claim, the main issue was whether all

7. Previously the IFC had commissioned an internal social impact review by Ted Downing, a University of Arizona anthropologist, that turned out to be quite critical. The resulting controversy led the American Anthropological Association to take up the issue publicly with the World Bank, leading to an earlier report by Johnston and Turner (1997). See also Hunter (1997a).

8. Downing reported that the situation among affected indigenous communities was "very, very bad" (personal communication, 12 May 1998). For Chilean critiques, see Opaso (1999); Jana (1999).

of those to be displaced by its construction would be taken into account. The bridge would change patterns of flooding and erosion, but resettlement plans had ignored the many thousands who live on shifting river islands, known as char people. According to Hanna Schmuck, an anthropologist with extensive local experience with the char people, they were at great risk because they had been completely left out of resettlement planning. According to Dana Clark of the Center for International Environmental Law, "the Panel's preliminary review found this to be true, and found that the Bank had failed to consult with them and failed to include them in resettlement benefits" (Clark 1999, 18). Their claim led to large-scale plans for recognizing and compensating the char people. Seen from Washington, this appeared to address the problem, but subsequent field surveys report dramatic problems with the adminstration of compensation. Therefore this is a case of partial rather than major claim impact.[9]

Concessions have also been limited in the Yacyretá dam case. The level of the reservoir was at least temporarily limited to seventy-six meters above sea level, in spite of powerful economic pressures to raise it to eighty-two or eighty-six. The Bank reportedly recognized that more people warranted compensation than had been counted in the original census, but there is no evidence of implementation as yet (Kay Treakle, Bank Information Center, personal communication, 20 Dec. 2000). According to Elías Díaz Peña of the Paraguayan environmental NGO Sobrevivencia (a Friends of the Earth affiliate), "The Panel's intervention . . . contributed to a process of opening dialogue (which was practically nonexistent before) between the EBY [the binational Paraguayan-Argentinian dam-building agency], the affected population and the government institutions from both countries" (Díaz Peña 1998, 1; 1999; Treakle 1998; Shannon 1999). Kay Treakle of the Bank Information Center, a Washington-based NGO, added that grassroots opposition in Paraguay had increased significantly and gained national allies since the panel claim. Local critics coalesced around the panel claim because "they had demands before but nowhere to put them. They didn't feel empowered until Umaña [then the panel chair] sat down with them" (Kay Treakle, Bank Information Center, interview, 9 May 1998). Although the construction project is already well under way, the international claim process has increased the local legitimacy and leverage of dam-affected peo-

---

9. Independent field surveys contradict the official claim by the NGO charged with administering compensation that it had achieved almost complete coverage of the first two years of losses by at least 12,000 claimants (the official counts vary). According to an independent survey of 725 households, only 57.11 percent received compensation for homestead erosion and only 47.6 percent for land losses suffered between 1996 and 1998, with few compensated for losses after that. Moreover, the amount of average compensation for lost land, livelihoods, and relocation was dramatically undervalued (only $140 per family), and the treatment by the NGO of the minority char people was widely experienced as discriminatory (Hanna Schmuck, personal communication, 29 October 2000).

ple in both Argentina and Paraguay. Local information centers were also set up, and some efforts were made at conflict resolution. In the big picture of the project, however, these concessions were at best partial.

The Itaparica claim also produced the promise of increased governmental attention to displaced people, but has produced very few tangible concessions. The Brazilian government, in order to convince the Bank's board to reject the claim, promised to allocate significant amounts of resources to complete the irrigation works promised to the thousands of smallholders displaced by the dam a decade before (Hall 1992; Vianna 1998a, 1998b, 2001; Rice 1998). Brazilian rural unions and their allies campaigned to participate in the decisions about how to allocate those resources. Since Brazil's financial crisis, however, the promised funds were cut. From an international point of view, moreover, the process through which the Bank's Board of Directors chose to accept an ad hoc promise from the Brazilian government in lieu of following through on the claim process set an important precedent (discussed later).

The panel claims involving India Eco-Development, urban water policy in South Africa linked to the Lesotho Highlands dam, Nigeria's Lagos Sanitation, and Brazil's Land Reform project have apparently not led to significant changes on the ground. In the first case, external inquires produced no independent evidence that villagers slated to be involuntarily relocated from zones designated to be parks were dealt with more gently. The two claims by the Lesotho campaign provided some public resonance for concerns about South African water policy issues affecting low-income communities, but did not affect the project (Patrick Bond, personal email communication, 4 May 1999; see also Letsie and Bond 1999b).[10] In the Lagos urban sanitation case, the panel members rejected the claims of human rights violations, with the result that a very limited official recognition of violations of the resettlement policy and a small fraction of the reportedly affected people were granted very modest compensation (interviews, World Bank Inspection Panel Secretariat, Nov. 1999, Washington, D.C.; see also "Inspection Panel Confirms" 1999, Washington, D.C.). The Brazilian claims against a market-style land-reform project were rejected by the panel as ineligible because the allegations that participants would be made worse off were considered hypothetical (the claim was subsequently refiled, with additional evidence of the potential for corruption in the implementation process) (interviews, World Bank Inspection Panel Secretariat and Brazilian Network on Multilateral Financial Institutions, Nov. 1999, Washington, D.C.). In response to the two claims, the government promised the Bank that it

10. This project later reappeared in the international headlines because of a World Bank investigation into corruption involving international contractors, but this was not related to the panel (see "Western Contractors" 1999). On Bank water policy issues more generally, see Moore and Sklar (1998).

would significantly reduce the interest rate for low-income land purchasers and that lands eligible for traditional expropriations would not be included in the Bank-funded part of market-based land-reform project. So far, however, the government has yet to follow up on these commitments. The most tangible impact of the panel claims appears to have been to reduce the size of the loan from a proposed $800 million to $202 million (Aurelio Vianna, Brazilian Network on International Financial Institutions, personal communication, 20 Dec. 2000; see also, Schwartzman 2000; Wolff and Sauer 2001).

The hardest fought battle around an Inspection Panel claim involved one in which Tibetans and their international allies filed a claim against China's proposed Western Poverty Reduction project. The project proposed to voluntarily resettle 58,000 poor Chinese farmers to a region that is historically home to Tibetan and Mongolian nomads. Critics charged that it would contribute to the long-standing Chinese policy of encouraging migration to dilute the ethnic Tibetan population, and senior Bank managers now privately admit it. The project's proposed forty-meter dam for irrigated agriculture also provoked environmental concerns. In spite of the Bank's vast and sophisticated public relations operations, this project managed to trip over one of the most well-known indigenous rights movements in the world, leading it to unite with the Bank campaign.

Controversy raged at the highest levels, cross-cut by other political tensions between the United States and the Chinese governments. The case turned into a make-or-break test for the Inspection Panel, in the face of Chinese government charges that investigating the Bank's own violations of its social and environmental policies violated national sovereignty. The transnational advocacy pressures were so effective and the violations of Bank policy so undeniable that both the U.S. and German governments voted against the project when it first reached the board, and the U.S. government reduced its annual Bank appropriations. The project was approved nevertheless, but on the condition that the Inspection Panel reassess it after six months. The April 2000 mass street protests against the World Bank and International Monetary Fund (IMF) encouraged the mass media to cover the case and energized the Tibetan solidarity movement. The Inspection Panel then produced a powerful indictment of the project's violations of Bank policies (Sanger and Kahn 2000; Sanghera 2000). By mid-2000, the campaign was able to mobilize vocal Tibetan exiles and their supporters downstairs at exactly the same time that the World Bank's Board of Executive Directors was meeting upstairs to decide whether to move ahead and fund the project. The board could actually hear the chants from the streets below.[11] This was the first street protest to target the board's loan-decision-

---

11. This report was confirmed by Dan Gross, senior World Bank anthropologist, on a panel at the American Anthropological Association meeting, 17 Nov. 2000, San Francisco.

making process so precisely. After the board rejected the Bank's proposed mitigation measures, China was obliged to withdraw the project proposal, in spite of the fact that it is the World Bank's largest single borrower. The *Financial Times* called it one of the Bank's "worst ever public relations disasters" (Sanghera 2000, 1; cf. Goodland 2001).

Some of the most important results of the claim process have been intangible. The process established the precedent of granting affected people direct access to an impartial international body. Many claimants report that this process has empowered them, even if they have not gained direct concessions on the ground. As World Bank President James Wolfensohn writes, "by giving private citizens—and especially the poor—a new means of access to the Bank, it has empowered and given voice to those we most need to hear. At the same time, it has served the Bank itself through ensuring that we really are fulfilling our mandate of improving conditions for the world's poorest people" (Umaña 1998, vii).[12] Indeed, the World Bank's executive directors even felt obliged to grant panel claimants a direct hearing, as a group, before making their 1999 decision to change the panel's mandate (World Bank 1999o). Yet it is precisely this granting of international standing that appears to have profoundly irritated the financial authorities of several major borrowing governments.

Even before the revision of the Inspection Panel's mandate, several factors inside and outside the institution constrained its potential impact. First, as already noted, the board often rejected the panel's recommendations. The panel is relatively autonomous, but it remains a Bank institution that serves at the board's discretion. Second, most civil society actors affected by Bank projects remain unaware of the panel and its pro-accountability potential. This is due not only to a lack of information about the panel, but also to a perception by those affected that most Bank-funded investments are exclusively nation-state projects. Even if they knew the Bank had provided funding, they would still need to be aware of the Bank's social and environmental safeguard policy commitments to know that compliance was even an issue (and therefore subject to accountability politics strategies). Third, many possible problems with many Bank projects are not directly subject to the panel's mandate. Fourth, even in cases where the affected people are informed about the panel and Bank policies and their concerns fit the panel's mandate, the costs and risks of filing a claim can be substantial. The costs involve the use of limited human resources to carry out the highly technical process of preparing, filing, and lobbying for a claim. The perceived risks also depend on whether potential claimants face the threat of reprisals at home. The panel's procedures and the Bank's extremely specialized policy language require both a command of English and a high level

---

12. Panel-watchers agree that without Wolfensohn's strong support, the panel would never have survived.

of familiarity with western-style legal culture. Finally, the motivation to use an institutional channel such as the Inspection Panel cannot be taken for granted because it requires an implicit acceptance of the Bank's legitimacy as a reformable institution.

SOCIAL AND ENVIRONMENTAL POLICY REFORMS

In principle, the panel's mandate is limited to investigating Bank noncompliance with its own safeguard policies. In practice, this usually involves focusing on Bank staff and management inattention to nation-state non-compliance with agreements to respect to the Bank's many environmental and social reform policies. Inherent in the Panel process, therefore, is a contradiction—that the Bank can and should condition its lending to nation-states on socially and environmentally responsible development investments. This is an assumption that many borrowing governments (and some Bank critics) reject. Transnational advocacy coalitions that support and use the panel, in contrast, contend the Bank and nation-states are economic and political partners and are therefore coresponsible for social and environmental costs.

Sharp debates over the Panel's actions have raised broader questions about the conflict inherent in the fact that, on paper, many of the World Bank's social and environmental standards are more rigorous than the actual practices of many governments. This gap leads to a permanent source of national-transnational friction. If the Bank does not promote an increase in social and environmental standards in the projects it finances, then a major disconnect (in Bank discourse) emerges between policy and practice. Many public interest watchdog groups stand ready to document and expose such inconsistencies and to bring them to the attention of those executive directors willing to listen. Conversely, when Bank managers and staff do choose to make reform policy compliance a priority in their bargaining agenda with borrowing governments, they must allocate limited political capital that might otherwise be used for their other priorities (such as promoting policy reforms of primary interest to foreign investors). The resulting national-transnational conflict slows the process of project design while the structural pressures to lend remain powerful—especially in cases of borrowers experiencing long-term net negative financial flows to the Bank.

To understand the political processes through which the social and environmental standards of Bank projects can be raised, the conventional external assumption that the Bank and its member states are monolithic actors must be put aside. The principal lesson from previous studies of institutional change at the World Bank is that the institution must be unpacked to understand the forces that favor or block reform. For example, Wade (1997) has persuasively documented the intense internal debates over whether to agree to policy reforms and then over whether to comply with them. Rich

(2000) has effectively documented how the Bank's internal lines of authority and staff incentives limit the influence of internal environmental and social policy analysts over project design and lending designs. I have shown how external advocacy campaigns empower insider reformists, increasing their leverage over Bank staff that would otherwise ignore the institution's social and environmental reform commitments (Fox 1998).[13] In a handful of cases, insider reform advocates have been able to draw on past reform commitments to take pro-reform initiatives even in the absence of immediate external pressures (Thorne 1998; Fox and Gershman 2000). Within this broader context, the next section assesses the dilemmas involved in assessing the Inspection Panel's indirect effects on World Bank reform practices.

SAFEGUARD POLICY COMPLIANCE — ANALYTICAL DILEMMAS

Panel claims had substantial direct effects in only four of the fifteen civil society claims in its first five years (Arun, Planafloro, China/Tibet, Pro-Huerta). It is quite possible, however, that the panel has also had important indirect effects on the World Bank that extend beyond the scope of the small number of projects that provoked formal claims. For example, we could hypothesize that the existence of the panel as a de facto court of last resort might make Bank staff and managers more circumspect in their attention to safeguard policy compliance. Some close observers report a climate of staff fear of claims. However, tracing any possible causal linkages between the panel's presence and increased safeguard policy compliance implies that we can first independently document patterns of improvement in policy compliance.

Assessing the degree to which hundreds of ongoing Bank projects actually comply with safeguard policies is not easy. Few comprehensive field-based assessments of Bank and borrowing government compliance with these reform policies exist. Many of the most reliable field-based assessments have been carried out by the Bank's own highly autonomous Operations Evaluation Department (OED), but most of their evaluations are desk reviews. Such studies are of limited usefulness because they are based on official project files that are created, by definition, by interested parties. Most

13. The Bank's policy on involuntary resettlement provides an instructive example of the interaction between pro- and antireform actors inside and outside of powerful institutions. The Bank's 1980 resettlement policy was its first to deal with social and environmental issues. Literally millions of people are evicted by Bank-funded infrastructure projects each decade, uniting environmental and human rights critics. By the early 1990s, the Bank had become a bit more circumspect and could point to some progress in terms of greater compliance with its own policies. External civil society pressure reinforced by donor government concern empowered internal reformists, who produced the most comprehensive assessment of Bank compliance with its own reform policies so far (World Bank 1994d). The specific pattern of impact of external criticism depended on the uneven presence and leverage of pro-reform factions within the Bank itself (Fox 1998).

field-based assessments of actual project implementation, moreover, cover specific projects rather than entire sectors or country portfolios. Most external critiques of the World Bank cover a wide range of projects and policies, but few isolate those projects approved after the reform policies were issued. This is in part due to the long lead time involved in project cycles. Most projects implemented in the mid-1990s were designed either before many of the reform policies or in the early years of their institutionalization. Most projects conceptualized since the environmental and social reform policies of the early 1990s were just beginning to be implemented in 1999.

Because the social and environmental policies did not apply retroactively, the fact that disastrous pre-reform projects are still ongoing is not an adequate test of the degree to which the newer reforms are being complied with. Independent assessments of the dynamics of Bank reform are continually challenged by the facts that the institution is an ever-moving target and actual project outcomes depend on complex state-society dynamics that are often far removed from the Bank itself (Fox 1997b). At the same time, the Bank's internal decision-making structures are changing. Its ongoing internal decentralization appears likely to weaken internal checks and balance that could encourage reform policy compliance. As one leading Bank environmental analyst recognized, "With the Bank's devolution of responsibility, however [to six regional operational vice presidencies], comes the need to ensure consistent compliance with the safeguard policies across the six regions" (Rees 1998, 60). As a result, a new Safeguards Compliance Unit was created, charged with auditing policy compliance, although its strategy and leverage are not clear. Rees's statement does add that the task force will "develop a framework to facilitate greater accountability, including the possibility of sanctions, for staff and managers responsible for noncompliance . . ." (60). More than a year later, it had not come to pass. As one Bank social development expert put it, "The big question is how do sanctions operate? No one ever lost their job for violating safeguard policies" (confidential interview, April 3, 1999, Washington, D.C.).

In spite of the massive empirical challenges involved in externally assessing compliance with reform commitments, two broad patterns are clear. On the one hand, the Bank does appear to be funding fewer obviously disastrous new infrastructure mega-projects. Potential disasters such as the Narmada dam receive much more scrutiny and are much more likely to be dropped early on in the project cycle.[14] On the other hand, the available evidence suggests that many projects continue to fall short of the Bank's own safeguard policies. For example, some high-impact projects appear to in-

14. Because Bank involvement provokes international scrutiny of social and environmental standards, national governments increasingly turn elsewhere to fund highly controversial projects, such as to bilateral aid agencies (e.g., China's Three Gorges dam).

clude planned safeguard provisions that high-level Bank environmental officials regard as public relations exercises designed to "buy time from our critics," according to an internal memo (quoted in Brown 1999).[15] Public interest groups also charge that the practice of miscategorizing projects continues to be widespread, which permits the avoidance of environmental and social impact assessments, consideration of alternative approaches, and mitigation measures (Kay Treakle, Bank Information Center, personal communication, June 1999).[16] Indeed, many Bank social and environmental staff members confide that they know of dozens of projects that fall far short of reform policies and therefore could be the subject of panel claims. Even if we made the reasonable assumption that safeguard policy compliance has improved to a substantial degree in recently designed projects, there is the ever-present problem of the counterfactual. Would the partial steps toward compliance have advanced as far in the absence of the panel?

Given the relatively small number of panel claims and their mixed record in terms of actual outcomes, it is likely that the panel's greatest impact has been indirect. In its early years, the panel members spent much of their time forwarding inquiries from project-affected groups to the particular Bank staff involved (Eduardo Abbott, World Bank Inspection Panel Secretariat, interview, April 1999, Washington, D.C.). Subsequent dialogue may have avoided the need for formal claims. More generally, the panel appears to have raised the potential public relations costs to the Bank of violating at least the most clear-cut of the safeguard policies, such as resettlement and environmental assessment.[17] Some insiders have dubbed the staff response in the project design process "panel-proofing" because they work from their checklists to make sure that they have a paper trail to demonstrate policy

15. This leaked report refers to the World Bank's promotion of an oil pipeline from Chad through Cameroon that would pass through vulnerable rainforest, affect indigenous populations, and subsidize Exxon (Shell subsequently withdrew). The implementation of the proposed mitigation commitments would depend on two corrupt and authoritarian regimes. After the pipeline project was approved, Chad's dictator spent his signing bonus on arms. See Farah and Ottaway (2000).

16. For example, the Bank clearly miscategorized the China Western Poverty Reduction Project as intermediate rather than high impact, although it turned out to have major environmental and indigenous rights implications. See Goodland (2001).

17. Other safeguard policies are easier to violate, such as the indigenous peoples policy. For example, the World Bank's huge portfolio of antipoverty projects in Mexico by definition affects many millions of indigenous people. The Bank's long-standing policy ostensibly requires their informed participation in any project that affects them. This includes projects that ostensibly help them, not only infrastructure-related damage control. Large amounts of Bank funding reach indigenous people in Mexico, but mainly through politicized patronage rather than informed participation, including apparent funding of the soft side of low-intensity conflict in Chiapas. This is an important example of a project risk that would not fit well with existing panel procedures, in part because of the difficulty of aggregating patterns of untold and invisible village-level material adverse effects. For details on rural civil-society monitoring efforts in Mexico, see the work of Trasparencia (www.trasparencia.org.mx) and Fox (1997a, 1997b, 2001).

compliance in the event of a challenge. Panel-proofing appears to be a contradictory process, in some cases leading to increased compliance, but in others promoting the pro forma fulfillment of administrative requirements rather than a focus on actual changes on the ground.

The panel clearly has had some impact on promoting a sustainable development agenda within the Bank, but the degree of its impact remains a matter of speculation. Robert Picciotto, director of Operations Evaluations Department, recognized that the Inspection Panel "played a very important role in putting the safeguard policies on the map" within the Bank. At the same time, however, he stressed that the safeguard policies are limited in their scope: "they are very important, they are everything for certain groups, but they are not everything for development. We don't have a safeguard policy on gender, for example" (interview, 13 April 1999, Washington, D.C.).[18] David Hunter, director of the Center for International Environmental Law (CIEL), made a related point: "The Panel can't get at stupid projects, claims must be linked to narrow policies" (interview, 5 April 1999, Washington, D.C.). Indeed, the Bank's environmental safeguard policies were originally approved on the condition that they apply only to project lending, excluding now-dominant structural adjustment lending from such scrutiny (Goodland 2000).

To assess the panel's indirect impact, we must also take into account the inherited pressures on managers and staff to lend funds to governments as quickly as possible, with as little friction as possible (Rich 1994, 2000; Wade 1997). President Wolfensohn's emphasis on a client focus (referring to borrowing governments) perpetuates these tensions. Wolfensohn has also highlighted the conflict between the pressure to lend and the need for quality results, and Bank management has carried out several major institutional changes in response, but the client focus appears to dominate thus far. What is clear is the magnitude of the challenge. According to a major internal study of unsatisfactory project performance, for example, staff continue to design projects with inadequate attention to beneficiary input. Staff suffer from "institutional amnesia, the corollary of institutional optimism and, despite lessons of experience, Bank staff are overoptimistic and tend to propose overambitious operations that are beyond local implementation capacity"[19] (Waldmeier and Suzman 1997, 1). According to one Bank staffer,

18. The Bank does have a gender policy, but it makes recommendations rather than establishing minimum standards ("Women's Eyes on the World Bank" 1997).

19. The 1997 Annual Review of Development Effectiveness found notable improvements, but at the same time found persistent problems in some areas of the Bank, including "pressure to lend; fear of offending the client . . . fear that a realistic, and thus more modest project would be dismissed as too small and inadequate. . . ." (quoted in Waldmeier and Suzman, 1997). According to Robert Picciotto, the 1998 Annual Review of Development Effectiveness showed continued improvememt, and OED's concerns led President Wolfensohn to create the Quality Assurance Group in the first place (Robert Picciotto, interview, 13 April 1999, Washington, D.C.).

the Board and management still focus on "staff/dollars lent," which encourages the cutting of corners (confidential interview, 1999, Washington, D.C.).[20]

Even if most Bank managers and staff were to do their utmost to comply with reform commitments, it would not take very many noncompliers to leave many high-impact projects in their wake. As a result, some internal and external participants in the reform process stress the importance of bolstering individual accountability—an issue excluded from the scope of the panel. For example, as one Bank social policy analyst argued, there has been "too much focus on structures rather than incentives and individuals. I would find 3 or 4 terrible cases and fire them, plus recruit those who believe in the policies" (confidential interview, 1999, Washington, D.C.).[21] OED Director Picciotto suggested that the threat of staff sanctions is not enough and that we need to look higher up. "You need to look at incentives in a broader way. Jim Wolfensohn would like to connect staff incentives with development results. The question is how to do it without unintended consequences. Development assistance is a team effort—individual staff behavior reflects the operating context, the skills imparted to him/her and the quality of support systems. Incentives and penalties should start with the managers. This is where the buck stops" (Robert Picciotto, interview, 13 April 1999, Washington, D.C.).[22] By 2001, new internal accountability mechanisms to promote reform policy compliance were announced, with uncertain effect.

Just as the Bank as an institution is a moving target, so too are its reform policies. The Inspection Panel was based on the premise that the reforms of the 1980s and 1990s set the standards against which the Bank could be held accountable. Management responded by arguing that these policies were too detailed and unwieldy and staff were therefore largely unfamiliar with them. Management began to "reformat" the policies, separating them into very brief mandatory sections (two pages) and a more extensive "recommended" good practice section. As one senior manager recognized in an internal memo: ". . . it has been hard for staff and managers to define clearly what is policy and what is advisory or good practice. *Our experiences with the Inspection Panel are teaching us that we have to be increasingly careful in setting policy that we are able to implement in practice*" (Alexander 1996, emphasis added).

Both external watchdog groups and insider Bank reformers agree that some important social and environmental policies are being diluted as key

20. Robert Picciotto argues that the pressure to lend within the Bank has decreased significantly in the late 1990s, but this staff quotation suggests that the perception may live on.
21. So far, no staffer or manager has ever been fired for violating safeguard policies, in spite of their damage to the Bank's public image.
22. The Inspection Panel's focus on operational managers coincided with the backlash against it. In the Singrauli case in India, the panel reportedly found that "the violations were even worse than initially thought and were primarily attributable to intense pressure from the bank's own senior regional managers to accelerate the loan approval process," according to Suzman (1998).

issues are moved from mandatory to recommended status (from Operational Policies to Good Practices). One Bank official concerned with accountability also expressed concern that the new policy language makes frequent reference to "in the judgement of . . . ," which blurs the definition of what is mandatory. We could argue, therefore, that accountability demands are having a perverse effect, driving a weakening of the very policy standards initially set by the Bank itself.

The Inspection Panel's effort to follow its mandated procedures also provoked a sustained backlash from some borrowing governments. The resulting ongoing conflict within the World Bank's Board of Directors suggests a picture of north-south relations that is much more nuanced than the conventional image of U.S. imposition. The board's September 1997 vote on the Itaparica claim was a major turning point. The Brazilian government effectively turned back the perceived northern threat to its sovereignty, using weak promises of ad hoc solutions (later broken). The U.S. executive director called a rare roll-call vote on whether or not to authorize an inspection (the vast majority of board decisions are made by consensus). As David Hunter of CIEL put it, to influence these board decisions "It helps to bring a big check, but clients have leverage too. The World Bank needs clients almost as badly as donors." More generally, Hunter added, "The credibility of the institution depends on not having a big split between donors and borrowers" (interview, 5 April 1999, Washington, D.C.).

The governments of Brazil and India led the counteroffensive to limit the panel's scope and autonomy. For example, their proposals excluded the Panel from examining any social-environmental problems that were jointly caused by governments and the Bank (which account for a large fraction of policy violations). The economic structure of the Bank-state relationship may be relevant to this debate. For most of this decade, both India and Brazil have been paying much more money to the Bank than the Bank has been lending to them. These flows are known as "net negative transfers." This has two implications. First, the Bank really does need both of these governments to continue borrowing in order to buffer the net negative transfer problem. If the Bank pushes too hard in favor of economically and politically costly social and environmental requirements, then these governments will be less inclined to borrow from the World Bank. Second, against the backdrop of these net negative flows, the panel's perceived political intrusion—indirectly recognizing the legitimacy of claims by groups that have not been heard by the state—is likely to be seen by economic policy makers as adding insult to injury. For example, when members of Brazil's broad civil society advocacy network that deals with international financial institutions met with Brazil's president, Fernando Henrique Cardoso, they criticized his government for pressuring the World Bank to block a panel inspection of the land reform project. President Cardoso, a former leftist sociology professor, "explained that he did that because 'in his day' it would have been unacceptable for a civil society group to ask an agent of 'imperialism' to get involved in internal issues" (reported in *Folha de São Paulo,* 10 July 1999, p. 3, translation by the author).

This is the context in which the Itaparica board vote was called, around the same time as India's Singrauli claim was being debated. The actual board vote is quite revealing of the hidden cleavages within the World Bank's Board of Directors. Recall that although the board is the ultimate body of authority that governs the World Bank, the executive directors have been widely assumed by outside observers to be powerless. For example, they have never rejected a loan proposed by management. Observers differ over whether it is Bank management or the U.S. government that really has the last word, and the answer no doubt depends heavily on whether the U.S. government is representing Wall Street versus environmental NGOs. Clearly, however, the Itaparica vote suggests that the issue of social and environmental policy compliance has turned the board into a more contested arena.

The actual Itaparica roll-call vote is detailed in table 6.4. Such votes are confidential (reportedly not even recorded in the official minutes). First, note the voting structure. It is widely known that the large donors are heavily weighted because of the one-dollar-one-vote system, but few are aware that many of the jurisdictions that hold Board votes include unusual combinations of countries. The heterogeneity of these groupings complicates the efforts of civil society organizations to hold their countries' financial authorities accountable for the votes of their board representatives. Most notable is the many votes that are held by representatives of blocs of countries that combine north and south or north and east (referring to the former Soviet bloc). In the Itaparica case, all the borrowing country blocs voted against the inspection, almost all the northern-only votes supported the Inspection Panel's recommendation (except for France).[23] The many votes that combined northern with eastern and/or southern countries were quite divided, often along difficult-to-predict lines. For example, the Italian government voted against the inspection, in spite of Italian civil society's sophisticated Bank reform campaign,[24] which has influence in parliament— perhaps because many of the world's dams involve Italian construction firms.

South Korea also voted against the inspection, although had Australia (its partner in the same voting bloc) been holding the seat that day, the whole

23. Reportedly the French government views the Inspection Panel as a U.S. creation and therefore opposes it on principle. France also lacks a powerful civil society Bank reform campaign, in contrast to England, Germany, Scandanavia, Switerland, and the Netherlands.
24. For details on the Italian World Bank campaign, see the Campagna per la riforma della Banca Mondiale website, http://www.unimondo.org/cbm/#.

Table 6.4

World Bank Board Votes on Itaparica Claim, September 1997

Executive Directors	Alternates	Casting Votes of	IBRD (% of total)[a]	Itaparica Claim Vote[b]
Northern Seats				
United States	United States		17.04	Yes
Japan	Japan		6.04	Yes
Germany	Germany		4.67	Yes
France	France		4.47	No
United Kingdom	United Kingdom		4.47	Yes
Sweden	Denmark	Denmark, Estonia, Finland, Iceland, Latvia, Lithuania, Norway, Sweden	3.27	Yes
Combined North and East/South Seats				
Belgium	Turkey	Austria, Belarus, Belgium, Czech Republic, Hungary, Kazakhstan, Luxembourg, Slovak Republic, Slovenia, Turkey	4.93	No
Netherlands	Romania	Armenia, Bosnia & Herzegovina, Bulgaria, Croatia, Cyprus, Georgia, Israel, Macedonia, Moldova, Netherlands, Romania, Ukraine	4.64	Yes
Venezuela	El Salvador	Costa Rica, El Salvador, Guatemala, Honduras, Mexico, Nicaragua, Panama, Spain, Venezuela	4.44	No
Canada	Barbados	Antigua & Barbuda, Bahamas, Barbados, Belize, Canada, Dominica, Grenada, Guyana, Ireland, Jamaica, St. Kitts & Nevis, St. Lucia, St. Vincent & the Grenedines	4.00	Yes
Italy	Portugal	Albania, Greece, Italy, Malta, Portugal	3.54	No
Switzerland	Poland	Azerbaijan, Kyrgz Republic, Poland, Switzerland, Tajikistan, Turkmenistan, Uzbekistan	2.96	Yes
South Korea	Australia	Australia, Cambodia, Kiribati, Korea, Marshall Islands, Micronesia, Mongolia, New Zealand, Papua New Guinea, Solomon Islands, Vanatu, Western Samoa	3.15	No

Southern Seats

	%	Vote[b]	Member countries
Mozambique	3.55	No	Angola, Botswana, Burundi, Eritrea, Ethiopia, Gambia, Kenya, Lesotho, Liberia, Malawi, Mozambique, Namibia, Nigeria, Seychelles, Sierra Leone, South Africa, Sudan, Swaziland, Tanzania, Uganda, Zambia, Zimbabwe
India	3.53	No	Bangladesh, Bhutan, India, Sri Lanka
Algeria	3.51	No	Afghanistan, Algeria, Ghana, Iran, Iraq, Morocco, Pakistan, Tunisia
Philippines	3.16	No	Brazil, Colombia, Dominican Republic, Ecuador, Haiti, Philippines, Suriname, Trinidad & Tobago
China	2.89	No	China
Saudi Arabia	2.89	No	Saudi Arabia
Russia	2.89	No	Russia
Kuwait	2.83	No	Bahrain, Egypt, Jordan, Kuwait, Lebanon, Libya, Maldives, Oman, Qatar, Syrian Arab Republic, United Arab Emirates, Yemen
Indonesia	2.64	No	Brunei, Fiji, Indonesia, Lao People's Democratic Republic, Malaysia, Myanmar, Nepal, Singapore, Thailand, Tonga, Vietnam
Argentina	2.41	No	Argentina, Bolivia, Chile, Paraguay, Peru, Uruguay
Comoros	2.07	No	Benin, Burkina, Faso, Cameroon, Cape Verde, Central African Republic, Chad, Comoros, Congo (Democratic Republic), Congo (Republic), Côte d'Ivoire, Djibouti, Equatorial Guinea, Gabon, Guinea, Guinea-Bissau, Madagascar, Mali, Mauritania, Mauritius, Niger, Rwanda, São Tomé & Principe, Senegal, Togo
Final Tally (%):	**YES 47.09** **NO 52.90**		

[a]IBRD, International Bank for Reconstruction and Development. From World Bank, 1997, *Executive Directors and Alternates of the World Bank and Their Voting Power.* World Bank Annual Report, 30 June, App. 2, 149.

[b]Actual executive director role call votes are confidential. Information on this roll call is based on interviews with Washingon-based public interest groups and policy makers (April 1999).

outcome might have been different, due to the closeness of the vote (Korea, Australia, and a dozen small countries hold 3.15 percent of the board's votes). The final tally was 52.9 percent against versus 47.09 percent in favor of the Itaparica inspection. The Panel—supposedly a tool of northern governments against southern governments—was successfully resisted by a coalition of Bank members from the south, east, and a divided north.

In short, U.S. hegemony has been overstated, at least insofar as its capacity to impose social and environmental reforms is concerned. This was underscored by the mid-1999 defeat of U.S. government efforts to block a socially and environmentally controversial loan to China, involving Tibet, by another loss of a roll-call vote.[25] As a compromise, the Bank's board assigned the Inspection Panel a monitoring role in project implementation, which contributed to China's withdrawal of the project in July 2000.[26]

According to both World Bank and advocacy NGO participants in the international debate over the panel's fate, the Itaparica claim vote was a turning point because it revealed the board's tenuous support for the panel. The Itaparica vote emboldened the Brazilian and Indian governments to go beyond their ad hoc defensive moves and instead to take the offensive to weaken the panel. The board created a working group to review the panel's procedures, including Brazil and India. They produced a set of recommendations that would have dramatically weakened it. The panel appeared to be destined for complete evisceration (Phillips 1999). However, an international campaign by organized claimants and their NGO allies led the board to decide to hear claimants' views directly, and a major consultation with them was held in Washington. Another key factor was that panel members themselves held firm and strongly defended their own independent sense of mission, bolstered by the fact that as a group they had succeeded in always making decisions based on consensus, remaining united in the face of many controversies. As a result, the board made some important changes in the proposed revisions. The China/Tibet loan was the first big test of the panel's capacity after this precarious board compromise over its role, and it emerged strengthened as a result.

Transnational advocacy efforts to increase institutional accountability target both the interests and the ideologies that sustain impunity. Constructing accountability therefore necessarily involves conflict. Understanding the dynamics of such conflict requires exploring the strategies and tactics of the multiple actors involved, as well as exposing the often-hidden fault lines and

25. As the *New York Times* editorialized, "approving this loan may violate the bank's own guidelines for assessing the social and environmental impacts of its projects" (Sanger 1999a). See also "Nepal" (1999).

26. For details, see the NGO Bank Information Center website, http://www.bicusa.org/asia/chinatibet.htm.

alliances. Like so many other examples of controversies over the role of the World Bank, the Inspection Panel experience opens a revealing window on the changing process of transnational conflict over both norms and practices. These conflicts unfold both within and among three intersecting arenas: the world's leading international development agency, diverse nation-states, and increasingly transnationally networked civil societies.

The World Bank's social and environmental policy reform process, including the panel experience, supports the proposition that the World Bank, nation-states, and civil societies (local, national, and international) are all internally divided over how to deal with the challenges of sustainable development and public accountability. The corollary of this proposition is that variation in the actual impact of both transnational advocacy pressures and World Bank lending on sustainable development will be driven by bargaining processes that cut across state, society, and international actors. The degree to which pro-sustainable-development policy makers within states are able to carry out reforms that increase institutional accountability will depend largely on their degree of support from outside allies. In other words, such reformist policy makers rarely dominate their states and therefore their influence rests on mutually reinforcing interaction with pro-reform actors internationally and within their own civil society. Similarly, the degree to which reformist forces within civil societies can influence their states' practices will depend largely on their capacity to form broader alliances, both internationally and within their own states. Internationally, the degree to which pro-accountability World Bank officials can comply with their own reforms will depend on their capacity to bolster pro-reform interlocutors in both states and societies. In short, no one set of pro-reform actors can get very far on its own.

The need for local roots is built into the Inspection Panel claim process, which relies on directly affected individuals being willing to make their claims on the record. Most often, only a small part of each local movement is aware of and engaged in the process of building transnational coalitions. The key transnational links often take the form of a handful of individuals who share social capital and trust with distinct movements in different countries and social sectors (Brown and Ashman 1996). The Internet and foundation-funded airplane tickets facilitate these transnational social relationships, but it is the cross-cultural diplomatic skills of individuals that generate the political trust necessary to sustain them.

North-south civil society coalitions combined southern mass protest and northern media coverage to put sustainable development reforms on the agendas of donor governments starting in the mid to late 1980s. At most, however, they usually manage to win over minority factions within the executive and legislative branches of their national governments. Northern policy makers responsive to transnational advocacy coalitions managed in turn to influence the World Bank through their formal governmental representation on the Board of Directors. As a multilateral organization, the Bank's board bridges representation from both donor and borrowing governments while being organizationally distinct from both individual governments and the World Bank apparatus itself. In other words, the main avenue for transnational advocacy leverage over the World Bank is through nation-states. In both north and south, the influence of advocacy groups over states is mediated largely by their media skills and their organized constituencies within their respective societies, which together shape their influence in branches of national governments that are usually excluded from the Bank-state partnership, such as legislatures (Fox and Brown 1998b; Fox 2000b).[27]

CONCLUSION

The Inspection Panel offers a powerful test case of the possibilities and limits for transnational advocacy networks to increase the public accountability of multilateral organizations. The panel is an institutional experiment that reflects the broader process of local, national, and transnational coalition-building and conflict that will determine the World Bank's impact on sustainable development. The panel experience is one among many indicators of this process of civil society pressure and institutional response, but both sides have staked it out as a critical battlefield. In terms of most of the actual claims, the panel's main contribution has been simply to listen to the claimants. This legitimation effect has been important, although not always sufficient to provide claimants with protection from authoritarian reprisals (as the Singrauli case suggests). So far, the panel has produced only a few on-the-ground solutions; indeed, solutions were not in its mandate. The most tangible progress was achieved in the panel's very first case, Nepal's Arun dam, and in the China Western Poverty Reduction and Argentina Structural Adjustment claims, with major partial changes in Brazil's Planafloro case. The first two projects were cancelled and the second two were improved. Within the World Bank, the panel has contributed most by raising the internal profile and legitimacy of the broader package of minimum safeguard policies, but it has also prompted somewhat perverse effects, such as panel-proofing and policy conversion.

At the international level, the panel was created by the board largely in response to international civil society pressures, but in practice it has been subject to a wide range of cross-cutting nation-state agendas from the south as well as the north. The panel has improved the Bank's public image and is a symbol of its commitment to its own policy reforms; at the same time as

27. In the south, Brazil has generated the most broad-based advocacy coalition to democratize the Bank-state relationship, bolstering public legislative oversight (Leroy and Couto Soares 1998; Barros 2001). Some Mexican public interest campaigns are pursuing a similar strategy of vertical integration (Fox 2001).

it has provoked a backlash from large nationalist borrowing governments. The Inspection Panel is a paradigm case both of the influence of transnational advocacy networks over international norms and policies and of their limited leverage over institutional behavior in practice.

One of this study's main findings is that, because of constraints on its mandate and its practice, the panel can deliver at most some degree of transparency and contributes to accountability only indirectly. The experience clearly shows that transnational advocacy networks can embed pro-transparency handles into international organizations, and these handles can be critical for opening doors that would otherwise remain closed. At the same time, these pro-transparency handles may remain out of reach of most who need them, or they may be too weak to sustain the pressure of trying to leverage a huge institution—breaking off in the hands of those who try to use them.

More generally, the experience reminds us that transparency is necessary but not sufficient for accountability. The future of the panel lies in many hands, but it still serves at the discretion of the World Bank's increasingly multilateral board. Ironically, it is this body of diverse nation-state representatives that will determine the fate of this experiment in institutional reform.

CHAPTER SEVEN

Corruption and Governance in Early Capitalism
World Bank Strategies and Their Limitations

Mushtaq H. Khan

One of the most dramatic changes in the World Bank's approach to development in the 1990s has been its new commitment to governance improvements and in particular to fighting corruption in some of the poorest countries in the world. Driven by evidence that corruption reduces growth and investment in developing countries, the Executive Board of the Bank approved its anticorruption strategy in September 1997, defining corruption as the "use of public office for private gain." According to the strategy, the Bank was to address corruption along four dimensions: preventing fraud and corruption in Bank projects, helping countries that request Bank assistance for fighting corruption, mainstreaming the concern with corruption in all of the Bank's work, and lending active support to international efforts in fighting corruption. These concerns were reflected in the *World Development Report* of 1997 and have been central to the subsequent concern of the Bank with governance and institutional reform. More recently, the Bank has argued that "there is nothing more important" than the fight against corruption (World Bank 2000d). The immediate effects of these policy announcements have been a much greater degree of concern with accountability within the Bank. At the same time, there has been a closer examination of the corruption and governance implications of Bank policies. Some older policies now have their anticorruption content more openly expressed; in other areas there are new emphases. Thus, Bank support for programs involving liberalization, reforms of the civil service, "rightsizing the state," and privatization was given renewed impetus with an emphasis on the anticorruption and governance improvement aspects of these reforms. In addition, there was a shift toward new areas for the Bank such as support for decentralization, devolution, and democratization and for greater civil society participation in monitoring developing country states.

Although the renewed implicit recognition of the importance of the state in economic development is very welcome, the Bank's approach to corruption and governance failures is fundamentally deficient in a number of ways. First, it is still based on a perception of economic development in which success is driven by efficient markets supported by noninterventionist states. This theoretical perception is not based on the historical evidence of late developers, particularly in Asia, and as a result the prescriptions it offers regarding the desired features of a state that can best carry out developmental functions is not necessarily appropriate for most developing countries.

Second, and closely related to the first problem, the empirical data showing a strong relationship between corruption and poor development are flawed. Although it is undoubtedly the case that corruption imposes large costs on investors and on society and that high levels of corruption undoubtedly undermine the social fabric if it goes on for too long, there is no evidence that successful developers first fought and won the battle against corruption and then developed. Rather, the evidence strongly suggests that in all the successful developers, from South Korea in the 1960s to China in 2002, corruption was rife during the period of early capitalist development. Why is there no example of a developing country that was corruption-free at an early stage of development? The answer that poverty breeds corruption is wrong; poor people are often scrupulously honest. Rather, the process of capitalist development itself generates powerful incentives and motives for corruption. Without excusing corruption, international agencies have to face up to the fact that the construction of capitalism, although it may be necessary for the long-term prosperity of poor countries, is itself an ugly and conflictual process. Attempts to attain a corruption-free, representative and accountable system of governance at this stage may not only not be achievable, but may divert attention from what actually needs to be done to improve the quality of state intervention to accelerate the transition and make it more socially acceptable.

The historical evidence tells us that the early stages of capitalist development are periods of great social disruption and of serious and sustained political instability in most countries. There is also very often a great deal of justified resentment and conflict as a new capitalist class emerges and begins to enjoy a life of conspicuous consumption and political influence. It is also a period when new areas of production and expertise are being developed and markets and institutions often need to be reconstructed to serve new needs and require careful regulation and support. This combination of social discontent, which creates strong incentives for clientelism and political corruption, and necessarily intrusive state regulation creates an environment where it is almost impossible to fight all corruption at the same time. Indeed to set the fight against corruption as a goal may exacerbate the sense of social injustice and instability because it is virtually impossible to achieve sustained reductions of corruption without overcoming the transition itself. The appropriate response must be to make sure that the most growth-reducing and antidevelopmental types of corruption are attacked first if the effort of governance reform is not to be dissipated in a series of futile gestures. The types of programs that the Bank still recommends, now in support of anticorruption, such as liberalization, downsizing the state, decentralization, and even democratization may not be relevant for addressing the problems of state failure or even for fighting corruption in most developing countries facing this transition (although democratization in particular may be desirable for other reasons).

Although all developing countries seem to have had a high degree of corruption, this does not mean that an analysis of corruption is unimportant. On the contrary, by examining the types of corruption in dynamic and not-so-dynamic developing countries, we can learn important lessons about which types of governance reforms are actually required to accelerate growth and attain relative prosperity. In successful developers, corruption could coexist with growth because it was part of a system of primitive accumulation through which a new class of capitalists emerged with strong state assistance and often in collusion with state leaders. State functionaries shared in some of the new wealth, but were also able to discipline capitalists to ensure that inefficiency did not sustain itself, infrastructure was not too badly constructed, and that domestic resources did not fly to foreign banks. In the less dynamic countries, although bureaucrats and politicians also captured wealth paradoxically they often captured a lot less in absolute terms because they failed to discipline capitalists, failed to maintain social order, failed to construct good infrastructure, failed to control capital flight, and, in the end, failed to generate growth. The subsequent sustainability of dynamic states has depended on how successful they were in institutionalizing the new power and wealth that capitalist development created while opening up (often very gradually) to greater popular participation in decision making. Thus, a historical examination of the data on corruption provides a very different set of prescriptions for states suffering from growth-reducing types of corruption and sustained state failure. It also suggests that none of the anticorruption policies of the Bank necessarily helps poorly performing countries to acquire the state capacities or political settlements that allowed dynamic countries to grow rapidly. Indeed, some of the new policies may actually make the transition period more difficult. The challenge for international agencies such as the Bank is to question the ideological self-image of capitalism that has been driving policy in ways that have made the construction of capitalism more difficult.

The first section of this chapter looks at the nature of the empirical evidence on which the Bank and other international organizations have based their anticorruption strategies. Although this evidence is often presented to support mainstream approaches such as that of the Bank, a closer look at the evidence shows that it is incompatible with the mainstream analysis of market-driven development. Rather it is consistent with a very different story about the nature of capitalist development and the role of the state. The next two sections examine the main components of the Bank's anti-corruption strategy, first looking at the strategy of reforming and downsizing the state and then examining the Bank's forays into apparently political areas such as reforms promoting decentralization, devolution, and civil society participation. Finally, the fourth section argues that although the Bank appears to have been willing to take on board political reform as part of its governance improvement strategy, the mainstream approach on which it is based ignores critical aspects of the role of the state during the capitalist transition. Taking on board the historical evidence provides a very different set of strategies involving the strengthening of state capacity in developing countries to promote accumulation, discipline the market, and maintain social order. Such strategies would hit hard at types of corruption that are based on unproductive groups capturing resources by using their political and social power. It would not necessarily remove or even seek to remove all types of corruption, and it would certainly not raise unviable expectations that this could be achieved if only the political will were there. A reduction of corruption across the board is unlikely without sustained economic development combined with the political and organizational reforms appropriate for more advanced economies.

THE ANOMALOUS EVIDENCE ON CORRUPTION

It is not surprising that the relationship between governance failures and corruption, on the one hand, and development, on the other, is complex and varies substantially across countries. This is because state policies, the organization and structure of societies, the level of economic development, and the types of technologies that are being used differ greatly among countries. Nevertheless, the dominant econometric relationships that have inspired much of the mainstream international interest in corruption reduction have been staggering in the simplicity of the relationship they have identified. Typically, they have sought to show a relationship between an index of corruption and a measure of developmental success, such as the rate of growth or the share of investment in the economy. There are serious measurement problems in trying to capture the extent of corruption in a country in one number. To make matters worse, corruption cannot be objectively measured and so the figures we have are actually subjective rankings of countries based on the perceptions of different groups of observers. Subjective indices are clearly not very satisfactory, and in addition they suffer from the serious problem that observers may perceive corruption to be more serious in poorly performing countries than in more dynamic countries even if objectively they have the same degree of corruption. This may then give rise to the misleading conclusion that higher corruption is associated with poorer economic performance. There is no need to discount these exercises completely, but we have to be aware of the limitations of the data.

The strongest empirical relationship that is observed is between corruption and per capita GDP. This relationship is unfortunately not very interesting because it tells us nothing about causality. It could be underdevelopment that was responsible for corruption rather than the other way around. A much more interesting relationship is between corruption and the rate of growth of GDP. If a relationship existed here, it would be much more compelling evidence that corruption had an effect on development. The econometric relationship here is much weaker, but Mauro (1995) provides the first regressions that show a significant relationship between these variables. The negative effect of corruption on growth was initially found to be weak, however, and disappeared when the investment rate was included as a variable explaining growth rates. In later work it was shown that some negative effect remained even when investment was included as an explanatory variable in the regressions (Mauro 1996). This result, and others that followed from it, provided the precise empirical basis for international agencies such as the International Monetary Fund (IMF) (where Mauro was based) and the World Bank to make corruption a direct policy target.

Apart from the size and significance of the effect of corruption on growth, a closer look at the data shows a much more important problem with the interpretation of the regression result. A graphical plot of corruption against growth shows that the asserted negative relationship is arguably based on an inappropriate exercise that combines countries at different levels of development. Countries have different levels of corruption depending on their level of development (remember that the strongest relationship of corruption is with the per capita GDP of a country). Thus, most advanced capitalist countries have much lower levels of corruption than most developing countries. Most advanced countries also have economies that work reasonably well and manage to chug along at a steady pace over the years.

In contrast, most developing countries (and particularly the poorest ones) have been in an economic mess since the 1980s or earlier, often with low or negative rates of growth. Their underdevelopment is associated with some of the highest corruption indices. A few developing countries, however, have done extremely well and have managed to far exceed the rates of growth achieved in the advanced countries. Of course, we expect developing countries to do this if they are ever to have a chance of catching up with the absolute living standards of the advanced countries. The problem is that these high-growth developing countries did not have significantly lower levels of corruption than other developing countries (allowing for the fact that

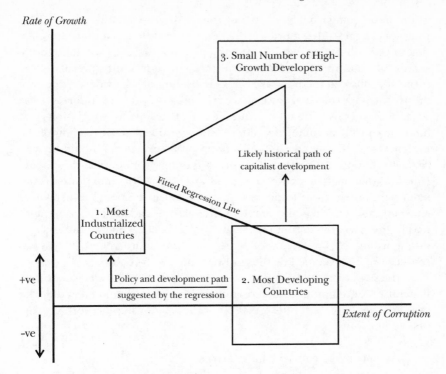

Figure 7.1 Relationship between Corruption and Growth

they were rapidly becoming richer) during their catching-up period. Figure 7.1 presents these observations in a simplified diagram.

The downward slope of the fitted regression line could be explained by the fact that relatively few countries were located in box 3, the group of underdeveloped countries that were growing rapidly enough to begin converging with the advanced countries. Regressions are based on numbers of observations and so the experience of the high-performance countries are swamped out as outliers, even though they are often very populous countries and even though their experience is of great significance for understanding the process of development.

The policy conclusions that the Bank and the IMF derive from these regressions is summarized in the arrow going leftward and upward from box 2 to box 1. Simply by looking at the negative slope of the line, it is concluded that in order to move toward the performance of the advanced countries, poorly performing countries must first reduce corruption, even though there is no historical observation of this ever happening. In contrast, a historical examination of the data suggests a quite different trajectory, shown by the arrow going from box 2 to box 3 and only subsequently to box 1. This trajectory suggests that a prior reduction of corruption is a misrepresentation of the conditions that led to developmental success, even though the successful countries must have gone through significant governance reforms that allowed them to take off. Our reading of the evidence does not reduce the importance of governance reforms, interpreted as reforms of the state, but forces us to treat with caution many of the policy conclusions that have uncritically become very widespread. Nor does such a reading of the evidence suggest that corruption is not a problem that we should be worried about. Rather it suggests that the real difference between developing countries that begin to converge with advanced countries and those that remain behind has more to do with political and institutional reforms that changed the *types* of corruption they suffered from and not just, or even primarily, the *extent* of corruption (Khan 1996a, 1996b). The importance of distinguishing between types of corruption and, more generally, types of rent-seeking is developed further in Khan and Jomo (2000).

In the next sections we evaluate how the World Bank has led other multilaterals in developing an anticorruption strategy in developing countries based on the dominant interpretation of the relationship between corruption and growth.

BANK ANTICORRUPTION STRATEGIES:
RIGHTSIZING THE STATE

Having identified corruption as a cause of underdevelopment with measurable effects on the growth rate and on investment, the Bank, together with other multilaterals, has identified a set of mechanisms through which corruption can be reduced. These mechanisms draw heavily from an implicit underlying neoclassical model of rent-seeking in which corruption and other forms of rent-seeking are driven by the ability of the state to create rents that distort the economy and reduce welfare and by the inability of society to discipline and punish those who seek to capture and share these rents both legally (through processes such as lobbying) and illegally (through processes such as corruption). The fight against corruption is therefore presented as a two-pronged one. The first prong is to limit the ability of the state to create rents, which in any case lower welfare. The second prong is to combine this with mechanisms that reduce the incentives of bureaucrats to be corrupt, for instance by increasing salaries (which are lost if the bureaucrats are caught and fired) and improving the monitoring and judicial systems (to improve the probability of their being caught and fired in the first place). The *World Development Report* of 1997 follows this scheme very closely, arguing that countries that have higher corruption have:

  1. A higher "policy distortion index" (that is, a greater divergence from a notional free market and lots of state-created rents). The

logic is that the greater the rents associated with state restrictions, the greater the incentives for businessmen and ordinary citizens to bribe to capture these rents or overcome these restrictions.

2. A lower opportunity cost of being caught in the act of corruption (in the form of lower civil service to manufacturing salary ratios). The lower the opportunity cost, the greater the incentive of bureaucrats to accept bribes because even if they are caught and fired they do not lose much.

3. A less meritocratic bureaucracy (more political appointments and fewer exam-based appointments). This means that bureaucrats have a short time horizon and are more willing to make money fast rather than being worried about their career prospects in the long run.

4. A lower predictability of the judicial system (measured by a lower probability of getting caught and being brought to justice). This too increases the incentive of corruption by making punishment less sure.

These observations, of course, mark no significant break with the policies that the Bank had been following for many years. Lowering the distortion index is entirely consistent with conventional Bank policies of rightsizing the state. These involved liberalizing the economy; getting rid of government interventions in the form of subsidies, tariffs and quotas; privatizing public sector enterprises that suffered from excess employment and distorted prices; and, in general, getting the state out of all activities that either distorted the market or that in theory the private sector could do. All that was now being added was the recognition that not only did these distortions have direct welfare costs that were well known, but in addition they had a much bigger indirect impact by encouraging corruption (and other forms of rent-seeking), making it even more important to attack these problems. However, the Bank did seek to distance itself from the more extreme neoliberals by recognizing the role of the state in providing essential public goods including law and order, primary education, health care, and some infrastructure. Thus, the emphasis was on rightsizing rather than downsizing the state, emphasizing the importance of getting the state to focus on its core tasks (even increasing its capacity to do these things) while getting it out of regulating and creating incentives for industrialization and catching up, for instance, which inevitably created rents and encouraged rent-seeking. At the same time, the Bank approach stressed the importance of having a well-trained professional bureaucracy that was well paid, together with a monitoring and accountability system that ensured that bureaucrats were held to account and fired or prosecuted if they failed to perform their duties or if they broke the law (World Bank 1997n).

Although the Bank approach may appear to be a balanced one, it is actually based on a very specific interpretation of the role of the state during development and of the institutional drivers of development. Underlying these prescriptions is the belief that free and unfettered markets are the best drivers of development in poor countries, provided that the state has created a basic legal framework and provided essential public goods. Any additional state intervention and the associated rents that such intervention inevitably creates are not only not necessary, but are a massive hindrance to development. But in fact the historical evidence of rapid late development tells a very different story. Despite significant differences in the details of policy interventions across the high-growth developing countries, a common feature characterizing virtually all of them was concerted rent-creating state intervention. State interventions were critical in managing the processes through which new capitalist classes emerged by acquiring capital and technology. The flow of real resources into the hands of newly emerging capitalists was orchestrated through a variety of mechanisms including state control over or ownership of banks; controls or distortions of prices, interest rates, and exchange rates; and directly through taxes and subsidies. Even more important, particularly in the dynamic economies, was the discipline that the state could impose on the newly emerging capitalist class to ensure that these resources were not significantly wasted and that potential capitalists who failed to become productive lost out and resources could be transferred to others. States also played an essential role in maintaining political stability through judicious resource transfers and redistributions, not always organized legally or publicly. Finally, states had to create new institutions for regulating markets and managing economic stability where preexisting economic institutions were largely inadequate. Aspects of these processes have by been well documented (Amsden 1989; Wade 1990; Aoki, Kim, and Okuno-Fujiwara 1997; Khan and Jomo 2000).

From the perspective of these historical observations, paring down the state to a corruption-free rump that somehow provides law and order in a poor and conflict-torn economy and that restricts itself to providing primary education and some essential infrastructure may be suggesting a blueprint that both is impossible to achieve (in its law and order objective) and will doom the poorest economies to at best a moderate economic performance. The provision of a semblance of political stability may be impossible in most developing economies without the hidden political transfers that are a source of political corruption. And a state that actually disengaged itself from the task of accelerating capitalist accumulation and disciplining emerging capitalists would doom the economy to much slower progress. But even more serious from my perspective, the evidence suggests that the policy package of rightsizing does not even achieve the limited objective of actually reducing corruption (regardless of the subsequent effects on growth).

The evidence of the 1980s and 1990s strongly suggests that liberalization and privatization are often associated with an increase in corruption rather than the reverse. This is most obvious in the case of Russia and eastern Europe. It is also the case in less well-recognized cases such as India, Pakistan, and Bangladesh, where the liberalization of the 1980s and 1990s were associated with very dramatic increases in corruption as reported in corruption indices. In a review of anticorruption strategies for the Operations Evaluation Department of the Bank, Huther and Shah (2000) look at the relevance of the main strategies in developing countries. They argue that some strategies such as introducing ombudsmen and raising public awareness of corruption are unlikely to have any effect on countries where governance is poorest. But although they accept that privatization had negative effects in Russia (Huther and Shah 2000, table 2), they still argue that reducing the size of the state, increasing citizen participation, and (somehow) improving the rule of law are still the best strategies in countries with the worst governance record. In fact, the systematic evidence that privatization and liberalization result in increased corruption is difficult to reconcile with the neoclassical perspective, but not with a perspective that recognizes that the environment for corruption is closely related to the stage and pace of the capitalist transition. Liberalization and privatization accelerate the creation of capitalists and dramatically increase the stakes for those who want to enter the new class or expand their stake in it. Corruption and rent-seeking are bound to increase in this context; the irony is that without a strong state regulating the process the outcome is not likely to be efficient, as the cases of Russia, Pakistan, and many other countries show.

What about the more pragmatic reforms suggested by the mainstream analysis—raising bureaucratic salaries and improving accountability? Here the theoretical justification has come under attack from within mainstream economics itself, and the evidence too is very disappointing. Higher salaries are theoretically expected to lower corruption because they increase the opportunity cost of corruption, provided there is some probability of being caught and fired (Gould and Amaro-Reyes 1983; Klitgaard 1988). High wages for bureaucrats operate like efficiency wages. It may be efficient to not only pay civil servants the market wage for their skill level but also a rent on top of that. This is because the work that bureaucrats do is often difficult to monitor and the rent (or efficiency wage) creates an additional incentive for honest service delivery, given a sufficiently high probability of getting caught and fired. This incentive mechanism breaks down if the probability of getting caught and/or of being actually fired when caught is very low (Besley and McLaren 1993; Huther and Shah 2000). In that case, the higher salary is just a bonus because the bureaucrat can continue to be corrupt. The cross-national empirical evidence shows, as expected, that there is very little if any relationship between bureaucratic pay increases and the reduction of corruption (Treisman 2000; Rauch and Evans 2000). And finally, coming back to our bigger picture of growth and development, there is, as we have already pointed out, little evidence that bureaucrats and politicians in fast-growing economies were actually squeaky clean. Just think of contemporary China or South Korea in the 1970s.

DECENTRALIZATION, DEVOLUTION, AND CIVIL SOCIETY

To complement its existing policies of liberalization and rightsizing, the Bank has been increasingly persuaded that it needs to support explicitly political reforms to increase the accountability of the state and to reduce the discretion available to bureaucrats. Thus, anticorruption strategies now include, in addition to the types of reforms discussed earlier, a commitment to decentralization to reduce the discretion available to bureaucrats and a commitment to more public oversight through support for democracy and a "vibrant" civil society (World Bank 2000d, 21). Driving these reforms is an underlying model of a developing economy in which society is composed of individuals with well-defined endowments who would go ahead and develop the economy according to their comparative advantage if left to their own devices. They only need the state to provide them with law and order and basic public goods, and this they can ensure by holding the state accountable. Decentralization and devolution enhance their ability to do this by bringing government closer to the final customers of state services. As before, we need to examine how sensible these strategies are in terms of the relevance of their underlying theories for the real situations in which they are being applied. We can also look at the evidence to see if corruption is lower and if welfare is higher in developing countries that have devolved and decentralized systems.

In the conventional service-delivery model of the state, the relationship between the electorate, politicians, and bureaucrats is as shown in figure 7.2. The electorate are the consumers of government services. They are supposed to elect and put pressure on politicians to translate their demands and requirements for services into policy. Politicians in turn are supposed to monitor and control the bureaucrats to ensure service delivery (but they may collude with bureaucrats to subvert the popular will). Note that the role of government in this perspective is simply to deliver services that the public collectively and democratically desires. Decentralization refers to administrative changes that give lower levels of government greater administrative authority in delivering services. Devolution involves, in addition, changes in political institutions so that electors vote for representatives at lower levels of government, who in turn have effective control over lower-level bureaucrats involved in service delivery. Clearly, no system is entirely centralized or devolved, but a devolved system has more aspects of service delivery and regulation managed by lower tiers of government, which are in turn answerable to lower-level politicians. Clearly not all services and regu-

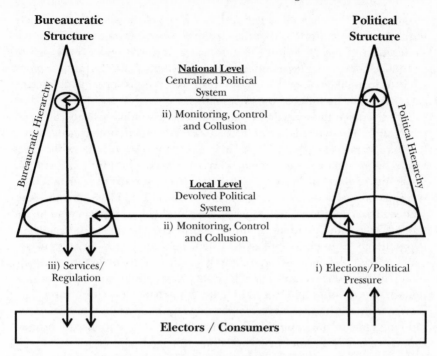

**Figure 7.2 Devolution, Decentralization, and Improvements
in Governance**

latory functions are suitable for devolution. Some government activities
such as building intercity highways may not be divisible to local government
without loss of efficiency. Thus devolution refers to a greater proportion of
divisible services being delivered through a devolved system.

If the state is primarily there to deliver services for the electors, decentralization and in particular devolution will plausibly improve accountability and governance by bringing government closer to the people. This will
make it easier for the people to monitor and discipline the state. Service delivery should improve and corruption should decline. But this plausible argument requires that a number of stringent conditions hold if it is to be true.
The effectiveness of governance from this perspective depends on the three
sets of relationships marked in figure 7.2: elections/political pressure; monitoring, control, and collusion; and services/regulation.

First, the arrows from the electorate to the politicians in the figure indicate the role of elections and other political processes in communicating the
objectives of the electorate to political representatives. How effective are
these processes in communicating the real interests of the electorate? To
what extent are these processes controlled by privileged groups within the

electorate? If the electors as consumers are to get the services they really want, the first condition is that the electoral process should reveal the real preferences of the electorate. To compare a devolved system with a more centralized one, the relevant question here is whether the electorate is more likely to formulate general social interests in elections for local politicians rather than for national or regional politicians.

Public choice theory tells us that democracy is unlikely to reveal social preferences if individuals in society have widely divergent preferences (Mueller 1989, especially 58–95). The view that democracy can allow the electorate to formulate clear demands even for service delivery ignores the possibility of deep divisions between classes and groups in society. These divisions are particularly intense during periods of rapid social transition. Under these conditions, democracy is even less likely to reflect common interests. Indeed, in developing countries democracy appears to systematically bypass the interests of the bulk of the voters. Instead, the political system typically reflects the interests of relatively small groups of organizationally powerful clients who control the electoral process financially and organizationally. For devolution to result in better governance even in terms of the service provision model, devolved elections have to result in a more accurate reflection of the popular will and break down the tendency toward the capture of political power by sectional interest groups.

Clearly devolution is likely to make some difference. The size of local constituencies is usually much smaller and so the same population will ultimately be electing a much greater number of politicians at the local level than at higher levels. Arithmetically, local politicians are likely to represent social interests to a greater extent simply because they are more numerous and a greater variety of interests are likely to be represented. On the other hand, the disparity of organizational and financial power can be as great in a village constituency as in a parliamentary constituency because the latter is simply an agglomeration of the former. So although local politicians are likely to reflect the interests of a more broad-based elite than national politicians, it will still be an elite nonetheless. More important for development, the interests of this local elite need not be more developmental compared to the elite represented at higher levels.

The evidence from India's considerable experience with local government suggests that service delivery has been most successful in states such as West Bengal and Kerala where elections have been contested in the context of centralized party structures with strong developmental and welfarist goals. However imperfectly, these centralized party structures were better able to represent general interests precisely because they were mass parties and had a high degree of centralization in terms of agenda setting and mobilizational power (see, for instance, Williams 1999). In other parts of India, where the electorate is fragmented, devolution has usually not resulted in a more accurate reflection of popular demands. Devolved political power has reflected the interests of relatively small groups of well-organized elites.

The second area where devolution could make a difference is shown by the arrows in figure 7.2 from politicians to bureaucrats, which describe the exercise of control by politicians over civil servants. This control can either ensure that the latter carry out their duties and deliver what the public requires or it can result in political intervention or collusion that benefits politicians and their clients and sometimes bureaucrats as well. In extreme cases in which politicians are excessively motivated by clientelism, the control exercised over bureaucrats by politicians can even be against the general interest. This argument has often been used and misused by dictators to subvert the political process, particularly in developing countries. The question for devolution and decentralization is whether local politicians are more likely to control local bureaucrats in the public interest and less likely to direct them or collude with them to benefit sectional interests compared to national politicians and higher-level bureaucrats.

There are a number of reasons why this expectation may not hold in many developing countries. First, local politicians usually lack sufficient constitutional powers to effectively sanction bureaucrats. This problem may be exacerbated by the fact that in most developing countries the educational and status gap between politician and bureaucrat may be far greater at the local government level than at higher levels. But more important, we have to ask if local politicians are more or less likely to engage in collusive corruption with bureaucrats compared to provincial and national politicians? There is no general answer to this question, which is valid everywhere. But given what we have already said about unequal access and clientelism at all levels of society, the propensity for collusion should be no less at the local than at the higher levels. In addition, there are many more points of interaction between politicians and bureaucrats in a devolved system compared to a centralized system, it is very difficult for the national press and senior investigators to watch what is happening at the local level, and it is often easier for local elites to intimidate their opponents and get away with overt corruption than it is for national politicians. For these reasons, local-level corruption is often no less and is sometimes proportionately much greater than corruption at higher levels. Clearly, there are no general reasons to believe that devolution will work to improve governance and reduce corruption in every case.

Third, the arrows in figure 7.2 from bureaucrats to the electorate shows the delivery of services, which in turn are the source of welfare improvements or welfare reductions for final consumers. For the electorate to be able to respond to government, there has to be a transparent chain of responsibility for specific services or interventions. The case for devolution and decentralization in terms of this relationship rests on the assumption that in devolved governments it is easier for the electorate to identify those responsible for particular decisions.

However, this expectation critically requires that there be no complementarities of local services with those provided by other units or funding requirements from higher levels of government. Otherwise, it would be relatively easy for local service providers to attribute their own failures to others or, indeed, their failures may actually be due to others. In either case, it would be very difficult for local consumers to decide without a lot of expenditure on information collection. In fact, bureaucrats in devolved systems frequently invoke these arguments even in sophisticated advanced economies, sometimes justifiably and sometimes not. If we move beyond the simplest service delivery to look at the types of activities that a developing country state has to engage in, such as maintaining law and order; accelerating the creation and consolidation of an efficient capitalist class; and encouraging technological progress, complementarities, and spillovers between localities and regions, there is no effective sense in which local monitoring of service delivery can attribute praise or blame to local bureaucrats. Not only that, the fragmentation of jurisdictions in the presence of complementarities can result in an excessive extortion of bribes by bureaucrats and politicians because bribe collectors in each jurisdiction are unaware of the negative effects of their activities in other jurisdictions (Treisman 2000; Shleifer and Vishny 1993).

These theoretical caveats are supported by empirical work that has sought to find a relationship between devolution and decentralization, on the one hand, and corruption, on the other. Treisman (2000) in a major cross-country study finds federal states to be more corrupt than unitary ones. Fjeldstad and Semboja (2000) find decentralized fiscal administration in Tanzania to be highly corrupt because of weak monitoring from above. Goldsmith (1999) points out how decentralized systems make it easier to hide corrupt practices in developing countries. On the other hand, some studies conducted for the Operations Evaluation Department of the World Bank have found that devolution has reduced some types of corruption. Crook and Manor (2000) report that in Karnataka, India, devolution reduced grand theft even though petty corruption increased. In a cross-country regression analysis that included both advanced and developing countries, Gurgur and Shah (2000) report that decentralization has a significant effect in reducing corruption. But they also point out that when the regressions are carried out for developing countries alone, there is no relationship between decentralization and corruption reduction. The latter result is more significant because including both advanced and developing countries in the same corruption regressions has problems that we have touched on earlier. Finally, the fact that a configuration of factors allowed devolution to result in better governance and lower corruption in some cases does not contradict the point that there is no general case in favor of devolution. To be fair, many Bank operatives in the field appear to be skeptical of the merits of pushing decentralization and devolution, but the official position has strong backers in the Bank.

There is a much stronger commitment in the Bank to the general proposition that greater civil society participation in monitoring government will improve governance and reduce corruption. The reasoning here is quite straightforward. The chances of catching the corrupt are supposed to increase with greater transparency. This increases the expected cost of corruption for the bureaucrat or the politician. If this is the case, we would expect countries with more freedom of information and more participatory politics to suffer less from corruption and poor governance. Once again, the underlying view of the relationship between state and society is the mainstream one in which individuals in society have to be vigilant to ensure that the state they have set up to deliver services does not rip them off. This picture has no analysis of divisions within society and how competing interests may quite legitimately try to exercise voice and influence over the state in their own interests. In reality, those who are monitoring the state may have specific interests of their own and not everyone in society may have the resources, the knowledge, or the organizational ability to exercise voice. If we take into account the real divisions that exist in the societies of developing countries, we have to ask which groups are most likely to exercise voice and influence as transparency and accountability increases and whether these groups are productive groups or not.

Without in any way diminishing the desirability of democracy and participation as political values, such an analysis will tell us if there is any reason to expect greater civil society participation in a particular country to actually result in general improvements in governance and corruption. In general, in most developing countries, capitalists are a very small group who lack social legitimacy because their wealth is often considered to be illegitimate and often actually is. They rarely play a predominant role in national politics or lead civil society organizations (although there are exceptions, such as Thailand). Nor is the vast bulk of the population, composed of workers and peasants able to play this role because they are typically too disadvantaged in terms of education and resources. Thus civil society organizations are dominated by the relatively narrow middle and lower-middle classes, who have the resources, the education, and the numerical strength to play a dominant organizational role. However well-meaning, inclusive, and humanistic their voice often is, these groups do not represent the interests of the whole society and more than that, they are often unaware of the harsh realities necessarily involved in the creation and operation of early capitalism. Their voice does little to change the underlying realities of primitive accumulation and political management in developing countries, but does add to the list of expectations that cannot be met. These considerations mean that the relationship between greater civil society participation and economic development can be quite complex and can vary greatly not only between developed and developing countries, but also within developing countries themselves, depending on the constitution and organization of social classes and groups (e.g., see Khan 1998b).

Once again, the importance of these considerations is borne out by the evidence. Although it is difficult to measure the degree of civil society participation or how vibrant it is, the presence or absence of democracy offers a measurable proxy. The evidence on the relationship between democracy and corruption underlines why it is important to have a good analysis of social structure in developing countries. Case study evidence provides many examples of democratic developing countries where corruption is rife. Not only that, they also provide evidence of corrupt politicians whose corruption is well known, winning elections against clean campaigners who seek to unseat them, not least in the biggest and most sustained democracy in the developing world—India. Similar examples can be found in neighboring Pakistan and Bangladesh. These cases cannot be explained by culture (which differs widely across the developing world) or by the lack of information because the corruption of particular leaders is often widely known and dissected in the press. Rather, we have to recognize that voting for machine politics patrons or mafia bosses is often a rational response on the part of voters in developing countries who can expect bigger payoffs and protection from supporting the right factions than from a clean campaigner who is delinked from the processes of political and economic accumulation. These case study insights are confirmed by Treisman (2000) in his cross-country regression analysis. He finds no evidence that corruption is lower in democracies. Democracy did have a small effect on corruption after many decades, but these long-term effects could have other explanations, because only successful economic developers are usually able to sustain long-lasting democracies.

It is worth repeating that international agencies are not necessarily wrong to support greater civil society participation in developing countries as an end in itself, but they are wrong to raise expectations that this will necessarily improve the quality of governance or reduce corruption. If improvements in the quality of state intervention are sought, as indeed they should be, attention has to be focused directly on what the state should be doing in a developing country trying to construct capitalism. The task of international agencies should then be to assist in developing state capacity in these areas. The focus on corruption is a damaging distraction even though corruption clearly imposes large social costs in developing countries. It is a damaging distraction because sustained reductions in corruption require development, and therefore the focus should be on improving the capacity of the state to govern in the interests of development. Such a strategy will have an incidental effect in reducing, as it must, growth-reducing types of corruption, but it is naïve to think that there will be substantial reductions of corruption in the short term.

AN ALTERNATIVE PERSPECTIVE ON REFORMING THE STATE

The Bank's approach to improving governance has been based on a service-provision model of the state in which the quality of provision is dependent on rightsizing the state so that it only delivers what the private sector cannot and on keeping bureaucrats and politicians under check through political decentralization and more civil society participation. We have indicated why this perspective on the state is inappropriate in a developing country context. We have also referred to some of the evidence that strongly suggests that the strategies being followed by the Bank are not likely to lead even to a reduction in corruption, let alone to the greater welfare that is supposed to follow from a market-led economy and a smaller cleaner state. Here we elaborate on the types of fundamental economic and political problems that a developing country state has to address and the types of capacity that it may have to develop if it is to carry out these tasks better.

In contrast to the service-provision view of the state, we argue that it is more appropriate to see the developing country state not only as the guarantor of social order, but as one of the key agencies involved in creating a completely new social order. The capitalist transition is not something that happens naturally, nor is it something that is widely supported, particularly in its early phases. The construction and deepening of a capitalist society involves both supporting and promoting an emerging capitalist class and ensuring that this process of support is sufficiently disciplined for resources not to be wasted by the emerging capitalists' turning into a class of unproductive conspicuous consumers. At the same time, the developing country state has to ensure that political stability is maintained at acceptable levels for the process of accumulation and investment not to get derailed. Both of these key areas of intervention open up massive opportunities for bureaucrats and politicians to share in or misappropriate some of the transfers that are necessarily involved in carrying out these tasks.

Looking first at the economics of transition, the developing country state does not just have to provide services such as clean water to citizens; more important, it has to aid and accelerate the creation of a class of capitalists. This in itself involves the state in deeply divisive decisions. If the right decisions are made, a class of capitalists will emerge that will help generate prosperity for their country. But regardless of their productivity, the beneficiaries of state interventions are inevitably enriched to rise beyond the reach of the average citizen. Although this is deeply divisive, no developing country state can sit back and be genuinely neutral in aiding all sections of society if economic viability depends on the rapid growth of the capitalist sector. Virtually all developing countries states have used mechanisms such as allocating land for industrial development, influencing relative prices particularly between agriculture and industry, managing taxes and subsidies, influencing exchange and interest rates, and so on to assist the emergence of the nascent capitalist class.

The implicit transfers to the emerging capitalist class as a result of these policies has a significance that is well beyond even the very large sums involved because the individuals who emerge from this process as potential capitalists are able to permanently differentiate themselves from the rest of society. What would they be willing to pay to be beneficiaries of state policies at this stage? When society is differentiating into new classes in this way, the standard analysis of how much rent-seekers will be willing to pay becomes deficient. Rent-seekers in this context will be willing to pay not only a fraction of the rent they can capture from the state, but perhaps a very large fraction given the long-term benefits they can hope to get by positioning themselves as emerging capitalists in the transition society. The transition state has to follow a difficult path. It cannot be expected to give no support at all to emerging capitalism without derailing development very significantly; on the other hand, if it does intervene, it has to try and ensure that the emerging capitalists cannot influence the allocation of resources in ways that derail technology acquisition and productivity growth.

Ironically, if the state can ensure that emerging capitalists are efficient, it does not matter too much for economic dynamism if bureaucrats and politicians make some money in the process. Capitalists, too, are usually only too happy to share some of their gains, particularly in the early stages of development. The real danger is when inefficient capitalists succeed in bribing or influencing the state to capture resources. When this happens, the cost to society is much greater than the resources wasted in corruption. The state may be systematically creating a class of conspicuous consumers rather than productive capitalists and wasting a huge amount of social resources in pampering a protected and unproductive class. Subsidies may be permanently captured by infant industries that refuse to grow up, and so on. The social costs of these policies are likely to dwarf the direct economic cost of the bribes. The institutional and political characteristics that have enabled a few developing country states to ensure that growth remained high during this transition period are not easy to summarize because what worked in each country depended on the internal social and political balance (for a discussion of some of these conditions see Khan and Jomo 2000).

Some general features of the dynamic countries do, however, stand out. States that were able to discipline capitalists at this stage seem either to have had a very strong capacity to override coalitions that formed to protect particular inefficient capitalists or sectors or to have had allies in society who shared an interest in ensuring that the emerging capitalists continued to get resources but did not waste them. Building these capacities and alliances was not simple, and most developing countries did not succeed. However, lessons can be learned from the successful countries to promote progress toward greater developmental commitment in countries performing less well. This certainly does not mean that Nigeria, say, should be encouraged to attempt South Korean industrial policy, but it does mean that appropriate policies and state capacities have to be developed in Nigeria if it is to manage the transition at the fastest rate that is feasible given its political and historical conditions. But such an agenda could not be further from an agenda of rightsizing the state.

The second and equally important challenge facing the developing country state is the maintenance of political stability in a context of intense social conflict and widespread resentment of the wealth and power of emerging capitalists. This resentment is widespread in developing countries, not least because the processes of state support that assisted their emergence are widely known. This explains the apparent paradox that political instability is often greater in more open developing societies where information about the effects of government policies is more freely available and the possibilities of expressing dissent are greater. In these contexts, the maintenance of political stability usually involves political clientelism in which powerful clients of political parties and the state have preferential access to resources and in return help to maintain stability. This, in turn, very often involves political corruption because these resources obviously cannot be publicly accounted for and audited. Political corruption of this type, although necessary for political stability, can be very damaging for the economy because these networks can also protect inefficient capitalists for a mutually beneficial price. The comparative evidence suggests that clientelism is not always consistent with a successful transition. Dynamic countries either suppressed clientelism or had fairly centralized versions of clientelism (Khan 2001; Khan and Jomo 2000).

These observations suggest an extremely important area of political reform in developing countries. Responding to the problems posed by clientelism requires a sustained long-term reform of political processes. This involves not just trying to reform political parties, but also a political leadership that is willing to engage in difficult political struggles against the mafia-like patrons and protection rackets that are widespread in developing countries. In areas such as this, international agencies could potentially play an important role in assisting developing country states. But here we find a real incomprehension of the problems faced by these states and an unwillingness on the part of international agencies to address the problems of real politics. In contrast to the anodyne support for civil society and democracy, a program of support for political reform that can make developing country states less vulnerable to clientelism would have directly positive effects for the economy. It would target precisely those types of political corruption that have seriously negative economic effects and enable developing country states to maintain a higher level of efficiency during the difficult phase of early capitalism. For the fight against clientelism to succeed, developing country states would have to maintain political stability through other means, and this would very likely require much more expenditure on transparent social programs and redistribution. But such strategies are not likely to find much favor in western countries committed to shrinking the developing country state and reducing international aid for developing countries.

CHAPTER EIGHT

Reassessing the Role of the World Bank in Sub-Saharan Africa

John Sender

The World Bank is not well regarded in many sub-Saharan African countries. This is in part because of the perception that it has behaved arrogantly toward many of its African borrowers. It has also become unpopular because it has been unable, despite the best intentions of some of its officials, to distance itself effectively from an intimate association with the short-run stabilization measures demanded by the International Monetary Fund (IMF). Since the 1980s, the Bank has been regarded as an increasingly fervent advocate of the policy prescriptions of the Washington Consensus that encompassed the economic views of the U.S. Treasury, the IMF, and the Bank.

This chapter begins with an overview of the scale and significance of the World Bank's activities in Africa, focusing on the direct and indirect influence of its concessional loans in this region and on its role in producing and disseminating socioeconomic statistics and in defining the agenda for policy debates in the period since the publication of the Berg Report (World Bank 1981). The second section introduces evidence concerning the failure of the Bank to assist in promoting economic growth in sub-Saharan Africa, focusing on trends in private and public sector investment and on the rate of growth of agricultural exports. The third section examines the Bank's response to this evidence of failure, as shown by its attempts to reassess the analytical framework for its operations. These reassessments show that the Bank's commitment to neoclassical economic theory has prevented it from developing a conceptual framework that would enable it to understand the potential for growth and the dynamics of poverty in sub-Saharan Africa at the end of the 1990s.

The aim of this chapter is not to reinforce negative perceptions in Africa of the role of the Bank or to support those political forces and nongovernmental organizations (NGOs) that reject proposals for a more generous replenishment of the International Development Association (IDA). Rather, the aim is to suggest that far more work needs to be done to improve the Bank's analysis of growth and poverty issues in specific African countries before the strong argument for dramatically expanding IDA flows to the region can be made more convincing.

The World Bank Group is the largest source of development assistance to Africa; its investment portfolio in Africa, which was first established in 1951, has reached a total of $18 billion. Most flows of new assistance to the region are channeled though IDA, amounting to an average of $2.5 billion per year since 1992. Commitments by IDA have been growing; they increased by approximately 17 percent in 1998 compared to commitments in 1996 (World Bank 1998m). This type of concessional flow is of considerable importance to low-income sub-Saharan economies because they are unable to attract external capital inflows on a significant scale from any other sources. Compared to other developing regions and in absolute terms, sub-Saharan Africa attracts negligible amounts of direct investment, bond lending, international bank lending, or other private flows (Organization for Economic Cooperation and Development [OECD] 1998b, chart III-2; Husain and Underwood 1991). Moreover, the proportion of gross domestic investment (GDI) and the proportion of imports of goods and services that are financed by aid is very much higher in sub-Saharan Africa than in any other developing region. Approximately 28 percent of GDI in sub-Saharan Africa was financed by aid in 1997, whereas in all low- and middle-income economies the proportion was approximately 3 percent; aid as a percentage of imports of goods and services in 1997 was four times greater in sub-Saharan Africa than in low- and middle-income economies (World Bank 1999p, tables 6–10). Growth in some important sub-Saharan African economies is even more dependent on concessional flows to finance GDI than these regional aggregates suggest. For example, in 1997 aid flows amounted to 84 percent of GDI in Uganda, 69 percent in Tanzania, and 50 percent in Senegal; aid was much greater than GDI in Malawi, Mozambique, Niger, Rwanda, Zambia, and Sierra Leone (World Bank 1999p, table 6.10).

Strategic interests and historical ties have a significant influence on the pattern of allocation of aid by bilateral donors to sub-Saharan African economies, for example in the franc zone (Burnside and Dollar 1997, 26; McGillivray and White 1993). Nevertheless, the World Bank, together with the IMF, has achieved a great deal of influence on the disbursements made by bilateral and multilateral donors; it has often been the case that non-Washington donors will not disburse aid to a sub-Saharan African country until that country has signed agreements with the Bank and the IMF.[1] The number and scope of the conditions attached to these loans has expanded a great deal since the early 1980s (Mosely, Harrigan, and Toye 1995; Kapur

---

1. The Bank notes that "other donors pay attention to structural adjustment programs when making decisions about aid allocations" (World Bank 1998d, 50).

1997). The Bank may, therefore, be regarded as a gatekeeper influencing the flow of much larger amounts of aid than it disburses on its own account.[2] Moreover, there are other, less direct ways in which the Bank has affected the pattern of aid flows in sub-Saharan Africa.

The Bank has, since the publication of the Berg Report (World Bank 1981), established a hegemonic position as the dominant source of economic and policy analysis for sub-Saharan Africa. Not only the amount of aid, but also the objectives, rationale, and conditions attached to all aid flows are profoundly influenced by the perceptions and activities of the World Bank.[3] Indeed, most donors to, and governments in, sub-Saharan Africa must rely on economic and other statistical data collated, processed, or collected by the Bank in formulating development policy. The alternatives to the data made available in Bank publications, including African development indicators, living standards measurement surveys, reports of the poverty monitoring and analysis team, policy working papers, policy research reports, discussion and technical papers, country economic studies, country poverty assessments and assistance strategies, staff appraisal reports, and performance audit reports, are far less technically competent or simply do not exist.[4] Between 1985 and 1997, for example, the Bank was involved in eighty-seven completed household surveys, including living standard measurement surveys, priority surveys, and income-expenditure surveys in forty African countries (Tjønneland et al. 1998, 25). It has, as a result of this work, established itself as the main source of measurement and analysis of poverty in this region.[5]

The detailed empirical work of Bank economists on African trade data is also valuable as a guide through some particularly unreliable published statistics (Yeats 1990, 1998). However, these efforts to publish more reliable data and technically sophisticated analyses, together with the Bank's ability to broker access to external capital inflows, are not sufficient to account for the full scope of its influence on economic policy making in sub-Saharan Africa. In addition, the Bank has devoted resources to molding the intellectual outlook of a new generation of African economists through its support to the African Economics Research Consortium, as well as through the

2. An estimate of aid/GDP suggests that somewhat more bilateral aid is allocated toward those countries that follow the policy advice of the Washington institutions (Burnside and Dollar 1997, 27).

3. "Most members of the OECD Development Assistance Committee . . . seem to take the World Bank approach as their point of departure" (Tjønneland et al. 1998, 16).

4. A useful source covering many Bank publications on sub-Saharan African is Mohan (1999).

5. This is in marked contrast to India, for example, where far more frequent and higher quality rural/poverty surveys and analytical work have been completed without the assistance of the Bank. See, for example, Sen and Ghosh (1993) or the remarkable flow of survey-based articles in the Bombay publication *Economic and Political Weekly*.

training offered by the Economic Development Institute in Washington and the lucrative career paths it provides by offering consultancy and other employment opportunities.[6]

The Bank itself recognizes its capacity to influence policy; it now regards its central task as providing the knowledge to devise development strategies (World Bank 1998o). Others have emphasized the Bank's ability to influence policy debates in developing countries, but have been disquieted by the degree of monopoly it has over research, as well as by its attempts to "disguise a multimillion dollar ideological operation as research" (Taylor 1997, 147; Amsden 1997; Tjønneland et al. 1998, 72). Of course, some of the attempts to challenge the hegemonic position of the Bank, including those that have achieved a degree of popularity among Africa's nationalist intelligentsia and the NGO community, could easily be ignored by the Bank (Sender and Smith 1986b); they were ineffectual largely because of their strong residual attachment to dependency theory, resting on "the importation of André Gunder Frank into Africa" (Hopkins 1988).[7] Because dependency theorists have so little to contribute to the detailed formulation of macroeconomic and fiscal policy, the political consequence in Africa, as in much of Latin America, was that the key short-term economic debates continued to take place within the narrow framework set by the neoliberal orthodoxy (Roxborough 1992). However, even when more politically realistic and relatively detailed alternative macroeconomic strategies have been proposed in Africa, for example by the Macroeconomic Research Group in South Africa at the request of the African National Congress (Macroeconomic Research Group [MERG] 1993), their influence on policy has been remarkably small; the World Bank, with the strong support of the large corporations based in South Africa, was easily able to persuade the post-Apartheid government to follow orthodox development strategies (Marais 1998).

Since the 1980s, the World Bank has been remarkably successful in brushing aside or gesturally accommodating criticisms of its policy prescriptions for Africa. The Bank has persisted in proposing the liberalization of domestic and international markets, macroeconomic stabilization, and privatization. It has concluded that African economic performance has been disastrous in the postindependence era and that poverty and stagnation in

6. In addition, "the World Bank is funding 'think tanks' around the world that subscribe to its values and ideology. These in turn are likely to shape how reality is perceived and *measured*" (Standing 1999, 15).

7. Dependency theory attempts to explain sub-Saharan Africa's economic performance largely by reference to deteriorating terms of trade (external forces) and the immutable structural barriers to the development of a "genuine" form of capitalism in the region rather than by reference to the domestic balance of political forces in particular countries. Examples of this line of argument can be seen in Leys (1996); UNCTAD (1998, 117, 121); Mkandawire (1998), 19–21.

Africa are the direct consequences of following a policy regime that impeded the operation of market forces. Its view, first strongly expressed in the Berg Report (World Bank 1981), was that the economic performance of every country in sub-Saharan Africa could rapidly be improved by a reliance on market forces and the reduction of state intervention and expenditure to a minimum. The influence of these views has, for all the reasons already discussed, been profound. It is, therefore, important to examine the empirical evidence concerning the impact of the Bank's recommendations.

THE BANK'S ECONOMIC IMPACT IN SUB-SAHARAN AFRICA

The consequences of the World Bank's policy prescriptions have always been predicted by heterodox economic theory to be harmful to the development prospects of sub-Saharan Africa. A key prediction was that the consequences of following deflationary macroeconomic policy in the name of stabilization would be a dramatic reduction in investment rates and growth. In fact, private sector investment in sub-Saharan Africa has not behaved in any way like the Washington analysis of incentives anticipated. Between 1990 and 1996, private investment in Africa remained below the levels reached in the 1970s and 1980s, following the trend in public investment, which, as a share of GDP in the 1990s, fell to less than one-half the level reached in the 1970s (Glen and Sumlinsky 1998). Public investment as a share of GDP in sub-Saharan Africa is now much lower than in any other region of the world. This has had negative effects on both the volume and the productivity of private investment in the region because of the well-established complementarity between these two categories of investment (UN Conference on Trade and Development [UNCTAD] 1998, 125).

Moreover, those sub-Saharan African economies that followed the consensus policy advice most closely and, therefore, were defined by the World Bank as "core adjusters" in 1993, because they were believed to have followed Bank policy advice most successfully, failed to grow as fast as a number of other, less compliant African countries over the subsequent five years (UNCTAD 1998, 124–26). Of course, there are serious methodological difficulties in attempting to establish a clear relationship between the World Bank's structural adjustment programs and declines in investment or growth; but it is not acceptable merely to shrug aside the claims for such a relationship by asserting that current lower levels of investment are more efficiently allocated than the higher levels achieved in Africa in the past or on the grounds that the decline represents an "investment pause" that will rapidly be reversed once stabilization has been achieved.[8] The acceleration in the

8. Nor is the Bank's suggestion that aid has not systematically influenced fiscal, monetary, and trade policies in sub-Saharan Africa (based on econometric analysis of a panel of fifty-six countries, many of which are outside Africa, as well as the invention of several contentious proxy variables) at all convincing (Burnside and Dollar 1997). It is obvious that the Bank has

annual average growth rates of GDP in sub-Saharan Africa from 1.7 percent in 1980–90 to 2 percent 1990–96 (World Bank 1998n, table 4.1) has not been accompanied by the levels of investment required to sustain accelerated growth.

Nor is it acceptable for World Bank officials to continue to claim that "countries that pursue appropriate policies have a better chance of economic success than those that do not" (Stiglitz 1997, 1), when the "appropriate" policies are defined as those recommended by the Washington Consensus. This claim is supported only by reference to the Bank's own contentious study of the impact of adjustment policies in sub-Saharan Africa (World Bank 1994a); it ignores the work that has thoroughly discredited this particular study (Mosley, Subasat, and Weeks 1995). In addition, far too little attention has been given to the accumulation of evidence suggesting a causal relationship between the macroeconomic stabilization programs of the IMF and declines in investment ratios (Bird 1996, 1758). During the period 1990–95, sub-Saharan African economies defined by the IMF as recent strong performers have consistently shown lower investment to GDP and private investment to GDP rates than the average for sub-Saharan Africa (Fischer, Hernandez-Catá, and Khan 1998, table 2).

Heterodox economists have also questioned the generalized empirical propositions concerning the inefficiency of public enterprises in developing countries (Chang and Singh 1993; Nolan and Xiaoqiang 1999); the theoretical arguments in favor of privatization have been criticized for even longer, but have not adequately been addressed in the analytical work of the World Bank (Bayliss and Fine 1998). By the end of the 1980s, most countries in Africa had been persuaded to accept World Bank assistance for privatization programs (Ariyo and Jerome 1999, 202). Unfortunately, it is surprisingly difficult to assess the impact of privatization in sub-Saharan Africa; the difficulties are not merely a result of the familiar methodological problems involved in the choice of an appropriate counterfactual—what would have been the welfare and economic consequences of not privatizing? It is certainly not satisfactory to base claims for the success of privatization in Africa on the number of transactions that have been completed. Besides, even the data required to assess outcomes on the basis of this trivial criterion have not been systematically collected (Bennell 1997). Despite its continued advocacy of privatization, the Bank has not made sufficient efforts to obtain the empirical evidence required to analyze the economic impact of the history of privatization efforts in the region as a whole or in a range of individual countries, such as Mozambique, where its demands for privatization have been most insistent (Cramer 1999).

---

had a far greater influence on policy formulation and implementation in some sub-Saharan African countries than in others; it is also obvious that the Bank's influence is not at all easy to quantify. We cannot conclude, therefore, that its influence has usually been insignificant.

Economists who had spent some time in rural Africa also predicted that the consequences of following Bank market liberalization policies for the rate of growth of agricultural exports would be disappointing (Sender and Smith 1990, chap. 6). Agriculture is an extremely important source of foreign exchange earnings, contributing over 50 percent of total exports by the 1990s in twenty sub-Saharan African countries (UNCTAD 1998, 135). A slow rate of growth of agricultural exports, therefore, limits the capacity to import and to achieve adequate rates of economic growth. Unfortunately, the Bank's predictions concerning the effects on the rate of growth of agricultural exports of policies to remove price distortions paid little attention to the fact that nonprice factors are extremely important in determining rates of growth of marketed agricultural output (Cleaver 1985; Berthelemy and Morrison 1989). In fact, the rate of growth of the volume of agricultural exports was either negative or less than 1 percent in twenty sub-Saharan African countries during the period 1985–96, when structural adjustment lending by the Bank was at its peak. The volume of agricultural exports from the region as a whole was lower in 1996 than it had been in the early 1970s (UNCTAD 1998, 143–44); no fewer than twenty-two sub-Saharan African countries recorded a lower volume of agricultural exports in 1997 than they had in 1970 (Food and Agriculture Organization 1999). The growth rates of total agricultural production were much more impressive over this period (Sender 1999), suggesting that attempts to increase the relative farm-gate prices of export crops through exchange rate liberalization, devaluations, and minimization of the role of the state in output and input marketing failed to achieve the incentive effects anticipated by orthodox analysis.

ANALYTICAL LIMITATIONS OF THE BANK'S RESPONSE
TO CRITICISM

In the late 1990s, the analytical framework for the lending operations of the Washington institutions has been re-examined at a senior level in the World Bank. Joseph Stiglitz, the senior vice president and chief economist of the Bank has set himself, in a series of publications in 1997 and 1998, the task of defining an "An Agenda for Development for the Twenty-First Century" (Stiglitz 1997, 1998c, 1998d). He aims to provide the foundations for "an alternative paradigm, especially one relevant to the least developed country" (Stiglitz 1998d, 5)—a new intellectual consensus of particular relevance to sub-Saharan Africa. In addition, the World Bank has been engaged in an initiative to reassess its analysis and policies designed to address poverty in preparation for the publication of a new World Development Report in 2000–2001 (World Bank 1999d). I discuss these new approaches here because a precondition for reinventing the Bank's relationships with Africa, as well as for the more persuasive arguments that are required to increase the Bank's resources to support African development, is a coherent analysis of the determinants of poverty and of the appropriate forms of state intervention in low-income economies.

At first blush, the Stiglitz critique of the Washington Consensus appears fundamental, signifying a real shift in policy and in the analytical methods underlying policy formulation. One interpretation of Stiglitz's papers, as well as of a range of other World Bank work in the period since the publication of *The East Asian Miracle* (World Bank 1993c), is that they represent an intellectual and ideological upheaval in the Bank, perhaps even "the demise of the Washington consensus" (Fine 1999a, 1). However, other long-standing critics of the Washington Consensus have been less impressed with scope and nature of the internal reexaminations of the old orthodoxy, dismissing the new post-Washington Consensus as "a repackaging and updating of neoliberalism" (Hildyard 1997, 2).

The conclusion reached by Stiglitz is that "[a]lthough the Washington consensus provided some of the foundations for well-functioning markets, it was incomplete and *sometimes* even misleading" (1998c, 17, emphasis added). Thus, he argues that the problem was that the consensus was too narrow; it was reasonably well conceived, but incomplete. He does not discard the core analytical methods and policy conclusions of the consensus, nor does he admit that it was fundamentally misconceived.

The limited implications for policy change are well illustrated in his discussions of the role of the state in development. Stiglitz correctly notes that the Washington Consensus policies "were based on a rejection of the state's activist role and the promotion of a minimalist, non-interventionist state." As an alternative, he offers the far from novel neoclassical argument that "government has an important role to play in responding to market failures, which are a general feature of any economy with imperfect information and incomplete markets" (1998c, 10). But he then adds the crucial qualification that not all governments have the capacity to respond effectively to market failures and that the role of the state should match its capability. In effect, static and ahistorical conceptions of capacity and capability provide a renewed rationale for a matching, minimalist state in sub-Saharan Africa, where state capacity is said to be small and capability is rapidly diminishing (World Bank 1997n, 14).[9] Moreover, given the initial condition of an assumed deficiency of capacity, the available policy options for state intervention are reduced to the familiar, limited menu that the World Bank should try to get governments better focused on the fundamentals—education, health, roads, law, and order.

Insisting that African states lack the capacity for anything other than a

9. This negative assessment of sub-Saharan African states has been clearly expressed: "The drastic impairment of the state looks very serious . . . while its past and current weaknesses are being compounded over time" (Aron 1997, 25).

limited range of interventions to support the familiar fundamentals provides support for another set of politically convenient arguments. World Bank publications by Burnside and Dollar (1997) and Dollar and Svensson (1998) reach the comforting conclusion that where structural adjustment lending has failed or in the many cases where aid has not had a positive influence on economic growth the blame lies with the incapacity of the unfortunate countries concerned rather than with the quality of aid policy design and implementation in Washington. The argument, as already noted, is that aid has not affected the policies adopted in poor countries, but some countries have demonstrated the capacity to adopt "good" growth-supporting policies. These capable countries were not always rewarded by aid flows for their espousal of consensus policies, especially by the bilateral donors whose disbursement policies are described as "inconsistent," but "when good policy and aid flows happen to coincide the outcome has been very good" (Burnside and Dollar 1997, 30). The policy implication, consistent with the conclusions reached by Stiglitz, is that there is no need to change fundamentally the policy prescriptions associated with aid. The Bank can continue to recommend the same old consensus policies, but aid should be directed only to those countries that have already demonstrated the capacity to adopt good policies.

This amounts to an attempt to shift the blame, to deny the connection between the content and design of the Bank's structural adjustment lending and the high proportion of such policy reform programs that have failed by any criteria.[10] It has been established that a large number of adjustment loans were unsuccessful in low-income countries, particularly in Africa, and it is suggested that adjustment lending failed because "African countries have characteristics that are not conducive to reform." The problem lies with the nature of African states, too many of which have not been democratically elected, are politically unstable, and "ethnically fractionalized" (Dollar and Svensson 1998, 16–17).[11] The policy conclusion is that, because so many

10. In a data set covering 220 reform programs sponsored by the World Bank, more than one-third were judged to have failed. Here the criterion of failure was whether the World Bank's own Operations and Evaluation Department was of the opinion that they had failed to meet their policy reform objectives in terms of trade liberalization, privatization, and so on. Objective outcome criteria, such as investment or export growth, were not used (Dollar and Svensson 1998, 14).

11. World Bank economists have attempted to explain cross-country differences in public policies, political stability and long-run economic growth by using a variable that is supposed to capture "ethnic diversity." This attempt has been criticized in detail by McIlwham (1998); some additional critical points are provided by Rodrik, whose equations suggest that "ethnic diversity may even be good for growth within Africa" (1998, 19). Another problem said to constrain poor African countries is that "people are wedded to traditional ways of thinking" as opposed to the "scientific ways of thinking" that predominate in advanced societies (Stiglitz 1998d, 6). Perhaps the Bank's econometricians will soon find a variable to proxy for such psychological defects, which will further improve their ability to account for cross-country differences in growth rates.

African states will continue to lack capacity or fail to exhibit the characteristics of promising candidates for adjustment support, they should not be selected as the beneficiaries of further adjustment lending. Thus, it is recommended not only that should African states match the scale and scope of their interventions to their limited capacity, but that allocating additional concessional flows is unlikely to improve the capacity of these states to promote development.[12] The minimalist state remains firmly on the policy agenda.

Inadequate state capacity in sub-Saharan Africa has been a self-fulfilling prophecy; the outcome of a bet rigged by those in a strong position to influence results. The Washington institutions have consistently demanded initiatives that impair governments' capacity for policy formulation and implementation. In Africa, civilian government employment accounts for a relatively small proportion of total employment compared to any other region of the world, but the Washington institutions insisted that African states were overextended by the 1980s. The policies they promoted in a continuing attempt to reduce fiscal deficits resulted, by the early 1990s, in a fall in government employment both in absolute terms and relative to the population.

Following structural adjustment, there has been a marked decline in the ratio of civil servants to the population in all sub-Saharan African countries for which time series are available. By 1996, only 1 percent of the population were civil servants, which is considerably lower than in other developing countries, where nearly 3 percent of the population is employed by the government, or than in the OECD economies, where approximately 7 percent of the population is employed by the government. The real wages of civil servants have fallen dramatically since 1989 for the majority of poor African countries covered by the data, with well-documented and predictable effects on their morale and efficiency in state institutions. Moreover, in several of those countries that experienced the strongest declines in average real wages in the civil service, this was associated with further decompression of upper-grade scales, encouraging the exit of the most highly qualified personnel. By late 1997, the IMF, whose programs have regularly included both targets for substantial reductions in the civil service wage bill and limits on the number of employees in the civil service, reached the surprising conclusion that "there is still scope for further downsizing" (Lienert and Modi 1997, 32). The failure of econometric research to discern any significant relationship between central government employment and the size of the fiscal deficit has not tempered the enthusiasm of both the Bank and the IMF for downsizing (Schiavo-Campo, Tommaso, and Mukherjee 1998).

While arguing how difficult, if not impossible, it would be for weak states

---

12. Stiglitz endorses the static concept of "absorptive capacity" (1998d, 19).

in sub-Saharan Africa to intervene to pursue national industrialization strategies, the Bank has demanded that these same ineffectual states attempt a range of other complex tasks, including the immediate and simultaneous implementation of fiscal discipline, financial deepening, privatization, good governance, democratization, and the liberalization of all trade and capital flows. These inconsistent policy recommendations appear to rest on the belief that the abstract model of better functioning markets, of an undistorted market-orientated economic system, is in some sense natural and, therefore, much easier to transplant into poor economies in sub-Saharan Africa than other systems in which nonmarket institutions, such as powerful associations of producers, strong trade unions, and proactive military and state agencies, have played such an important role. The assertion is that, in the absence of a long list of special, unusual, perhaps even one-off initial conditions, states in the 1990s would be well advised only to attempt what comes "naturally," as if the evidence from the Soviet Union had not demonstrated the monumental difficulties of big bang, or shock therapy, attempts to establish a textbook, "natural" market economy in the absence of efforts to sustain powerful institutions to direct and regulate market forces (Chang 1997; Nolan 1996).

Stiglitz, does list some mechanisms whereby the capability of states may be enhanced; his list is much more interesting for what it does not include, than for what it does. Most important, he does not recognize the possibility of dynamic processes of "institutional learning" in poor economies (Chang 1993, 154) or of any scope in the medium-term in Africa for conscious efforts to import, modify and rapidly invent, and then reinvent the institutions crucial for dynamic industrialization. The Bank's case for defining a limited role for African states in the twenty-first century continues to rest on the assertion that "In other parts of the world, building effective bureaucracies has been a very slow process . . . requiring, quite possibly, decades or even generations to be institutionalized" (Brautigam 1996, 101). The consensus, static view on African state (in)capacity still insists that "Institutions are not very plastic: they are the products of their environments and the negative impact of past distortions will persist" (Aron 1997). There is a great deal of evidence, however, from Korea in the early 1960s and from Taiwan in the 1950s, that contradicts this view (Cheng, Haggard, and Kang 1996).

Stiglitz claims that in successful economies intervention to inhibit particular imports was not significant (1998d, 12). He also asserts that "Import substitution was a highly ineffective strategy for economic development" (1998c, 8). The historical evidence, however, does not provide strong support for these claims. In the successful east Asian economies, the long history of protection from external competitors of new domestic industries producing for the home market is well documented (Amsden 1989; Shin 1996). Amsden has also criticized consensus attempts to portray the results of state intervention to promote industrialization through protection and subsidies outside east Asia as a failure (1997, 470–72).[13] A strong case for selective state intervention in certain key import-substitution and export-oriented industries to achieve an accumulation of capabilities and know-how has been made for sub-Saharan Africa. The argument is that, as in east Asia, such interventions "will allow governments to learn how to design sectoral policies, to find out what incentives are effective and for what purpose. . . . More sophisticated policies needed for promoting the next generation of industries can build on these experiences" (UNCTAD 1998, 222). However, it appears that the key mechanism for learning by doing, which has facilitated the transfer of technology in all late-industrializing economies, is explicitly rejected in the post-Washington Consensus.

In addition, the new consensus remains wedded to an analytical framework that ignores the specific role of the manufacturing sector in economic development. The new growth theory underpinning Stiglitz's policy recommendations is based essentially on the old aggregate production function models of the 1950s and 1960s, to which have been added variables representing investment in education and research and development and the assumption that there are increasing returns to investment itself (Eatwell 1994). No attempt has been made to come to grips with the conceptual limitations of aggregate production functions as tools for understanding the structural changes associated with growth (Harcourt 1972) or with analyses that focus on the crucial role of the manufacturing sector as a source of dynamic increasing returns (McCombie and Thirlwall 1994, chap. 2). Thus, although Stiglitz indicates that it may be desirable to develop sector-specific strategies (for the health care sector or agriculture), direct interventions to promote manufacturing or the subsector-specific industrialization strategies that he admits were followed in a number of successful late-industrializing economies are not on the recommended policy agenda for Africa (1998d, 12, 28).

In the new consensus, the only novel intervention recommended to facilitate technological transfer, adaptation, and assimilation is supply-side support for tertiary education (Stiglitz 1998c, 11). Unfortunately, even developing countries with high levels of scientific knowledge comparable to that of advanced countries "have not obeyed a Say's Law: their supply of educated people has failed to generate demand necessary to employ it" (Amsden 1997, 470). Stiglitz does not mention that many other policies have been required to create the industrial production capacity to absorb young educated workers. For example, although he notes that successful

13. In common with many publications by economists working at the World Bank, Stiglitz's work contains remarkably few references to any empirical or analytical work that has not been carried out by or under the auspices of the Washington institutions themselves. For some examples of the Bank's surprisingly limited coverage of the available literature, see White and Bhatia (1998); World Bank (1996j).

economies have engaged in what he terms "mild financial restraint," he fails to pay sufficient attention to the central policy role played by the preferential allocation of subsidized credit to selected manufacturing enterprises (Stiglitz 1998c, 11); these enterprises were identified in South Korea, for example, at the subsectoral level by a highly interventionist industrial policy, supported both by state ownership of banks and mandatory deposits from financial institutions (Chang 1993; Harris 1987).

In sum, the post-Washington Consensus, like the old Washington Consensus, retains a very limited conception of the role of the state in promoting growth in poor economies. The grudging and qualified tone of the critique is evident in the following speculative conclusion: "Perhaps had these [East Asian miracle] countries followed all of the dictums of liberalization and privatization, they would have grown even faster . . ." (Stiglitz 1998d, 12).

Unfortunately, the first cut of the Bank's report entitled "Attacking Poverty" (World Bank 1999d) also does not contain many unambiguous examples of a new approach. There are few indications that the old analytical framework, the old familiar policy stance, has been reassessed or that the lessons of decades of experience have successfully been incorporated into genuinely new policy directions. As is the case with the new paradigm proposed by Stiglitz, some apparently new arguments turn out, on closer inspection, to be qualified or downplayed elsewhere in this document.

For example, many economists would welcome the fact that the "Attacking Poverty" report appears to distance the Bank from the deflationary policies characterizing much of its policy lending over the previous fifteen years. They would applaud the statement that "Given a macro-economic crisis, . . . [a] pro-poor response strategy would be one which is output expansionary, and which protects public spending . . ." (World Bank 1999d, sec. 6.2). They would also welcome the recognition (chap. 8) that the role of fiscal and monetary policy in the face of economic shocks should be to induce investment and growth rather than fetishizing price stability or a stable, small fiscal deficit as the overriding goal. Nevertheless, the impact of these macro-economic policy conclusions is somewhat qualified elsewhere in the document, where it is suggested that perhaps deflation will not hurt the poor (in the long run) and that the safety nets established alongside austerity packages will actually be capable of protecting the poor. But the degree of protection likely to be offered to the poor by these instruments may be doubted. The Bank's efforts and lending to support social action programs and social funds have been relatively small, emerging in the late 1980s as a tardy and limited response to criticisms of its economic reform policies; few attempts have been made to assess the abysmal record (from the point of view of the rural poor) of Washington-sponsored "safety net mechanisms" (Tjønneland et al. 1998, 23). Furthermore, the report assumes that the familiar orthodox policies of financial market deregulation and privatization should always be pursued in poor countries (World Bank 1999d, chap. 8). The fact that it faintly echoes the post-Washington Consensus platitudes concerning the need for "care" in implementing these policies (and notes the possibility of "mixed results" for the poor) can be interpreted as a thin gloss superimposed on a fundamental adherence to the tenets of the neoliberal faith.

Some economists and NGOs might also welcome the report's emphasis on empowerment, voice, and broad participation, particularly the participation of women.[14] However, the use of these politically correct phrases cannot conceal the report's failure to come to grips with the dynamic processes through which the poor have historically struggled, with varying degrees of success, to improve their position. This failure arises from an initial analytical failure to define the characteristics of the poor accurately, but is exacerbated by the report's fuzzy and inadequate recommendations concerning the institutional reforms and the other policy interventions that are required to enable the poor not merely to participate in decision making (whatever that means), but, more important, to oppose and to struggle more effectively against those political forces that oppress them.

Some examples will help to make the analytical and policy problems clearer. When a poor young rural woman resists the efforts of the male relatives in her landless household to force her to marry an elderly local landowner by committing suicide, it could perhaps be said that she is participating in and influencing a decision about the allocation of village labor resources. (And there are some neoclassical economists who would not blush or hesitate to use such a formulation.) Similarly, poor casual harvest workers who join together to beat up any laborer who agrees to accept a piece-rate below the negotiated norm could also be said to be participating in local-level economic decision making. Yet these two rather brutal agrarian examples of the real political economy of local-level participation are clearly not what the Bank has in mind.[15] The Bank pays no attention to some other forms of participation or defensive strategies that might become available to the rural poor, such as demonstrating for the state-employed labor inspector to enforce payment of the legislated minimum harvest wage or pursuing legal redress against the sexual abuse of young women through an accessible court that is independent of local male notables. Interventions to support such defensive strategies are not discussed in this report.

The point is that the report is far too vague about the type of participation or voice the Bank wishes to encourage and the specific forms of intervention that may be required to facilitate effective defensive strategies by the

14. The Bank's president also praises empowerment, participation, recognition of women, and the positive role of civil society (Wolfensohn 1998).
15. On the analytical implications of the coercive features of rural societies see Bhaduri (1986). On suicide in an African rural context, see Sender and Smith (1990).

poor. This vagueness stems, in part, from an initial failure to define precisely the characteristics of the poor people it wishes to empower. It is one thing to offer financial and institutional support to a group of entrepreneurial women who are married to the largest farmers and most influential political men in a rural area, to enable them to club together to flood the local market with their basketwork or soft toys; it is quite another thing to allocate resources to support the formation of trade unions among landless agricultural laborers. The Bank has published no proposals for the support of rural or other trade unions in sub-Saharan Africa. It is willing to proclaim its support for "greater community voice and management" for "beneficiary involvement" (World Bank 1998d, 85), but those organizations established to represent the specific interests of workers are either not mentioned or are regarded as likely to aggravate poverty because they impede the efficient operation of the labor market. A major deficiency of the report is its refusal to analyze processes of differentiation in rural areas, confining itself to practically useless generalizations, such as "Rural areas will continue to account for significant numbers of the poor . . ." (Chapter 7), or platitudes about "the energy of the informal sector" (93).

This report recommends only two types of institutional reform to give the homogeneously conceived poor and women "a greater say" (93).[16] First, decentralization from central to local government levels is recommended, although it is admitted that the results of such reforms for the rural poor have been mixed—"mixed results" in World-Bank-speak means that there is no persuasive evidence that policies had the results that the World Bank anticipated. Second, the report recommends land reform, although it is by no means clear that the poorest rural women have benefited from most land reform programs nor is it clear what policies are to be promoted in the many countries where redistributive land reforms are not politically feasible in the medium term. In addition, if some rural people acquire new assets as a result of donor policy interventions, the fact remains that many of the poorest households will continue to lack access to the means of production and will depend for their survival, in the short as well as the long run, on the irregular and pitifully low wages they can command in casual and unregulated labor markets.

---

16. The institutional recommendations made by World Bank officials in other contexts appear to be inconsistent with the claim that "participation matters" and that "the people must be consulted and involved" (Wolfensohn 1998, 14). Although the people may be trusted to assist with the minor matter of the design of rural water supply projects, for example, it is dangerous if powerful interest groups in sub-Saharan African countries attempt to influence other decisions that may affect their well-being. Good macroeconomic management in reforming countries may depend on the removal of the important macroeconomic decisions from public debate. It is suggested that this can be achieved by adopting "commitment technologies," including the creation of autonomous central banks and tariff bindings with the World Trade Organization (WTO) (Collier and Gunning 1999).

In rural sub-Saharan Africa, the Bank continues to focus its efforts on supporting farmers and the rural self-employed, undertaking no research into the conditions of hired labor on farms and "often ignoring the landless and those with insufficient access to land" (Tjønneland et al. 1998, 21). The fact is that there has been a huge expansion of wage labor in rural Africa since the 1950s. A growing number of microsurveys suggest that many of the poorest rural women survive only on the basis of the wages they receive as casual workers (Sender and Smith 1990; Sender and Johnston 1996; Cramer and Pontara 1998; Guyer 1997; Peters 1996). The design and sampling methodology of the national household surveys supported by the World Bank ensure that these statistically representative surveys are an unreliable guide to identifying the poorest people in rural areas (Standing, Sender, and Weeks 1996, chap. 7).

The methods proposed by the report to identify or characterize the poor invite a rather cynical response. The international aid bureaucracy regularly wishes to demonstrate that a large proportion of its expenditures is directed toward the poor. If the poor are broadly or vaguely enough defined, that is, in terms of the arbitrary mix of lead indicators listed in chapter 1 of "Attacking Poverty," to include most members of the rural or female or child population, for instance, then it will be easy to defend almost any pattern of expenditure in a country as pro-poor. Such window-dressing efforts are familiar to anyone who has looked at Bank project appraisal reports or country poverty profiles in which approximately one-half of the population is conveniently "poor."

At the same time, the bottom line of Bank exercises of this type is the global quantitative guesstimate of the total number of millions of people who are "poor" or the percentage of the "poor" living in particular countries or regions (World Bank 1999d, par. 1.4). Presumably, it is thought that an up-to-date pseudoscientific estimate of these large numbers or percentages will, by publicizing the immense scale of the problem, prick the conscience of the donors' funders. In fact, the authors of this report do not appear to be willing to rely on the conscience of their funders. They suggest that there is a link between failures to achieve poverty reduction and the outbreak of wars and between "social stability" and poverty reduction (chap. 4). They highlight the risk of "social explosions" if funds are not made available to take advantage of the opportunities for poverty reduction. Not only are the poor a moral affront, they are also dangerous.

Thus, to an outside observer this new report on poverty appears to be geared toward the need to generalize and to justify the operations of the Bank across a huge range of countries rather than being designed to engage in a serious discussion of the dynamics of poverty. Such a discussion would require far more historical detail concerning political and economic processes in specific places and an analytical framework that focused on national and local political struggles to an extent that would be diplomatically embarrassing for international bureaucrats.

CONCLUSION

In its arguments for a minimal state and for a reduction in the volume of aid to miscreant states in sub-Saharan Africa, the World Bank has not addressed the task of promoting rapid structural change and economic growth. Growth requires far higher and sustained levels of investment geared toward expanding exports, especially processed and manufactured exports, as well as investment in a manufacturing sector that expands to cater for rising domestic incomes and demand. There are no grounds for believing that the required levels of investment in manufacturing can be achieved without substantial state support to and protection of a new class of domestic capitalists. The inability of sub-Saharan African states to provide such support or the impossibility of improvements in their capacity to provide such support and orchestrate the appropriate interventions cannot simply be assumed.

There is a case for caution and for demanding adherence to transparent conditions when lending to governments that persistently fail to achieve a reasonable acceleration in export or investment growth; these are, after all, the key objective determinants of their capacity to repay. There are no respectable arguments for allocating loans on the basis of shifting indices supposed to capture good macroeconomic policies or on the basis of a government's coerced gestures toward the espousal of Washington-approved policy rather than on the basis of a careful monitoring of objective outcome measures (Spraos 1986).

The Bank's proposals concerning the forms of state intervention that are required to reduce the vulnerability of the poor in sub-Saharan Africa (World Bank 1999d, chap. 5) are also inadequate. Three positive suggestions can be made concerning areas where it may be particularly important to narrow the gaps in the Bank's current analysis and research on poverty. First, there is quite a lot of evidence that the poorest people are particularly vulnerable to sudden increases in the real price of basic food grains, either because small farmers are net purchasers of food or because the poorest landless laborers face great difficulties in negotiating real wages that keep pace with rising food prices (Ghose 1989). There is, therefore, a case for promoting appropriate forms of regulation of markets for basic food grains, as well as for proceeding with considerable caution before abandoning state procurement and fair-price distribution institutions.

Second, a key strategy adopted by poor people in the face of serious threats to their survival is migration. In the case of sub-Saharan Africa, this often entails cross-border or other forms of long-distance migration in search of casual or seasonal wage employment. It should not be assumed that the vulnerability of the poor is best alleviated by efforts to keep them self-employed wherever they happen to be. There is, therefore, a need to discuss support for policies that would reduce some of the legal and financial barriers to mobility currently faced by very poor and vulnerable people.

Third and finally, the attack on poverty requires the widespread dissemination of far more accurate and far more detailed time-series data—demographic, anthropometric, socioeconomic, agronomic, and, in particular, labor market—if coherent policies are to be devised. The resources devoted to institutional support for regular and methodologically consistent surveys and to establishing the reputation and credibility of the state agencies responsible are woefully inadequate. The Bank is in a very strong position to highlight all of these data inadequacies in sub-Saharan Africa, as well as to insist on intervention to strengthen the capacity of relevant local institutions. This could usefully be a major theme of the forthcoming World Development Report.

CHAPTER NINE

The World Bank's Speculation on Social Capital

Ben Fine

One aim of this chapter is to examine critically the treatment of social capital in the work of the World Bank. As such, it is primarily an intellectual exercise, but is it merely academic? A second aim, in the broader context of assessing the operational impact of the World Bank, is to examine the relationship between the Bank's research and its own policies, as well as the more general influence it exerts on the research and policy environment, and vice versa.

Broadly, there are two opposing stereotypical views on the relationship of the Bank's research and policies. On the one hand, research is seen as highly influential in setting policy perspectives and priorities, trickling down to affect, if not to determine, internal operations; such research can also have a seepage effect on operational activity outside the World Bank. On the other hand, the World Bank's research is seen as irrelevant to the loans made and how they perform, with such research and operations functioning (whatever the individual effect) in essentially different worlds. This second approach tends to be informed by two very different stances on the source of the independence between research and policy: either those directly responsible for making loans in the World Bank proceed oblivious to any intellectual turmoil that surrounds them, not least because they are practical and steeped in local knowledge and experience, or on a grander scale policy is determined by external economic and political conditions, with research being used at most to rationalize (or even contradict) what is done in practice. Despite some common features across the World Bank's research and research environment, the role of research is uneven across issues and its impact cannot be predetermined. It certainly does not inevitably fall at one or the other of the two extremes outlined.

This chapter uses such discussion as background to a critical account of an idea that has come to the fore in World Bank research—social capital. This idea is analytically located in the more general, continuing weaknesses in the way in which economy and society, and the relationship between them, have been constructed and construed in World Bank research. In a nutshell, the economy is perceived to be based on market relations. Under the Washington Consensus, market relations are understood to work well and policy should be devoted to removing social impediments to the market, such as excessive government intervention and correspondingly induced rent-seeking. With the post-Washington Consensus, emphasis is placed both on the presence of market imperfections and the role of the social as nonmarket forms of handling them. In other words, the social is the economic by other (nonmarket) means. From this perspective, policy should be designed so that the social ensures that economic policy is implemented and that market imperfections are addressed through nonmarket forms. This framework allows economists to address the social and social scientists to be taken seriously by economists. But it only does so at the expense of perceiving the economy (and market) as nonsocial, at least at first. As a result, issues of economic power, interests, structures, and developmental tendencies can only be introduced as a social afterthought, if at all. In short, although the attempt to integrate economic and social analysis into the research agenda of the World Bank is to be welcomed, it is likely to remain inadequate, not least because of the failure to challenge the economic analysis itself. Indeed, the placing of social capital on the research agenda of the World Bank is a remarkable reflection, if not resolution, of its failure to understand the economic as both social and capital. This is not remedied by an ex post adding on of (noneconomic) social capital. The particular spin put on social capital by the World Bank is uncovered by a selective account of contributions.

RESEARCH AND THE WORLD BANK

This section provides commentary on the significance of research in the functioning of the World Bank by charting a course between two stylized extremes: research as critical and research as irrelevant.

Is the World Bank's research merely presentational froth, a conduit for predetermined policies, a sideline with little or no impact on operational outcomes? Gustav Ranis, for example, identifies two "circulatory systems," one around the president's office, the research wing, and the chief economist, the other around operating departments concerned with, "being polite but getting on with the lending" (1997, 79).

Alternatively, the World Bank can be perceived to exercise an influence far beyond the conditions attached to the loans that it makes (whatever the role of research in determining these) as both an educational and a knowledge bank. With a research budget in the region of $25 million,[1] Ranis

---

1. De Vries (1996, 238) reports that the World Bank distributes 1 million books and papers, has a catalogue list of five hundred titles, and publishes on a scale equivalent to a sales vol-

(1997, 75) also observes of the World Bank that "Its dissemination efforts, especially in the Third World, are prodigious and overwhelming. At the same time the Bank has paid relatively little attention to the output of other national and international organizations. . . . Indeed even much relevant output by academia is largely ignored" (1997, 75). This luxury (or is it disdain?) follows from the sheer weight of research, backed up with the power to lend:

> In analyzing the Bank's influence on development economics it
> must be recognized that the Bank's size gives it a unique position.
> The Bank employs around 800 professional economists. . . . These
> resources dwarf those of any university department or research in-
> stitution working on development economics. There are more than
> 3,000 additional professionals in the Bank. The size of the Bank's
> lending program (of the order of $15 billion to $20 billion a year)
> allows it to exert considerable influence on the thinking and policies
> of borrowing countries. The weight of the number of development
> economists, the research budget, and the leverage from lending
> means that the Bank's potential influence is profound, and that the
> Bank cannot be seen as just one of a number of fairly equal actors in
> the world of development economics. (Stern and Ferreira 1997,
> 524)

Further, the World Bank has sought to incorporate governments into the formulation of adjustment policies so that the policies will be indigenously owned. Although presented as a means of democratizing and enhancing policy formulation by local participation, it is a moot point whether this is more accurately perceived as a form of repressive tolerance and a sophisticated means of ensuring implementation. Gerald Helleiner puts it most delicately:

> The World Bank now says that it is encouraging local program own-
> ership, "insisting that the materials we use as the basis for . . . lend-
> ing decisions be the product of Africans," hiring local African
> consultants rather than foreigners wherever possible, and attempt-
> ing . . . to develop professional and analytical skills in public policy
> in Africa. These efforts are overdue, and they are probably biased in
> their orientations (toward orthodox Bank perspectives), but they
> have been welcomed in Africa. (1994, 10–11)

---

ume of between $10 million and $30 million. Significantly, however, the public relations budget is two to three times that for research, provoking the speculation about which is the dog and which is the tail.

A blunter assessment is given by Arnold Harberger. Having pointed to the low weight of the World Bank loans relative to other flows and what is needed, he observes:

> The Bank must recognize that ultimately its role is that of a teaching institution. It teaches developing countries lessons they have to learn about economic policy. In part it does so by training young people from developing countries. . . . In part it does so through what people from developing countries learn when they occupy staff jobs. In part it does so through Bank missions going to developing countries and working with the ministers and their staffs. (Harberger 1992, 93)

In this light, loans and operations might be seen as supplying a token demonstration effect to allow World Bank policy (and research) to prosper by other educational means.

In particular, the World Bank played its part in not only promoting the neoliberal Washington Consensus, but the consensus also set the analytical agenda for development studies—the market versus the state, heavily leaning on the market side. Even so, this might have been driven by the dictates of Reaganism and the like. As Ranis puts it more generally, in the warmer climes of adjustment with a human face:

> The Bank has shown a tendency not to innovate but to take over quickly the leadership on any given theme. . . . More current examples include the environment, women in development, military expenditures and governance. Subjects accepted as topical from either a functional or political point of view are quickly incorporated into Bank language . . . become part of the Bank's research and analysis agenda, and sometimes even of its stated lending criteria. (1997, 74)

Adopting an intermediate position between these two extremes, we find it useful to view the World Bank's research as both cause and effect. It does have an impact on its own and the broader policy environment in addition to being a response to its dictates. Consider the conclusion of Sebastian Edwards on trade policy, for example:[2]

---

2. For a stronger, if implicit, account of the World Bank's role in promoting openness in trade policy in terms of how we learned to embrace the Washington Consensus and abandon inappropriate theory and misleading stylized facts, see Krueger (1997). For a review of the tensions between the new trade policy and the new trade theory, see Deraniyagala and Fine (2001). Note that Kapur, Lewis, and Webb tell the story in a slightly different way: the departure of Robert McNamara as Bank president is followed by that of Hollis Chenery as chief economist. He is succeeded by Anne Krueger who, "in turn, replaces large fractions of the Bank's central economics establishment until she had a highly compatible staff" (1997, 22).

The Bank has contributed somewhat (but not a whole lot) to these policies. . . . ideas have had a role in the recent reform movement. And, over the years, the Bank has made a contribution to the intellectual debate on the consequences of alternative trade regimes. Although the quality of Bank research has not always been very high, and although no memorable pieces have been produced, I believe that the Bank has been able to accumulate an impressive body of evidence that points toward the benefits of liberalization policies. (1997, 47)

Further, Anne Kreuger suggests that the associated research work was of practical significance: "High marks must go to the analytical research that pointed to measurement techniques such as effective protection and cost benefit, which enabled policy makers and their analysts to obtain empirical quantification, however rough, of the relevant magnitudes" (1997, 19).

Another area in which the World Bank has been particularly prominent is in the human capital approach to the economics of education, which has been attached in the 1990s to the promotion of primary schooling, especially for girls.[3] As early as 1981, George Psacharopoulos describes the World Bank's 1980 policy paper on education in these terms: "It might not be an exaggeration to treat this Paper as a modern Bible on educational development" (1981, 141). As Phillip Jones accepts, "There can be no doubt as to the quality of much of the Bank's research output in the 1980s, evidenced by the number of articles by Bank staff gaining acceptance in leading academic journals" (1992, 229).

However, Jones heavily qualifies this praise by pointing to the overgeneralization of the research from the results of a few country studies, the failure to develop and draw on indigenous research capacity, and the wish to reduce the provision of education to a flow of financial costs and benefits.[4] Indeed, he adds, "It would be facile to criticize Psacharopoulos' research leadership as too focused, too bound to Bank requirements, insufficiently open-ended and insufficiently free-ranging, as it would be to criticize the highly repetitive nature of his publications" (Jones 1992, 227). And he ultimately sees the Bank's educational research as being driven by other imperatives:

The most powerful force for change in policy has been the desire to keep the Bank functioning as a bank. Its borrowers need to be confronted with new reasons for borrowing, whether on commercial or concessional terms. It is simply not in the scheme of things for the

3. For a critical assessment, see Fine and Rose (2001).
4. Note, however, that Stern and Ferreira (1997) make no mention of the World Bank's contribution to the economics of education and only mention human capital in a reference to new growth theory.

Bank officers to promote a fresh view about education and development if it did not have possibilities for opening up new patterns of lending. . . . In their daily work, loan officers are driven by (and to an extent their careers are dependent upon) their success in negotiating large numbers of sizable loans and in encouraging quick disbursements for each stage of projects. This latter aspect, encouraging as it does superficial evaluation so as not to slow down the rate of disbursements during a project, helps explain the relative lack of interest displayed by the Bank in matters of educational detail, especially in the classroom. Loan officers, but also research and policy analysts in education, display—as a group—a certain naiveté about process matters in education, not least the practical dimensions of teaching and learning, policy formulation, the management of educational change, and community motivation and participation. (220)

This contrasts with trade theory and policy, in which the World Bank research is generally considered to be influential and accepted, and explains what has been described as the ignorance, rejection, and/or manipulation of human capital theory for advocacy purposes by World Bank educational operatives. The theory is more or less irrelevant to them once loans have been agreed on. Unlike trade policy, which tells us (however well and however legitimately) what to do with tariffs, calculating rates of return on educational expenditure does not help to put an education project in place other than in principle.

Privatization provides a sharp contrast to education and trade as an illustration of World Bank research, both in its level of academic sophistication and in its influence on outcomes. Although consistently and aggressively pursued as a policy measure, the World Bank's research has remained impoverished at best and apologetic at worst. Analytically, it has fallen far short of the content of the approach that dominates the orthodoxy—with its conclusion that ownership as such does not matter relative to the conditions of competition and regulation.[5] Its empirical work has simply and primarily been self-serving. If the lessons from the existing literature had been learned and followed in advance, the policies would have been very different, particularly in terms of the desirability, sequencing, and integration of privatization or public sector reform with other policies.[6] I suspect that even its authors would not claim that research on privatization at the World Bank is at the intellectual frontier, let alone pushing it outward.

5. Fine (1990) terms this the new synthesis on privatization. See also Fine (1997).
6. For a review of World Bank thinking, see Bayliss (1999); Bayliss and Fine (1998); and references cited in these works.

So, as privatization shows, even though in the areas of education and trade the World Bank has been highly active in the wider academic environment and has wielded some influence, this is not so in all areas. Even in the research on education and trade, there is some doubt over quality, as already indicated by Jones (1992) and Edwards (1997), respectively. Even the generally favorable Barend de Vries is light in his praise: "Nevertheless one can say that the Bank is only to a limited extent a creator of new ideas. It absorbs ideas from many other places, integrates them in its operations practices, tests their practicality, and provides a forum for interchange among academics and government officials" (1996, 240). And even if policy is research-led, the research in the lead has become both internationalized and Americanized, with the two more or less synonymous in mainstream neoclassical economics (see Coats 1996a).[7] This leads Devesh Kapur, John P. Lewis, and Richard Webb to cast some doubt on the independence of the World Bank's economists:

> Economics would become the Bank's hallmark scholarly discipline, and the economists who heavily shaped Bank operations as well as its research were recruited from a wide array of countries. To a large degree, however, they were the product of the graduate economics departments of English-speaking, but especially American, universities. This fact, as it played into the Bank's consulting, research, technical assistance, and agenda setting, would enhance the US role in the institution beyond the apparatus of formal governance. (1997, 4)

Initially, then, it can be concluded that the role of research in the World Bank is complex, uneven, and shifting, depending on the issue concerned as well as on the internal and external environments, both intellectual and political.[8] In addition, a number of weaknesses can be identified: poor quality; poor engagement with alternatives (Americanization); excessive dissemination at the expense of independent research capacity building (ditto); poor coherence and integration in how research is used in the choice, de-

7. Particularly disturbing is the declining number of U.S. students taking doctorates in economics while the number studying in the United States from abroad continues to increase. Hodgson and Rothman (1999, n. 165) report that over 70 percent of the editors of the top thirty economic journals are located in the United States, almost 40 percent in twelve institutions alone. Two-thirds of articles are of U.S. authorship, the top twelve institutions accounting for over 20 percent. They conclude, "the degree of institutional and geographical concentration of editors and authors may be unhealthy for innovative research."

8. By way of comparison and despite claims to the contrary (Polak 1996), the IMF can be judged to have failed to be at the forefront of macroeconomic research despite its role in stabilization. This is a result of the obsessive, if institutionally determined, preoccupation with financial programming, both analytically and as a target. See Fine and Hailu (1999).

sign, monitoring, and assessment of activities; overgeneralization in order to rationalize loans and leave room for discretion despite the need for country and issue specificity; and limited engagement in self-criticism and assessment even when there are sea changes in approach. Further, the gaps between World Bank and high-quality academic research and between research of any quality and policy practice seem to be wider the more macroeconomic or program-based (as opposed to microeconomic or project-based) the issue concerned.[9]

So far, however, we have considered only research within economics. Now consider the relationship between economics and the other social sciences. The view is now prevalent that a long battle has been waged to have social factors taken seriously by the World Bank's economists.[10] Michael C. Cernea regrets the absence of cultural factors in the thinking of World Bank economists, who, "as the professional body presiding most often over the rites of project making, have done little to incorporate cultural variables into project models" (1991b, 6). Further, he continues, "the neglect of social dimensions in intervention-caused development always takes revenge on the outcome" (6). This is one reason why social science knowledge ultimately becomes incorporated into projects—the projects fail or otherwise can be enhanced by studied participation rather than by relying on dubious trickle-down effects. The imbalances that social science must seek to redress are those of the "econocentric," "technocentric," and "commodocentric" in-house cultures at the World Bank, that is, undue emphasis on getting prices and technology right and neglect of social actors, respectively (Cernea 1996, 15–16). He appears to be a heavily critical of economists. It is not so much that they are wrong as that they are one-sided, primarily as a consequence of their university training: "Many of the former students in economics . . . brought to the Bank—or to governments and the private sector elsewhere— biased, one-sided conceptual models. . . . Can we correct afterwards what the university has not done well at the right time?" (Cernea 1996, 17).

At times, particularly in Cernea's earlier work, it is a question of making given policies work better: "how can sociology and anthropology help improve resettlement?" (Cernea 1991a, 198). Yet this is but a short step from the position that social science must inform policy making in more than a limited way:

> For all these reasons—economic, social, moral, financial—social
> analysis is not only *instrumental* but . . . indispensable. It directly in-

9. I am grateful to Jonathan Pincus for suggesting this point to me.
10. In what follows, discussion is confined to a number of works by Michael C. Cernea. But see also Kardam (1993), favorably cited by Cernea (1994), who argues that the shift to accept the social within the World Bank was a result of internal and external factors, the former including successful advocacy in which the World Bank's Sociology Group is seen as key.

creases the successes of programs. . . . (It) *is not a luxury or a marginal add-on* to inducing development, but is as necessary *as the economic analysis is* for designing and ascertaining the feasibility and adequate goal-directedness of development programs. (Cernea 1996, 10)[11]

From painfully late beginnings, social theory has gained momentum and presence. Cernea (1996) observes that the first anthropologist was appointed to the World Bank only in 1974, compared to 1950 for the World Health Organization (see also Cernea 1991b, 22). Subsequently, however, Cernea notes:

> The group assembled during these twenty years is today the world's *largest group of this kind working in one place*—about 50–60 social scientists, who actually practice development anthropology and sociology. In addition, hundreds of social scientists from developing and developed countries are employed each year as short term consultants, largely due to the demand for social analysis *legitimized by the core in-house group.* (1996, 4, emphasis added)[12]

In retrospect, such growth and influence looks like a successful assault on the narrow and narrow-minded hegemony exercised by World Bank economists. Especially in view of the increasing prominence of adjustment with a human face, social science has also been promoted by external influence. As Cernea observes, under the slogan of putting people first the opportunities for social science are unlimited: "The range of entrance points for sociological knowledge and skills should be expanded to all segments of development planning, from policymaking to execution and evaluation, and from theorizing to social engineering" (1991b, 36).

Looking forward, however, the achievements of the social scientists are considerably less impressive. From the perspective of the post-Washington Consensus, there is nothing at all troublesome in the positions adopted by the noneconomists. The emphasis on market imperfections is positively embraced, as is the coexistence of economic and noneconomic factors. In addition, four distinct but closely related features of the work of these social

11. "My conviction, relying on experience inside a major development agency, is that social research findings will become effective guidance for future practice only if they result in the *formulation and adoption of new or improved policy guidelines.* Social science knowledge must be used not just to evaluate program results but to craft policies. Only new policies have compelling *authority* over *planning*" Cernea (1993, 15).

12. Cernea adds: "During the last eight to ten years, the Bank's corps of non-economic social scientists—mainly anthropologists, sociologists, and political scientists—has probably become *the largest group of this kind in the world that works together in one location actually practising development sociology and anthropology.* In this process they often break open new trails, chart untraveled territory, and push the frontiers of these disciplines forward" (1994, 3). Note how the World Bank's economists are emulated in relative weight of external academic presence, if not internally.

scientists are particularly disturbing: (1) there is an acceptance of the division between the economic and the social, (2) this division carries the implication that the economic is nonsocial, (3) the economic analysis of the World Bank (other than its omission of the social) is accepted uncritically, and (4) the social, even if pursued aggressively, serves primarily as an add-on to the economic. In a sense, in its interaction with economic engineering, social engineering has been pushed to its logical conclusion: for projects to be chosen, for them to be of higher quality, for implementation to be successful, and to clear up at the end, it is as well to incorporate what is involved at the outset.

In this light, it is hardly surprising that the noneconomists have accepted their marginal position, if only to press for it to be less marginal. This is illustrated by what is possibly their most active area of engagement—involuntary resettlement. The issue itself is self-marginalization, dealing with the consequences of projects that might otherwise be overlooked except for their putting impediments in their way. Paradoxically, that the economic is social emerges in the (economic) areas explicitly addressed by the poverty-induced resettlement literature, with Cernea (1991a, 195–96) listing them as landlessness, homelessness, joblessness, marginalization, food insecurity, increased morbidity and mortality, and social disarticulation (see also Cernea 1991b, 22–23).

These issues are often at the core of development economics. If they are social, so is economics in general. How can social sciences deal with these by relying on what might be termed noneconomics alone? How can they do so without challenging economics itself? Significantly, Cernea seems to offer only limited criticism of economics other than in its oversights. Indeed, Guggenheim and Cernea (1993) praise Schuh (1993) for emphasizing the role of family and household, even though the article they are discussing is entirely couched in the terms of mainstream economics with a reliance on the new household economics and human capital theory. As we show next, the introduction of the noneconomic into the economic has become entirely acceptable to mainstream economics without challenging, and even reinforcing, its underlying methodology. One of the ways of papering over the fundamental schism between a nonsocial economics and a social noneconomics has been to invent and deploy the notion of social capital, which World Bank noneconomists have heavily promoted. Social capital does not challenge the economics and economists of the World Bank and can have the effect of strengthening their position and scope. In this respect, heirs to Cernea should heed his advice because social capital does not assert new ideas, it merely consolidates the old: "For applied social scientists, quibbling only for improving practical fixes is never enough. Asserting innovative ideas does require intellectual wrestling and theoretical engagement" (1996, 16).

It appears, then, that the World Bank contains two worlds, one of economists and one of noneconomists. Social capital holds out the prospect of bringing these two worlds together, although it is a meeting, even a confrontation, that is based on entirely different intellectual backgrounds and dynamics. How does it turn out?

THE WORLD BANK'S SOCIAL CAPITAL

In the broader intellectual environment, social capital has shot to analytical prominence in less than a decade. Pierre Bourdieu, the left-wing social theorist, was an early contributor, emphasizing how social stratification is created, sustained, and endowed with meaning in view of different economic, social, and political access to "resources." He has dropped out of the picture, especially in the World Bank's approach, which explicitly draws on the crude functional and rational-choice sociology of James Coleman, who separately developed the notion of social capital to explain why those with more social capital in the form of family background gain a better education. It is simple to extend the scope of such inputs and outputs to fill an entire universe of cause and effect. Social capital is anything beyond an individual's own personal world that allows him or her to achieve something else—education, income, health, or whatever. And what is true for the individual is extrapolated to the village, community, or nation.

Within the realm of political science, social capital was anticipated in all but name by the theory of collective action (Olson 1965). But, in this area, by far the most significant input has been provided by Robert Putnam (1992). Explicitly appealing to the work of Coleman (1988), he has sought to explain the relative economic performance of northern and southern Italy by the presence of horizontal civic associations in the successful north as compared to the unsuccessful south. What has propelled the profile of Putnam's work is his attempts to explain aspects of the U.S. decline in terms of the erosion of its social capital (Putnam 1993, 1995, 1996). Oversimplifying, but not unduly, U.S. citizens have been reducing their engagement in horizontal civic associations, not least as a consequence of watching too much television.

On the basis of analyses such as those of Coleman and Putnam, there has been an explosive interest in social capital across the social sciences. The concept has inspired a number of survey articles and special journal issues (Foley and Edwards 1997; Harriss and de Renzio 1997; Wall, Ferrazzi, and Schryer 1998; Woolcock 1998). Michael Woolcock (1998), for example, points to seven distinct areas of application—economic development, (dys)functional families, performance in schooling, community life, (work) organization, democracy and governance, and collective action. In short, social capital certainly has had a life of its own both before and independent of how it has been used by the World Bank.

The scope of material covered by social capital—by discipline, content, method, and so on—is vast.[13] For economists, it is anything other than natural, physical, or human capital. According to the World Bank's own definition, frequently reproduced in one form or another:

> The traditional composition of natural capital, physical or produced capital, and human capital needs to be broadened to include social capital. Social capital refers to the internal social and cultural coherence of society, the norms and values that govern interactions among people and the institutions in which they are embedded. Social capital is the glue that holds societies together and without which there can be no economic growth or human well-being. Without social capital, society at large will collapse, and today's world presents some very sad examples of this. (World Bank 1998i)

For Christiaan Grootaert (1997), it thereby becomes the missing link in explaining economic development. This can be understood in two ways. First, conceptually the role of capital in economic growth, say, is already presumed to be understood as far as its natural, physical, and human components are concerned. They are stocks that aid production and that can either be added to or depleted. Easily overlooked but equally emphasized by the addition of social capital to the analysis is the presumption that capital in these other senses is individual. This is a consequence of the physicalist notion of capital that is employed in each of the three nonsocial variants, in the sense that they are perceived in terms of their physical productive properties alone. Insofar as capital (and, dare I say, capitalism) depends on social relations, these are now separately assigned to the component of social capital. Second, it is recognized that some sort of social arrangements are essential for the other capitals to function in practice (outside the world of Robinson Crusoe), so that social capital is the "glue that holds societies together."

In effect, social capital is so broad a concept that it not only transforms itself as it evolves in its various applications and networks, it also incorporates and transforms the literature on which it draws. It is also endowed with the magical property of repairing the ruptures across the social sciences and creating interdisciplinarity (Woolcock 1998, 160).[14] Given the background presented in the previous section, social capital in the World Bank can un-

---

13. As Woolcock puts it for individual motivation, "If social capital can be rational, pre-rational, or even non-rational, what is it *not*? At the very least, these different conceptualizations suggest that there may be various forms or dimensions of social capital" (1998, 156).
14. Alejandro Portes suggests that "the fungibility of diverse sources of capital reduces the distance between sociological and economic perspectives" (1998, 3). But see Fine (1999a) for an extensive discussion of the relationship between the fungibility (or fluidity) of capital and the confusion or enigma that surrounds it in the social sciences.

doubtedly be perceived as a key instrument used not so much in development as in social scientists' obtaining greater leverage over unyielding economists. Although my conclusion is that the economists are gaining more
than they are conceding, this is not my primary concern; such divisions are
likely to continue in the World Bank with greater or lesser impact on its operations and their outcomes, which often have only a limited connection to
Washington-based disputes. Rather, the importance of the evolution of social capital in the World Bank is more because of its influence on development studies as a whole. The World Bank has carved out a role for itself as
a knowledge bank. As such, it not only takes deposits selectively and decides
whether to pass them on, it also creates its own intellectual assets with which
it seeks to credit its own operations. Social capital incorporates all of these
processes and, in addition, in part reflects internal disputes over the significance of economic and social factors and economic and social theory. A
burning question is whether social capital, like bad money, is subject to Gresham's law and will drive more appropriate ideas and theories out of circulation or whether is it, as the more favorably inclined claim, more of a
neutral veil that facilitates the exchange and development of ideas. From
the evidence presented next, social capital, insofar as it metaphorically
adopts the form of money, is indeed subject to Gresham's law!

These observations can be illustrated by two examples from the literature. In an early contribution, Maurice Schiff (1992)[15] suggests that there
are positive externalities across groups of people formed over time. Consequently, when an individual leaves one group to migrate to another in pursuit of higher economic gains, a negative externality is imposed on the
abandoned community, whose productivity suffers. This can all be modeled
in a simple way. Schiff goes on to suggest that this is the way that the disso-
lution of native communities in Brazil as a consequence of the arrival of a
highway should be understood. Far from investigating the power and economic interests underlying the penetration of the rainforests, the highway
is seen as undermining the social capital of indigenous tribes by easing the
constraint on individuals' being able to leave. This example is as close to
purely speculative as we can get. It proceeds simply by extending neoclassical economics on a logical basis without regard to the realities of the object
of study.

The contribution of Paul Collier (1998), effectively Joseph Stiglitz's dep-
uty, is more derivative of the existing literature, which he sees as disparate,
ranging across many disciplines, and needing to settle down in agreed-on
definitions that he seeks to provide "from basic economic theory." In other
words, it is a matter of taking the noneconomic literature and incorporat-

15. This article is one of fifteen key readings on social capital selected by the World Bank's
Social Capital website: www.worldBank.org/poverty/scapital/.

ing it within economics as is. He begins with the social: "Social capital is 'social' because it involves some non-market process which nevertheless has economic effects. The economic effects are consequently not 'internalized' into the decision calculus of each agent by the prices faced in markets. In the language of economics, they are 'externalities' (Collier 1998). On the other hand, social capital is capital if it has the economic effect of sustaining a stream of income. On this basis, the notion of social capital is further refined according to, "the forms of social interaction, the particular type of externality which is being internalized, and the mechanisms of internalization." More specifically, "The building blocks of the analysis are thus the three externalities, the four types of social interaction, and the six mechanisms of internalization." These blocks are the externalities of knowledge of others' behavior, knowledge of the nonbehavioral environment, and collective action; social interaction in the form of hierarchies, clubs, networks, and observation; and internalization of knowledge through pooling and copying it, of opportunism through trust gained by repeat transactions or reputation built on gossip, and of free-riding through norms and rules. No doubt this list could be extended with some reference to network and organization theory or even to personnel management. In a less harmonious vein, notions of power and violence could also be added.

As it stands, Collier's contribution represents a compromise between the new microeconomics, which has inspired Stiglitz's post-Washington Consensus and is essentially concerned with more efficient contracting through nonmarket mechanisms, and the noneconomic social capital literature with its concerns about social organization and behavior. He does, however, lean heavily on the side of pure speculation rooted in received mainstream economic theory. The extent of the use and evidence of knowledge of social theory is particularly limited. Thus, although Collier's paper is considerably more sophisticated than Schiff's, essentially in its degree of disaggregation, both share two fundamental features: that the social, as capital, can only be introduced because it was left out in the first place in considering the economy and that economics is nonsocial because capital (and other assets) are conceived of primarily as physical (even where natural or human) and attached to individuals. This is, of course, entirely unacceptable because capital can only exist in the context of the glue of the social relations in which it is embodied. These can be added as an afterthought, as a corrective to their omission at the outset, although perceived as an innovative insight and extension.

Essentially, then, the differences between Schiff and Collier are simply ones of scope and terminology, with Schiff's Brazilian highways as idealized and abstract as Collier's more overtly abstract generalities. The policy implications derived by Collier are equally idealized and speculative:

The distributional consequences of civil society capital are likely to be mixed. Copying will tend to be progressive, except for barriers of social segmentation; pooling, repeat transactions and reputation will tend to be regressive; and norms and rules will tend to be progressive, except where the concentration of leadership among the higher income groups has the effect of marginalizing the interests and participation of the poor. (1998)

Obfuscating vernacular aside, did we not know all of this already?[16]

In short, there is a wonderful analytical complacency to be derived from the incorporation of social capital. Two separate loose ends can be tied up; the failure of economic analysis and its exclusion of social factors can resolve one another. The weaknesses of an unquestioned economic analysis can be remedied by the explanatory cure-all provided by social capital—the glue and missing link of economic performance. Social capital also has the advantage of being so amorphous that it both provides a general theory and allows for unlimited discretion in specific applications, whether theoretical, empirical, or for policy.

From an analytical point of view, then, social capital is something of a wonder drug. As a consequence, in principle, it has profound implications for policy choices. Build social capital, not schools, seems to be the lesson taken from the study of Tanzanian villages undertaken by Deepa Narayan and Lant Pritchett (1997). In the preface, Ismail Serageldin claims that:

> This study provides quantifiable evidence that village-level social capital—membership in groups with particular characteristics—significantly affects household welfare. In one telling statistic the study finds that one standard increase in village-level social capital increases household income per person by 20 to 30 percent. By comparison, a one standard deviation in schooling—nearly three additional years of education per person—increases incomes by only 4.8 percent. (1997, vii; but see also Narayan 1997, viii)

Thus, it bears emphasizing that social capital's associated policy framework provides for unlimited generality, on the one hand, and discretion, on the other. Only now this is attached to field research and even to operations. For example, attached to the World Bank's Social Capital Initiative have been

16. Collier continues: "What is the implication for a pro-poor public policy? The different distributional consequences of differing mechanisms of internalisation suggests that public policy should both promote most heavily those mechanisms which are most distributionally progressive, and should attempt to redress the regressive aspects of the other mechanisms" (1998). Who could disagree with such profundity?

twelve research projects. These are extremely diverse and add little of novelty to the analytical and policy arenas other than to impose social capital, often uncomfortably, as an organizing concept. Indeed, the proposals are marked by a degree of unanimity in being unable to define social capital satisfactorily and needing to operationalize it during the course of research.[17]

One project is concerned with the decline in the provision of health care in Russia and how social capital networks might be used as a remedy (Rose 1998). According to the project proposal, "The research findings will be used to design policy recommendations for the formulation of welfare and health promotion policies, especially regarding the ways in which informal social capital networks add value to policies, or substitute for government programs" (World Bank 1998i, 22). Such goals might be thought to be a little modest for a society of 150 million people, which has experienced an unprecedented a fall in male life expectancy between 1989 and 1995 of as much as six years (Field 1995).

Another project addresses the social capital of those whose lives and livelihoods have been impaired by the mining operations of Coal India Limited (CIL). I have no expertise in this area, but have consulted both the project proposal (World Bank 1998i) and a number of documents from NGOs and local organizations that have long been in dispute with both the World Bank and CIL over rehabilitation. The two sources represent very different worlds. For the project proposal, the building of social capital will enhance the benefits of rehabilitation through community participation. In the proposal's thirteen pages, there is scarcely a hint of the conflict in the past about the desirability of many of the mining projects in the first place, let alone the roughshod ways in which rehabilitation and participation have previously been handled by alternative accounts. At best, we are told that "The notion of consulting project affected people (PAPs), target communities at large, local state authorities, and NGOs on social and environmental issues is entirely new to CIL. Moreover, previous interface between the key stakeholders in the mining areas—due partially to issues of power, equity, and access to resources—has not always developed under cooperative terms" (World Bank 1998i, 30). From the opposing perspective, this might be considered more than an understatement, certainly misleading and mutually inconsistent (CIL both new to consultation and facing lack of cooperation). As one commentator has put it:

> The problem seems to be that in micro projects (building a village
> road) the people are encouraged to decide and implement, but in

17. For Grootaert and van Bastelaer, "The Social Capital Initiative aims to contribute to both the conceptual understanding of social capital and its measure. Although there is a significant and rapidly growing literature on social capital and its impact . . . , it has not yet provided an integrated and generally accepted conceptual and analytical framework" (1998).

the wider macro context (issues of future livelihood, legal recognition, land and water control), their opinions are ignored. The Bank, government and CIL are selective as to when/on what terms they will give participation. It is they who claim power to decide. Thus, in the context of macro projects (and peoples' economic dispossession, felt helplessness), the micro-project participation is largely irrelevant. Everybody, from top company management to village simpleton, knows this.

Further, the Berne Declaration reports as follows:

Participants of the March 1995 workshop complained that no representatives of project-affected people were able to attend, and that such consultations must rather take place in the project areas proper. The responsible Bank representative claims that the consultation process was as inclusive as possible, and that no groups were purposely excluded. Affected NGOs do not agree. The report of the March 1995 workshop lists one group which was excluded because it was "too radical." At least three other grassroots groups reported to Northern NGOs that they had never been consulted and that their letters to Coal India and the World Bank had never been answered, although they had worked with people affected by coal mines for many years. Two of them, the Jharkhand Janadhikar Manch (JJM) and the Chotanagpur Adivasi Sewa Simiti (CASS) from Bihar, prepared detailed, state-of-the-art critiques of Coal India's resettlement and rehabilitation policy and of the new Bank projects. (1998)

In short, if we allow the term, it would appear that there is no shortage of social capital in this sector. The kindest interpretation of the project to promote more and better social capital might be that this is a wish to wipe a dirty slate clean; the unkindest interpretation might be that this is a cynical disregard for the past and a wish to promote social capital of the "right" type to filter and minimize opposition to predetermined coal projects.

BRINGING THE SOCIAL BACK IN OR INTERROGATING THE ECONOMIC?

I hope enough has been said to convince the most hard-boiled of NGO activists and World Bank operators in the field that World Bank research does matter. It does so in a number of ways, which are well illustrated by social capital. First, the research tends to be organized under an umbrella of the most general kind. This has the advantage of opening avenues for the business of the Bank as a bank—a rationale by which to lend to its customers. Investments to build social capital are unlimited in scope. In addition, they leave considerable room for discretion and for more extensive intervention in civil society.

Second, in setting analytical agendas, research can have the effect of dictating the terms under which opposition is posed. In this respect, the World Bank has moved from an opposition between market and state. Now, in the wake of the post-Washington Consensus, we are all to be channeled into a dialogue of correcting market imperfections and building social capital. When set against the Washington Consensus, this seems to have the potential advantage of both skirting criticism and incorporating critics.

Third, this dialogue continues to reflect a sharp dichotomy between the economic and the noneconomic that has only been reinforced by the introduction of social capital. Indeed, this can be understood as an initiative to smooth the way for otherwise only marginally changed economic policies to be implemented without challenging their efficacy and desirability. This is evident in the cited case of CIL, but it applies equally and more generally to research around social capital itself. At best, social capital refines economic performance through spillover effects to an otherwise unreconstructed economy. In practice, the focus of the World Bank in its work on social capital has been even narrower, tending to divert attention from the role of the state and core economic analysis.[18] On the one hand, topics are excluded despite the gargantuan range otherwise covered by the social capital initiative—families, communities, civil society, public sector, ethnicity, gender, crime and violence, economics, trade and migration, education, environment, finance, health, nutrition and population, information technology, poverty and economic development, urban development, water supply, and sanitation. On the other hand, the initiative is closely aligned with the Bank's focused on local-level institutions (World Bank 1998j).

Fourth, because this is not inevitable—some of the social capital literature does address what would previously have been termed the economics and politics of the developmental state (see Evans 1996)—it follows that the World Bank has some effect in steering research for both internal and external purposes. This has clearly been much more important in some areas than in others, especially in trade policy and the economics of education, and the World Bank has never been able to dictate or determine either re-

18. See Edstrom (1999), who is sector manager for Social Development at the World Bank: "Whether considering the distributional impacts of the financial crisis in East Asia, of structural adjustment in Africa, of privatization in Eastern Europe and the Former Soviet Union, or of large infrastructure projects anywhere in the world, we know that, to be sustainable, development needs to be broadly inclusive. We acknowledge that too often in the past, the World Bank focused too much on the economics of growth, without a sufficient understanding of the social, the political, the environmental, and the cultural aspects of development. Nonetheless, the Bank has recognized, albeit later than some of our sister agencies in the United Nations, that development must be people-centred—that is, people must be the focus of the development agenda."

search or policy directions without opposition. Nevertheless, its influence is arguably excessive.

I am acutely conscious that these are heavy criticisms. In addition to my introductory remarks, I recommend the following goals, if not the means to achieve them. First, the quality of World Bank research needs to be considerably improved by greater internal and external debate, by meeting the highest standards of the disciplines and areas that it claims to cover, and by peer review. Second, given the weight of World Bank research and researchers, diverse approaches need to be encouraged and intellectual independence and originality guaranteed. Third, research should be debated openly in the context of the closest attention to project formulation, implementation, and monitoring. Fourth, capacity building in and teaching for research should be geared toward achieving similar levels of openness and originality.

CHAPTER TEN

Conclusion

Jonathan R. Pincus and Jeffrey A. Winters

At an earlier stage in the evolution of the World Bank, reforms conducted largely from within were adequate to the task of adjusting the institution to the challenges and opportunities of the era. But the time for incrementalism and reform has long passed. Internally the World Bank has lost its sense of focus and direction, whereas externally it no longer fits a rapidly evolving global political economy. The World Bank is in urgent need of a much deeper reinvention, possibly assisted by the institution's senior management, but designed and imposed from without by the Bank's shareholders. In our opening chapter, we set forth competing visions of reinvention, assessing the strengths and weaknesses of each along three dimensions— operations, concepts, and power. We strongly favored the last vision, reinventing the World Bank as a development bank. While operationally and conceptually the World Bank *qua* development bank would reaffirm the importance of public sector capital flows and address many of the institution's most serious problems raised in this book, we also noted that existing power relations and interests render this path toward reinvention an unlikely prospect. As conflicts and controversies over the Bank's operations and scope continue to fester in the years to come, it is much more likely that we will muddle along with a status quo institution making forays into becoming a knowledge bank and other areas beyond its capability. Alternatively, if sufficient conservative political forces could be mobilized under a Republican administration in the United States, there is a somewhat lesser possibility that the path of reinvention toward what we called a niche bank would be followed. Neither of these options, in our view, will settle the deep problems of the Bank nor contribute in significant ways to spurring growth and reducing poverty in poor countries.

The contributors to this volume, although not necessarily agreeing with our call for a development bank, all provide important information and analyses supporting our main observations. Although focused on the presidency of James Wolfensohn, Bruce Rich (chap. 2 in the volume) emphasizes that the problems of the Bank extend far beyond any single individual, including its powerful president. Sharply criticizing Wolfensohn's choices and priorities, he develops his argument about the almost chronic failures of the Wolfensohn presidency in a way that makes it impossible ultimately to assign him much of the blame. Rich depicts a Bank president simultaneously doing too much and too little, not because he has some personal defect but because those with the power and responsibility to reinvent the Bank from without have been derelict. The process of reinvention is much too encompassing for any chief executive of the institution to undertake successfully.

The historical sections provided by Devesh Kapur (chap. 3 in this volume) help us understand why this is so. Although most World Bank presidents have left only a faint impression on the institution, occasionally aggressive individuals such as Robert McNamara and Wolfensohn define their presidencies through industrious institutional reorganization. McNamara was decidedly more effective in changing what the Bank was and did than Wolfensohn, although less because he was a more capable reformer than because he exerted his influence on the institution at a much earlier stage of its development, when reforms conducted from within were still sufficient to solve most problems. He also benefited from an international environment that was supportive of his ambitious plans to expand the scope of the organization and provide the large capital increases required to boost the amount of lending in tandem with his operational aspirations.

By the time the energetic Wolfensohn appeared on the scene, the geological layering of the Bank was vastly thicker and more riddled with fault lines than anything McNamara had faced. Perhaps an analogy to the engineering of computer operating systems is more appropriate. The increasingly attractive user interface of Microsoft's Windows software cannot disguise the fact that successive versions of the program have added layer upon layer of code over an aging, and essentially unchanged, DOS architecture. The operational limitations of the program cannot be overcome on the basis of incremental change; what is needed is a decisive break with the past. In the same way, another round of reforms and patches will not resolve the Bank's current pathologies, which are attributable more than anything else to the institution's loss of focus resulting from years of incremental change. These attempts at internal reform may produce a few public relations victories, but they will not solve the endemic conceptual and operational shortcomings that are the root cause of the Bank's decreasing effectiveness as a development agency.

Jonathan Pincus (chap. 4 in this volume) and Ben Fine (chap. 9 in this volume) offer critiques of two major elements of the status quo or knowledge bank. Both arguments favor reinvention as a development bank instead. Through an analysis of the Bank's involvement in the Integrated Pest Management project in Indonesia, Pincus presents an operations story showing that the World Bank is ill-suited to micro- or even mezzolevel participatory development work. In response to pressures from critics, the Bank has moved into a bewildering array of development efforts having to do with farmers, women, fishermen, court systems, and rule of law. The Bank lacks the staff, structure, mode of operation, and expertise to train 1 million farmers to use natural pest control techniques on Java or elsewhere. As an institution designed to work primarily through central governments from capital cities (if not from Washington, D.C.), the Bank nearly destroyed an Indonesian farmer training program that was up and running successfully largely because the project under Bank tutelage reinforced the state's vertical structures and bureaucratic predations.

Fine takes a different tack in challenging the direction of reforms underway in the 1990s at the World Bank. Through an analysis of the Bank's remarkably unsophisticated intellectual treatment of social capital, Fine raises serious questions about the Bank's capacity to position itself on the cutting edge of knowledge about poverty and development. Although the World Bank is a widely appreciated source of cross-national data, its research has lacked intellectual rigor and originality. This is largely the result of ideological constraints placed on the Bank by its shareholders and imposed internally by a slavish acquiescence to the confines of neoliberal economic theory. World Bank research on poverty and development has obtained its hegemonic status within the profession on the basis of the institution's financial clout rather than the quality of its output. This hardly provides a firm basis from which to launch a knowledge bank. A development bank, as we envision it, would not have a knowledge component but would instead unbundle this enterprise to ensure that it was critically and intellectually independent of the lending and development arms of the institution.

Although John Sender (chap. 8 in this volume) and Mushtaq Khan (chap. 7 in this volume) take on quite different subjects, they develop a parallel critique of the World Bank. Sender's review of the Bank's record of operations in Africa argues that basic concepts about limiting the role of the state have undermined the ability of the Bank to be effective in alleviating poverty. Khan points out that the Bank's approach to corruption is subverted by a general misunderstanding of how capitalist development has unfolded historically and, echoing Sender, by a more specific bias against the developmental role of the state. Both Sender and Khan concentrate their arguments within the operations and concepts dimensions of this volume's framework of analysis.

In different ways, Jeffrey Winters (chap. 5 in this volume), Jonathan Fox (chap. 3 in this volume), and Devesh Kapur (chap. 3 in this volume) grapple with the question of power, control, and accountability. In his examination of criminal debt, Winters points out that the World Bank is legally liable for a share of tens of billions of dollars in corrupted loan funds and yet has managed to saddle indebted populations around the world with a repayment burden for funds they never received. Like the problem of corruption itself, this is a matter of power. And the question of who will pay for these losses is a power play at many levels simultaneously—horizontally between richer-creditor and poorer-debtor shareholders, but also vertically between indebted populations and their own abusive elites in collusion with the Bank's management. Fox and Kapur also elaborate these horizontal and vertical dimensions of power in their chapters. Careful to consider poor people as distinct from poor countries, Kapur is nevertheless most concerned with the horizontal question of whether changes in governance at the World Bank have affected which states are really in charge. He does not find the institution to be evolving in the direction of more balance and democratization among shareholders. Fox, meanwhile, considers the interactions between these horizontal and vertical dimensions of power. His analysis of the Itaparica case elaborates on the formation of north-south coalitional lines and supports his conclusion that the entire Inspection Panel exercise represents an imperfect effort at accountability.

This volume, perhaps inevitably, raises more questions than it answers. Our objective, however, is not to produce a blueprint for reform but instead to assemble an independent scholarly assessment of the World Bank as it exists today and to illuminate key obstacles lying in the path of reinvention. We have argued the reinvention project comprises three distinct yet closely interrelated dimensions of operations, concepts, and power. We have considered several competing visions of reinvention and examined their implications for the mismatch between the Bank's ambitions and operational capacity, the conceptual framework through which the Bank approaches the core issues of economic development and poverty reduction, and the power dynamics that both motivate the reinvention project and place constraints on the range of possible outcomes.

The lens of operations, concepts, and power leads to some clear, although troubling, conclusions. Efforts to reinvent the World Bank as a knowledge bank fail to resolve the inherent contradictions between the Bank's operational ambitions and capabilities and will thus further intensify the perennial problems of goal proliferation and institutional paralysis. In the absence of enlightened leadership from the United States, this remains the most likely outcome in the foreseeable future. Similarly, proposals for greater operational selectivity that inspire the idea of the niche bank—although attractive to U.S.-based aid skeptics—are conceptually and operationally flawed. As the 1990s financial crises have shown, private investment is an inadequate substitute for public sector development banking and the need to respond to recurrent episodes of financial distress would quickly overwhelm attempts to achieve operational focus on the basis of the neoliberal vision of unfettered markets and minimal public intervention. At the opposite extreme, the Left populist contention that the Bank should either be radically democratized or shut down essentially replicates the ambiguous position of the Bank's current management. Although the issue of internal governance is crucial, adding more voices to the already cacophonous demands for consultation will lead to neither greater accountability nor responsiveness to local communities. In the absence of a prior rationalization and reordering of institutional priorities, efforts to increase participation will only widen the gap between the Bank's ambitions and operational capacities.

We have argued against the currently fashionable proposals for a knowledge or niche bank and in favor of a return to the World Bank's roots as a development bank. Unbundled, streamlined, and more transparent, the World Bank as development bank would undertake a much narrower range of lending activities while maintaining a strong commitment to public capital flows for development across a broad range of countries. The World Bank as development bank would focus its energies on designing and implementing projects and loan programs in which it has an established comparative advantage. This would include physical investments amenable to external supervision and balance-of-payments support negotiated in tandem with bilateral donors and linked to programs specifically tailored to the requirements of individual countries. Policy advice, research, and evaluation would be carried out by a range of independent agencies to minimize moral hazard and conflict-of-interest problems.

This is an operationally and conceptually coherent vision of reinvention, but it is politically improbable. The experience of the 1990s does not provide much reason for optimism that the development bank can be achieved on the basis of internal reforms. Reinvention, as we have argued, will not come from within—rather, it must be imposed. Yet it is difficult to escape the conclusion that the institution's major shareholders are as unlikely to impose limits on the Bank as the Bank is to restrain itself. Barring a major realignment of shareholders' attitudes and expectations, the World Bank will in all likelihood stumble forward along its current dysfunctional path.

References

Adams, Patricia. 1991. *Odious Debts: Loose Lending, Corruption, and the Third World's Environmental Legacy.* Toronto: Probe International.

African Development Bank. 1998. *African Development Report.* Oxford: Oxford University Press.

Aguilar, Mario A., Jit B. S. Gill, and Livio Pino. 2000. *Preventing Fraud and Corruption in World Bank Projects: A Staff Guide.* Washington, D.C.: World Bank.

Alexander, Myrna. 1996. Conversion of Remaining ODs. Internal memo, 15 March OPRDR, World Bank, Washington, D.C.

Amsden, Alice H. 1989. *Asia's New Giant: South Korea and Late Industrialization.* New York: Oxford University Press.

——. 1997. "Bringing Production Back In—Understanding Government's Economic Role in Late Industrialization." *World Development* 25(4): 469–80.

Anderson, Robert S., Edwin Levy, and Barrie M. Morrison. 1991. *Rice Science and Development Politics: Research Strategies and IRRI's Technologies.* Oxford: Clarendon Press.

Aoki, Masahiko, HyungKi Kim, and Macahiro Okuno-Fujiwara. 1997. *The Role of Government in East Asian Economic Development: Comparative Institutional Analysis.* Oxford: Clarendon Press.

Aparico, Teresa, and John Garrison. 1999. "The Challenges of Promoting Participatory Development in the Amazon." In *Thinking Out Loud: World Bank Latin American and Caribbean Region Civil Society Papers,* edited by Kerianne Piester. Fall. Available from www.worldbank.org/laccs; INTERNET.

Ariyo, Ademola, and Afeikhena Jerome. 1999. "Privatization in Africa: An Appraisal." *World Development* 27(1): 201–13.

Armijo, Leslie Elliott, ed. 1999. *Financial Globalization and Democracy in Emerging Markets.* New York: St. Martin's Press.

Aron, Janine. 1997. Africa in the 1990s: The Institutional Foundations of Growth. Working paper series 97-15, Centre for the Study of African Economics, Oxford.

Bandow, Doug, and Ian Vasquez, eds. 1994. *Perpetuating Poverty: The World Bank, the IMF, and the Developing World.* Washington, D.C.: CATO Institute.

Barros, Flávia. ed. 2001. *Banco Mundial, participação, transparência e responsabilização.* Brasilia: Rede Brasil, sobre Instituições Financeiras Multilaterais.

Baum, Warren C. 1982. *The Project Cycle.* Rev. ed. Washington, D.C.: World Bank.

Bayliss, Kate. 1999. Privatization, the World Bank and Africa: Time for a Rethink. Mimeographed.

Bayliss, Kate, and Ben Fine. 1998. "Beyond Bureaucrats in Business: A Critical Review of the World Bank Approach to Privatization and Public Sector Reform." *Journal of International Development* 10(7): 841–55.

Bennell, Paul. 1997. "Privatization in Sub-Saharan Africa: Progress and Prospects During the 1990s." *World Development* 25(11): 1785–1803.

Berg, Elliot. 2000. "Aid and Failed Reform: The Case of Public Sector Management." In *Foreign Aid and Development: Lessons Learnt and Directions for the Future*, edited by Finn Tarp and Peter Hjertholm. London: Routledge.

Berne Declaration. 1998. "Mainstreaming Sustainability: The World Bank and the Rehabilitation of the Indian Coal Sector." Available from http://www2.access. ch/evb/BD/coal.htm; INTERNET.

Berthelemy, Jean-Claude, and C. Morrison. 1989. *Agricultural Development in Africa and the Supply of Manufactured Goods*. Paris: Organization for Economic Cooperation and Development.

Besley, Timothy, and McLaren, John. 1993. "Taxes and Bribery: The Role of Wage Incentives." *Economic Journal* 103: 119–41.

Bhaduri, Amit. 1986. "Forced Commerce and Agrarian Growth." *World Development* 14(2): 267–72.

Bird, Graham. 1996. "Borrowing from the IMF: The Policy Implications of Recent Empirical Research." *World Development* 24(11): 1753–60.

Bourdieu, Pierre. 1980. "Le Capital Social: Notes Provisoires." *Actes de la Recherche en Sciences Sociales*, no. 31: 2–3.

Bowles, Ian, and Cyril Kormos. 1995. "Environmental Reform at the World Bank: The Role of the US Congress. *Virginia Journal of International Law* 35(4): 777–839.

Bradlow, Daniel D. 1996. "A Test Case for the World Bank." *American University Journal of International Law and Policy* 11(2).

Bramble, Barbara, and Gareth Porter. 1992. "NGO Influence on United States Environmental Politics Abroad." In *The International Politics of the Environment*, edited by Andrew Hurrell and Benedict Kingsbury. New York: Oxford University Press.

Braun, Ann R. 1997. *Report of a Technical Audit Conducted for the World Bank of the Indonesia Integrated Pest Management Training Project*. Jakarta: World Bank.

Brautigam, Deborah. 1996. "State Capacity and Effective Governance." In *Agenda for Africa's Economic Renewal*, edited by Benno Ndulu and Nicolas van de Walle. New Brunswick, N.J.: Transaction.

Bread for the World Institute. 1996. "The Debt Initiative: Sham or Historic Breakthrough?" *News and Notices for World Bank Watchers*, 15 November.

Brecher, Jeremy, Tim Costello, and Brendan Smith. 2000. *Globalization from Below: The Power of Solidarity*. Boston: South End Press.

Broches, Aron. 1959. "International Legal Aspects of the Operations of the World Bank." *Recueil des Coursde l'Académie de Droit International* 297(3): 302–408.

———. 1995. *Selected Essays: World Bank, ICSID, and Other Subjects of Public and Private International Law*. Martinus Nijhoff Publishers, Dordrecht, The Netherlands.

Brown, L. David, and Darcy Ashman. 1996. "Participation, Social Capital and Intersectoral Problem-Solving." *World Development* 24(9): 1467–79.

Brown, Paul. 1999. "World Bank Pushes Chad Pipeline." *The Guardian*, 11 October.

Bureau of National Affairs. 1996. "Analysis and Reports: International Finance: World Bank to Team with Critics to Look at Economic Adjustment." Washington, D.C. 4 November.

Burnside, Craig, and David Dollar. 1997. Aid Policies and Growth. Macroeconomics and Growth Division, Policy Research Department, paper 1777, World Bank, Washington, D.C.

Canadian International Development Agency (CIDA). 1997. "Our Commitment to Sustainable Development." Available from http://w3.acdi-cida.gc.ca; INTERNET.

Caplen, Brian. 1999. "The Scalp-Hunters of Capitol Hill." *Euromoney* 365 (September): 170–77.

Carnegie Endowment for International Peace (CEIP). 2001. *The Role of the Multilateral Development Banks in Emerging Market Economies*. Available from www.ceip.org/econ; INTERNET.

Caufield, Catherine. 1996. *Masters of Illusion: The World Bank and the Poverty of Nations*. New York: Henry Holt and Company.

Cavanagh, John, Daphne Wysham, and Marcos Arruda, eds. 1994. *Beyond Bretton Woods: Alternatives to the Global Economic Order*. London: Pluto Press.

Cernea, Michael C. 1991a. "Involuntary Resettlement: Social Research, Policy, and Planning." In *Putting People First: Sociological Variables in Rural Development*, edited by Michael Cernea. 2d ed. Oxford: Oxford University Press.

——. 1991b. "Knowledge from Social Science for Development Policies and Projects." In *Putting People First: Sociological Variables in Rural Development*, edited by Michael Cernea. 2d ed. Oxford: Oxford University Press.

——. 1993. "Anthropological and Sociological Research for Policy Development on Population Resettlement." In *Anthropological Approaches to Resettlement: Policy, Practice, and Theory*, edited by Michael Cernea and Scott Guggenheim. Boulder: Westview Press.

——. 1994. *Sociology, Anthropology and Development: An Annotated Bibliography of World Bank Publications, 1975–1993*. Environmentally Sustainable Development Studies and Monographs Series, no. 3. Washington, D.C.: World Bank.

——. 1996. *Social Organization and Development Anthropology: The 1995 Malinowski Award Lecture*. Environmentally Sustainable Development Studies and Monographs Series, no. 6. Washington, D.C.: World Bank.

Chang, Ha-Joon. 1993. "The Political Economy of Industrial Policy in Korea." *Cambridge Journal of Economics* 17(2): 131–57.

——. 1997. "Markets, Madness and Many Middle Ways—Some Reflections on the Institutional Diversity of Capitalism." In *Essays in Honor of Geoff Harcourt*, edited by Philip Arestis, Gabriel Palma, and Malcolm Sawyer. Vol. 2. London: Routledge.

Chang, Ha-Joon, and Ajit Singh. 1993. "Public Enterprises in Developing Countries and Economic Efficiency—A Critical Examination of Analytical, Empirical and Policy Issues." *UNCTAD Review*, no. 4: 45–82.

Cheng, Tun-jen, Stephan Haggard, and David Kang. 1996. *Institutions, Economic Policy and Growth in the Republic of Korea and Taiwan Province of China*. Project on East Asian Development: Lessons for a New Global Environment, no. 2. Geneva: UNCTAD.

Chossudovksy, Michel. 1997. *The Globalization of Poverty: Impacts of IMF and World Bank Reform.* London: Zed Books.

Clark, Dana. 1999. *A Citizen's Guide to the World Bank Inspection Panel.* 2d ed. Washington, D.C.: Center for International Environmental Law.

Cleaver, Kevin M. 1985. The Impact of Price and Exchange Rate Policy on Agriculture in Sub-Saharan Africa. World Bank staff working paper, no. 728, World Bank, Washington, D.C.

Coats, Alfred. 1996. "Comments." *History of Political Economy* 28(suppl.): 369–79.

Cohen, Robin, and Shirin Rai, eds. 2000. *Global Social Movements.* London: Athlone.

Coleman, James S. 1988. "Social Capital in the Creation of Human Capital." *American Journal of Sociology Supplement* 94: S95–S120.

Collier, Paul. 1998. Social Capital and Poverty. Social Capital Initiative working paper 4, World Bank, Washington, D.C.

Collier, Paul, and Willem Gunning. 1999. "Explaining African Economic Performance." *Journal of Economic Literature* 37(1): 64–111.

Cramer, Christopher. 1999. "Privatization and Adjustment in Mozambique: A 'Hospital Pass'?" *Journal of Southern African Studies* 27: 79–103.

Cramer, Christopher, and Nicola Pontara. 1998. "Rural Poverty and Poverty Alleviation in Mozambique: What's Missing from the Debates?" *Journal of Modern African Studies* 36(1): 101–38.

Crook, Richard, and Manor, James. 2000. Democratic Decentralization. Operations Evaluation Department, working paper series no. 11. Washington, D.C.: World Bank.

Dahl, Robert A. 1999. "Can International Organizations Be Democratic?" In *Democracy's Edges,* edited by Ian Shapiro and Casiano Hacker-Cordon. Cambridge, UK: Cambridge University Press.

Danaher, Kevin. 1994. *50 Years Is Enough: The Case against the World Bank and the International Monetary Fund.* Boston: South End Press.

de Tray, Dennis. 1998. "World Bank Is Doing All It Can for Crisis-Hit Indonesia." *Jakarta Post.* September 24.

de Vries, Barend. 1996. "The World Bank as an International Player in Economic Analysis." *History of Political Economy* 28(suppl.): 225–44.

Department for International Development (DFID). 1997. Eliminating World Poverty: A Challenge for the 21st Century. White Paper on International Development, Department for International Development, London. Mimeographed.

Deraniyagala, Sonali, and Ben Fine. 2001. "New Trade Theory Versus Old Trade Policy: A Continuing Enigma." *Cambridge Journal of Economics* 25(6): 809–25.

Dewatripont, Mathias, Ian Jewitt, and Jean Tirole. 1999. "The Economics of Career Concerns, Part II. Application to Missions and Accountability of Government Agencies." *Review of Economic Studies* 66 (1): 199–217.

Díaz Peña, Elías. 1998. Statement by Elías Díaz Peña to the World Bank Board of Executive Directors. Washington, D.C., 3 February. Center for International Environmental Law. Available from www.ciel.org; INTERNET.

Dollar, David, and Jakob Svensson. 1998. *What Explains the Success or Failure of Structural Adjustment Programs?* Macroeconomics and Growth Group. Washington, D.C.: World Bank.

Dunne, Nancy, and Sathnam Sanghera. 2000. "China Drops Plea for World Bank Aid over $40 Million Tibetan Scheme." *Financial Times,* 8 July.

Eatwell, John. 1994. "Institutions, Efficiency and the Theory of Economic Policy." *Social Research* 61(1): 35–54.

Edstrom, Judith. 1999. Addressing Social Development by the World Bank. Statement delivered by sector manager, Social Development, World Summit for Social Development. February 16, New York.

Edwards, Sebastian. 1997. "Trade Liberalization Reforms and the World Bank." *American Economic Review* 87(2): 43–48.

Einhorn, Jessica. 2001. "The World Bank's Mission Creep." *Foreign Affairs* 80(5): 22–35.

Evans, Peter. 1996. "Introduction: Development Strategies across the Public-Private Divide." *World Development* 24(6): 1033–37.

Environmental Defense Fund. 1998. Letter from 126 NGOs from 35 countries to Mr. James D. Wolfensohn, 7 December, drafted in coordination with Indonesia NGOs, Washington, D.C.

Farah, Douglas, and David B. Ottaway. 2000. "World Bank Reassesses Chad Pipeline Deal." *Washington Post,* 5 December.

Feeney, Patricia. 1998. *Accountable Aid: Local Participation in Major Projects.* Oxford: Oxfam.

Feyzioglu, Tarhan, Vinaya Swaroop, and Min Zhu. 1998. "A Panel Data Analysis of the Fungibility of Foreign Aid." *World Bank Economics Review* 12(1): 29–58.

Fidler, Stephen. 2001. "The Man Who Broke the Bank." *Foreign Policy* 126: 40–50.

Field, Mark. 1995. "The Health Crisis in the Former Soviet Union: A Report from the 'Post-War' Zone." *Social Science and Medicine* 41(11): 1469–78.

Fine, Ben. 1990. "Scaling the Commanding Heights of Public Enterprise Economics." *Cambridge Journal of Economics* 14(2): 127–42.

——. 1997. "Privatization: Theory and Lessons from the UK and South Africa." *Seoul Journal of Economics* 10(4): 373–414.

——. 1999. "The Development State Is Dead—Long Live Social Capital." *Development and Change* 30(1): 1–19.

——. 2001. "Neither the Washington nor the Post-Washington Consensus: An Introduction." In *Development Policy in the Twenty-First Century: Beyond the Post-Washington Consensus,* edited by Ben Fine, Costas Lapavitsas, and Jonathan Pincus. London: Routledge.

Fine, Ben, and D. Hailu. 1999. Convergence and Consensus: The Political Economy of Stabilization and Growth. Mimeographed.

Fine, Ben, and P. Rose. 2001. "Education and the Post-Washington Consensus— Plus Ca Change?" In *Development Policy in the Twenty-First Century: Beyond the Post-Washington Consensus,* edited by Ben Fine, Costas Lapavitsas, and Jonathan Pincus. London: Routledge.

Fischer, Stanley, Ernesto Hernandez-Catá, and Mohsin S. Khan. 1998. *Africa: Is This the Turning Point.* IMF paper on policy analysis and assessment, 98/6. Washington, D.C.: International Monetary Fund,

Fisher, William, ed. 1995. *Toward Sustainable Development? Struggling over India's Narmada River.* Armonk: M. E. Sharpe.

Fjeldstad, Odd-Helge, and Joseph Semboja. 2000. "Dilemmas of Fiscal Decentralization: A Study of Local Government Taxation in Tanzania." *Forum for Development Studies* 27(1): 7–41.

Florini, Ann, ed. 2000. *The Third Force: The Rise of Transnational Civil Society.*

Washington, D.C.: Japan Center for International Exchange/Carnegie Endowment.

Foley, Michael W., and Bob Edwards. 1997. "Escape from Politics? Social Theory and the Social Capital Debate." *American Behavioral Scientist* 40(5): 550–61.

Food and Agriculture Organization. 1999. FAOSTAT internet accessible database, www.apps.fao.org. Rome.

Fox, James J. 1993. "Ecological Policies for Sustaining High Production in Rice: Observations on Rice Intensification in Indonesia." In *Southeast Asia's Environmental Future: The Search for Sustainability*, edited by Harold Brookfield and Yvonne Byron. Oxford: Oxford University Press.

Fox, Jonathan A. 1997a. "Transparency for Accountability: Civil Society Monitoring of Multilateral Development Bank Anti-Poverty Projects." *Development in Practice* 7(2): 167–71.

———. 1997b. "The World Bank and Social Capital: Contesting the Concept in Practice." *Journal of International Development* 9(7).

———. 1998. "When Does Reform Policy Influence Practice? Lessons from the Bankwide Resettlement Review." In *The Struggle for Accountability: The World Bank, NGOs and Grassroots Movements*, edited by Jonathan A. Fox and L. David Brown. Cambridge, Mass.: MIT Press.

———. 2000a. Assessing Binational Civil Society Coalitions: Lessons from the US-Mexican Experience. Chicano/Latino Research Center working paper, no. 26, University of California, Santa Cruz. Available from http://www.irc-online.org/bios/pdf/index—docs.html; INTERNET.

———. 2000b. "The World Bank Inspection Panel: Lessons from the First Five Years." *Global Governance* 6(3): 279–318. Available from http://www2.ucsc.edu/cgirs/conferences/humanrights/index.html; INTERNET.

———. 2001. "Vertically Integrated Policy Monitoring: A Tool for Civil Society Policy Advocacy." *Nonprofit and Voluntary Sector Quarterly* 30(3): 616–27.

Fox, Jonathan A., and L. David Brown. 1998a. "Introduction." In *The Struggle for Accountability: The World Bank, NGOs and Grassroots Movements*, edited by Jonathan A. Fox and L. David Brown. Cambridge, Mass.: MIT Press.

———, eds. 1998b. *The Struggle for Accountability: The World Bank, NGOs and Grassroots Movements*. Cambridge, Mass.: MIT Press.

———. 2000. "The World Bank and Social Capital: Lessons from Ten Rural Development Projects in Mexico and the Philippines." *Policy Sciences* 33(3–4): 399–419.

Gavin, Michael, and Dani Rodrik. 1995. "The World Bank in Historical Perspective." *American Economic Review* 85(2): 329–34.

General Accounting Office (GAO). 1996. *World Bank: U.S. Interests Supported, but Oversight Needed to Help Ensure Improved Performance*. Report no. GAO/NSIAD-96-212, National Security and International Affairs Division, Washington, D.C.: General Accounting Office.

———. 2000. *World Bank: Management Controls Stronger, but Challenges in Fighting Corruption Remain*. Report no. GAO/NSIAD-0073, Washington, D.C.: General Accounting Office.

George, Susan. 1988. *A Fate Worse than Debt*. Harmondsworth: Penguin.

German Federal Audit Office. 1994. FZ-Massnahme mit Nepal; Wasserkraftwerke (WKW) Arun III. 19 December.

Ghose, A. K. 1989. "Rural Poverty and Relative Prices in India." *Cambridge Journal of Economics* 13(2): 307–31.

Gilbert, Christopher, Andrew Powell, and David Vines. 1999. "Positioning the World Bank." *Economic Journal* 109: 598–633.

Glen, Jack D., and Mariusz A. Sumlinski. 1998. *Trends in Private Investment in Developing Countries: Statistics for 1970—96.* IFC Discussion Paper 34, Washington, D.C.: International Finance Corporation.

Goldsmith, Arthur A. 1999. "Slapping the Grasping Hand: Correlates of Political Corruption in Emerging Markets." American Journal of Economics and Sociology 58(4): 866–83.

Goodland, Robert. 2000. *Social and Environmental Assessment to Promote Sustainability.* World Bank environment paper, no. 74. Washington, D.C.: World Bank.

——. 2001. Environmental and Social Lessons to Be Learned from the World Bank's Fiercest Controversy, World Bank Group invited address, 18 September, Washington, D.C.

Gould, David J., and Jos A. Amaro-Reyes. 1983. The Effects of Corruption on Administrative Performance: Illustrations from Developing Countries. World Bank staff working paper, no. 580, World Bank, Washington, D.C.

Government of Indonesia and United Nations Food and Agriculture Organization. 1991. *Midterm Review, Training and Development of Integrated Pest Management in Rice Based Cropping Systems.* GOI-FAO Review Mission, UTF/INS/067/INS, July, Jakarta.

Grootaert, Christiaan. 1997. Social Capital: The Missing Link? Social Capital Initiative working paper 3, World Bank, Washington, D.C.

Grootaert, Christiaan, and Thierry van Bastelaer. 1998. "Expected Contributions from the Social Capital Initiative." IRIS. Available from http://wbln0018.worldbank.org/essd/essd.nsf/d3f59aa3a570f67a852567cf00695688/d9236b2cb5147fa9852567ed004c4a2f?OpenDocument; INTERNET.

Guggenheim, Scott, and Michael Cernea. 1993. "Anthropological Approaches to Resettlement: Policy, Practice, and Theory." In *Anthropological Approaches to Resettlement: Policy, Practice, and Theory,* edited by Michael Cernea and Scott Guggenheim. Boulder: Westview Press.

Gurgur, Tugrul, and Anwar Shah. 2000. Localization and Corruption: Panacea or Pandora's Box. Paper presented at the IMF Conference on Fiscal Decentralization, 21 November Washington, D.C. Mimeographed.

Guyer, Jane. 1997. *An African Niche Economy: Farming to Feed Ibadan, 1968–88.* London: Edinburgh University Press, for the International African Institute.

Gwin, Catherine. 1997. "U.S. Relations with the World Bank, 1945–1992." In *The World Bank: Its First Half Century.* Vol. 2, *Perspectives,* edited by Devesh Kapur, John P. Lewis, and Richard Webb. Washington, D.C.: Brookings Institution.

Haas, Ernst. 1980. "Why Collaborate? Issue Linkage and International Regimes." *World Politics* 32(3): 357–405.

Hair, Jay D., Benjamin C. Dysart, Luke J. Danielson, and Avra O. Rubaleava. 1997. Pangue Hydroelectric Project (Chile): An Independent Review of the International Finance Corporation's Compliance with Applicable World Bank Group Environmental and Social Requirements. Internal document, April 4, World Bank, Santiago, Chile.

Hall, Anthony. 1992. "From Victims to Victors: NGOs and the Politics of Empowerment at Itaparica." In *Making a Difference: NGOs and Development in a Changing World,* edited by Michael Edwards and David Hulme. London: Earthscan.

Hammig, Michael D. 1998. USAID and Integrated Pest Management in Indonesia: The Investments and Payoffs. Report prepared for USAID, Jakarta.

Hansen, Henrik, and Finn Tarp. 2000. "Aid Effectiveness Disputed." *Journal of International Development* 12: 375–98.

Harberger, Arnold. 1992. "Comment." In *Adjustment Lending Revisited: Policies to Restore Growth,* edited by Vittorio Corbo, Stanley Fischer, and Steven B. Webb. Washington, D.C.: World Bank.

Harcourt, Geoff. 1972. *Some Cambridge Controversies in the Theory of Capital.* Cambridge, UK: Cambridge University Press.

Harris, Laurence. 1987. "Financial Reform and Economic Growth: A New Interpretation of South Korea's Experience." In *New Perspectives on the Financial System,* edited by Laurence Harris, J. Coakley, M. Croasdale, and T. Evans. London: Croom Helm.

Harriss, John, and Paolo de Renzio. 1997. "'Missing Link' or Analytically Missing?: The Concept of Social Capital, An Introductory Bibliographic Essay." *Journal of International Development* 9(7): 919–37.

Head, John W. 1996. "Evolution of the Governing Law for Loan Agreements of the World Bank and Other Multilateral Development Banks." *American Journal of International Law* 90(2): 214–34.

Helleiner, Gerald. 1994. "From Adjustment to Development in Sub-Saharan Africa: Consensus and Continuing Conflict." In *From Adjustment to Development in Africa: Conflict, Controversy, Convergence, Consensus?* edited by Giovanni Cornia and Gerald Helleiner. London: Macmillan.

Hildyard, Nicholas. 1997. The World Bank and the State: A Recipe for Change? Bretton Woods Project, London.

Hirschman, Albert O. 1970. "The Search for Paradigms as a Hindrance to Understanding." *World Politics* 22(3): 120–41.

———. 1984. "A Dissenter's Confession: The Strategy of Economic Development Revisited." In *Pioneers in Development,* edited by Gerald M. Meier and Dudley Seers. Oxford: Oxford University Press.

———. 1995. *Development Projects Observed.* Washington, D.C.: Brookings Institution Press. (Original edition, 1967).

Hjertholm, Peter, and Howard White. 2000. "Foreign Aid in Historical Perspective." In *Foreign Aid and Development,* edited by Finn Tarp. London: Routledge.

Hodgson, Geoffrey, and Harry Rothman 1999. "The Editors and Authors of Economics Journals: A Case of Institutional Oligopoly?" *Economic Journal* 109(2): 165–86.

Hopkins, Anthony G. 1988. "African Entrepreneurship: An Essay on the Relevance of History to Development Economics." *Geneve Afrique* 26(2): 7–28.

Human Rights Watch. 1998. World Bank Should Monitor Abuses in India. Press release, 21 April.

Hunter, David. 1997a. "Extending the Inspection Panel to the IFC and MIGA." In *The World Bank Inspection Panel: A Three Year Review,* edited by Lori Udall. Washington, D.C.: Bank Information Center.

———. 1997b. "The Planafloro Claim: Lessons from the Second World Bank Inspection Panel Claim." Center for International Environmental Law. Available from www.ciel.org; INTERNET.

Husain, Ishrat, and John Underwood, eds. 1991. *African External Finance in the 1990s*. Washington, D.C.: World Bank.

Huther, Jeff, and Anwar Shah. 2000. Anti-Corruption Policies and Programs: A Framework for Evaluation. Policy Research working paper 2501, Operations Evaluation Department, World Bank, Washington, D.C.

"Inspection Panel Confirms World Bank Forced Evictions in Lagos." 1999. *SERAC@WORK* 2(1).

International Bank for Reconstruction and Development (IBRD). 2001. "Ten Things the Bank Does." Available from http://www.worldbank.org/tenthings/seven.htm; INTERNET.

International Development Organization. 1998. *Additions to IDA Resources: Twelfth Replenishment, a Partnership for Poverty Reduction*. Washington, D.C.: World Bank.

International Finance Corporation. 1998. *Annual Portfolio Performance Review*. Washington, D.C.: World Bank.

Jana, Dario. 1999. "El Etnocidio del Pueblo Pehuenche en el Alto BioBio de Chile." International Rivers Network. Available from www.irn.org; INTERNET.

Johnston, Barbara, and Terence Turner. 1997. "The Pehuenche, the World Bank Group and ENDESA S.A." American Anthropological Association. Available from www.aaanet.org/committees/cfhr/rptpehuenc.htm; INTERNET.

Jones, Phillip. 1992. *World Bank Financing of Education: Lending, Learning and Development*. London: Routledge.

Jones, Sidney, and Mike Jendrzejezyk. 1998. World Bank Projects in the Singrauli Region of India. Memo to World Bank President James Wolfensohn and World Bank Executive Directors, 16 April. Unpublished manuscript.

Kapur, Devesh. 1997. "The New Conditionalities of the International Financial Institutions." In *UNCTAD Research Papers for the Group of Twenty-Four*. Vol. 8, *International Monetary and Financial Issues for the 1990s*. New York: UNCTAD.

———. 2000. "Who Gets to Run the World." *Foreign Policy* 121: 44–50.

———. 2001. "Expansive Agendas and Weak Instruments: Governance Related Conditionalities of International Financial Institutions." *Journal of Policy Reform* 4(3): 207–41.

———. 2002. "The Common Pool Dilemma of Global Public Goods: Lessons from the World Bank's Net Income and Reserves." *World Development*. 30(3).

Kapur, Devesh, John P. Lewis, and Richard Webb, eds. 1997. *The World Bank: Its First Half Century*. Vol. 1, *History*. Washington, D.C.: Brookings Institution.

Kardam, Nüket. 1993. "Development Approaches and the Role of Policy Advocacy: The Case of the World Bank." *World Development* 21(11): 1773–86.

Kaufmann, Daniel. 1997. "Corruption: The Facts." *Foreign Policy* 107(summer): 114–31.

Keck, Margaret, and Kathryn Sikkink. 1998. *Activists beyond Borders*. Ithaca: Cornell University Press.

Kenmore, Peter E., F. O. Carino, C. A. Perez, V. A. Dyck, and A. P. Guiterrez. 1984. "Population Regulation of the Rice Brown Planthopper (*Nilaparvata lugens stal*) within Rice Fields in the Philippines." *Journal of Plant Protection in the Tropics* 1(1): 19–37.

Khagram, Sanjeev. 2000. "Toward Democratic Governance for Sustainable Development: Transnational Civil Society Organizing around Big Dams." In *The Third Force: The Rise of Transnational Civil Society,* edited by Ann Florini. Washington, D.C.: Japan Center for International Exchange/Carnegie Endowment.

Khan, Mushtaq H. 1996a. "The Efficiency Implications of Corruption." *Journal of International Development* 8(5): 683–96.

———. 1996b. "A Typology of Corrupt Practices in Developing Countries." *Liberalization and the New Corruption. IDS Bulletin* 27(2): 12–21.

———. 1998. "The Role of Civil Society and Patron-Client Networks in the Analysis of Corruption." In *Corruption and Integrity Improvement Initiatives in Developing Countries.* OECD/UNDP. New York: UNDP Management Development and Governance Division.

———. 2001. "The New Political Economy of Corruption." In *Development Policy in the Twenty-First Century: Beyond the Post-Washington Consensus,* edited by Ben Fine, Costas Lapavitsas, and Jonathan Pincus. London: Routledge.

Khan, Mushtaq H., and Jomo, K. S. 2000. *Rents, Rent-Seeking and Economic Development: Theory and Evidence in Asia.* Cambridge, UK: Cambridge University Press.

Kilby, Christopher. 2000. "Supervision and Performance: The Case of World Bank Projects." *Journal of Development Economics* 62: 233–59.

Killick, Tony. 1998. *Aid and the Political Economy of Policy Change.* London: Routledge.

Klitgaard, Robert. 1988. *Controlling Corruption.* Berkeley: University of California Press.

Kraske, Jochen. 1996. *Bankers with a Mission: The Presidents of the World Bank, 1946–91.* New York: Oxford University Press.

Krueger, Anne O. 1997. "Trade Policy and Economic Development: How We Learn." *American Economic Review* 87(1): 1–22.

———. 1998. "Whither the World Bank and the IMF?" *Journal of Economic Literature* 36(4): 1983–2020.

Kurian, Priya. 1995. "The US Congress and the World Bank: Impact of News Media on International Environmental Policy." In *International Organizations and Environmental Policy,* edited by Robert V. Bartlett, Priya Kurian, and Madhu Malik. Westport, Conn.: Greenwood.

Lachica, Eduardo. 1994. "Environmentalists Are Opposing Plans of World Bank to Build Dam in Nepal." *Wall Street Journal,* 12 September.

Lensink, Robert, and Oliver Morrissey. 1999. *Uncertainty of Aid Flows and the Aid-Growth Relationship.* CREDIT research paper 99(3), University of Nottingham, Nottingham.

Lensink, Robert, and Howard White. 1999. "Assessing Aid: A Manifesto for the 21st Century?" *Sida Evaluation Report.* Swedish International Development Cooperation Agency, 99/17:13. Available from http://www.sida.se/Sida/articles/3600–3699/3637/assessing.pdf; INTERNET.

Leroy, Jean-Pierra, and Maria Clara Couto Soares, eds. 1998. *Bancos multilaterais e desenvolvimento participativo no Brasil: Dilemas e desafios.* Rio de Janeiro: FASE/IBASE.

Letsie, David, and Patrick Bond. 1999. Social, Ecological and Economic Characteristics of Bulk Water Infrastructure: Debating the Financial and Service Delivery Implications of the Lesotho Highlands Water Project. South Africa. Unpublished manuscript.

Levine, Ross, and David Renelt. 1992. "A Sensitivity Analysis of Cross-Country Growth Regressions." *American Economic Review* 82(4): 942–63.

Leys, Colin. 1996. *The Rise and Fall of Development Theory.* London: James Currey.

Lienert, Ian, and Jitendra Modi. 1997. A Decade of Civil Service Reform in Sub-Saharan Africa. IMF working paper. Fiscal Affairs Department, International Monetary Fund, Washington, D.C.

Linser, Wolfgang. 1991. "Statistics on Pesticide Production." Ministry of Finance, Jakarta. Mimeographed.

Lipton, Michael, and Richard Longhurst. 1989. *New Seeds and Poor People.* London: Unwin Hyman.

Lloyd, John. 1998. "A Country Where the Awful Has Already Happened." *Financial Times,* 24 October.

Loos, Jane. 1998. Options to Reduce Negative Impact from Corruption on Bank-Financed Activities. Office memorandum to Mr. Jean-Michel Severino, vice president, EAP, 19 October, World Bank, Washington, D.C.

Loveard, Keith. 1997. "The Dark Side of Prosperity: A World Bank Critic Alleges Waste and Graft." *Asia Week,* 15 August.

Macklin, Michael. 1992. *Agricultural Extension in India.* World Bank technical paper 190, Washington, D.C.: World Bank.

Macroeconomic Research Group (MERG). 1993. *Making Democracy Work: A Framework for Macroeconomic Policy in South Africa.* Capetown: Oxford University Press and Scandinavian Institute of African Studies, Uppsala.

Marais, Hein. 1998. *South Africa: Limits to Change, the Political Economy of Transition.* London: Zed Books.

Marshall, Katherine. 1999. Conference on Reinventing the World Bank at Northwestern University (with SOAS), May 14–16 1999. Confidential internal memorandum, 25 May, World Bank, Washington, D.C.

Masebu, Peter. 1999. "Another Call To Write off Africa's Bilateral Debts." *Africa News,* 2 November.

Mason, Edward S., and Robert E. Asher. 1973. *The World Bank since Bretton Woods.* Washington, D.C.: Brookings Institution.

Matlack, Carol. 1997. "What Happened to the Coal Miners' Dollars? At Least $100 Million from a World Bank Loan Is Lost." *Business Week,* 8 September.

Mauro, Paolo. 1995. "Corruption and Growth." *Quarterly Journal of Economics* 10(3): 681–712.

———. 1996. The Effects of Corruption on Growth, Investment and Government Expenditure. IMF working paper, International Monetary Fund, Washington, D.C.

McCombie, J. S. L., and Anthony P. T. Thirlwall. 1994. *Economic Growth and the Balance of Payments Constraint.* London: St. Martin's Press.

McConnell, Mitch. 2000. Statement of U.S. Senator Mitch McConnell on FY2001 Appropriations for International Financial Institutions. Press release, 6 April.

McGillivray, Mark, and Howard White. 1993. Explanatory Studies of Aid Allocation among Developing Countries. Working Paper Series, Institute of Social Studies, The Hague.

McIlwham, Fiona. 1998. "Africa's Growth Tragedy" Reconsidered. Master's thesis, Department of Economics, School of Oriental and African Studies, University of London.

Meltzer, Allan H. et al. 2000. "Report of the International Financial Institution Advisory Commission." Available from http://phantom-x.gsia.cmu.edu/IFIAC; INTERNET.

Mikesell, Raymond, F. 2000. "Bretton Woods: Original Intentions and Current Problems." *Contemporary Economic Policy* 18(4): 404–14.

Millikan, Brent. 1998. "Planafloro: Modelo de Projeto Participativo." In *Bancos multilaterais e desenvolvimento participativo no Brasil: Dilemas e desafios,* edited by Jean-Pierre Leroy and Maria Clara Couto Soares. Rio de Janeiro: FASE/IBASE.

———. 2001. "O Painel de Inspeção de Banco Mundial e o pedido de investigação sobre o PLANAFLORO," in *Banco Mundial, participação, transparência e responsabilização,* edited by Flavia Barros. Brasilia: Rede Brasil, sobre Instituições Financeiras Multilaterais.

Millman, Joel, and Jonathan Friedland. 1997. "World Bank Finance Arm Tends to Aid Least Needy." *Wall Street Journal,* 23 September.

Mills, C. Wright. 2000. *The Power Elite.* 2d ed. Oxford: Oxford University Press.

Mkandawire, Thandika. 1994. "Adjustment, Political Conditionality and Democratization in Africa." In *From Adjustment to Development in Africa,* edited by Giovanni Cornia and Gerald Helleiner. London: Macmillan.

———. 1998. *Thinking about Development States in Africa.* Project on Economic Development and Regional Dynamics in Africa: Lessons from the East Asian Experience, study no. 9. Geneva: UNCTAD.

Moberg, David. 2000. "Silencing Joe Stiglitz." *Salon.* Available from http://www.salon.com/news/feature/2000/05/02/stiglitz/index.html; INTERNET.

Mohan, P. C., ed.. 1999. *Bibliography of Publications: Africa Region, 1993–8.* Technical paper 425. Washington, D.C.: World Bank.

Moore, Deborah, and Leonard Sklar. 1998. "Reforming the World Bank's Lending for Water: The Process and Outcome of Developing a Water Resources Management Policy." In *The Struggle for Accountability: The World Bank, NGOs and Grassroots Movements,* edited by Jonathan A. Fox and L. David Brown. Cambridge, Mass.: MIT Press.

Morse, Bradford, and Thomas Berger. 1992. *Sardar Sarovar: Report of the Independent Review.* Ottawa: Resource for the Future International.

Mosely, Paul, Jane Harrigan, and John Toye. 1995. *Aid and Power: The World Bank and Policy Based Lending.* Vol. 1. 2d ed. London: Routledge.

Mosely, Paul, Turan Subasat, and John Weeks. 1995. "Assessing Adjustment in Africa." *World Development* 23(9): 1459–73.

Mueller, Dennis C. 1989. *Public Choice II: A Revised Edition of Public Choice.* Cambridge, UK: Cambridge University Press.

Multilateral Investment Guarantee Agency (MIGA). 1997. *Annual Report.* Washington, D.C.: Multilateral Investment Guarantee Agency.

———. 1998. *Annual Report.* Washington, D.C.: Multilateral Investment Guarantee Agency.

———. 2000. *Annual Report.* Washington, D.C.: Multilateral Investment Guarantee Agency.

Naim, Moises. 1996. "From Supplicants to Shareholders: Developing Countries and the World Bank." In *The International Monetary and Financial System,* edited by Gerald K. Helleiner. London: Macmillan.

Narayan, Deepa. 1997. *Voices of the Poor: Poverty and Social Capital in Tanzania.* Washington, D.C.: World Bank.

Narayan, Deepa, Robert Chambers, Meera Kaul Shah, and Patti Petesch. 2000. *Voices of the Poor: Crying Out for Change.* New York: Oxford University Press, for the World Bank.

Narayan, Deepa, Raj Patel, Kai Schafft, Anne Rademacher, and Sarah Koch-Schulte. 2000. *Voices of the Poor: Can Anyone Hear Us?* New York: Oxford University Press, for the World Bank.

Narayan, Deepa, and Lant Pritchett. 1997. Cents and Sociability: Household Income and Social Capital in Rural Tanzania. Policy research working paper 1796. World Bank, Washington, D.C.

Ndikumana, Leonce, and James K. Boyce. 1998. "Congo's Odious Debt: External Borrowing and Capital Flight in Zaire." *Development and Change* 29(2): 195–217.

"Nepal: More Dam Trouble." 1993. *Economist,* 16 October.

Nolan, Peter. 1996. *Russia's Fall, China's Rise.* London: Routledge.

Nolan, Peter, and Wang Xiaoqiang. 1999. "Beyond Privatization: Institutional Innovation and Growth in China's Large State-Owned Enterprises." *World Development* 27(1): 169–200.

Nye, Joseph S., Jr. 1990. *Bound to Lead: The Changing Nature of American Power.* New York: Basic Books.

——. 2001. "Globalization's Democratic Deficit: How to Make International Institutions More Accountable." *Foreign Affairs.* July/August: 2–6.

Olson, Mancur. 1965. *The Logic of Collective Action.* Cambridge, Mass.: Harvard University Press.

Opaso, Christian. 1999. The Bio-Bio Hyodrelectric Project: A Lesson Not Fully Learned by the World Bank. Paper submitted to the World Commission on Dams. International Rivers Network. Available from www.irn.org; INTERNET.

Organization for Economic Cooperation and Development (OECD). 1998. *OECD/DAC Development Cooperation Report.* Paris: OECD.

Oxfam. 1995. *A Case for Reform: Fifty Years of the IMF and the World Bank.* Oxford: Oxfam Publications.

Pack, Howard, and Janet Rothenberg Pack. 1990. "Is Foreign Aid Fungible? The Case of Indonesia." *Economic Journal* 100: 188–94.

Pasic, Amir, and Thomas Weiss. 1997. "The Politics of Rescue: Yugoslavia's Wars and the Humanitarian Impulse." *Ethics and International Affairs* 11: 105–31.

——. 1999. Yacyretá Hydroelectric Project: The Struggle for Participation. Paper presented to the World Commission on Dams, 15 June. International Rivers Network. Available from www.irn.org; INTERNET.

Peters, Pauline. 1996. Failed Magic or Social Context? Market Liberalization and the Rural Poor in Malawi. Development Discussion Paper 562, Harvard Institute for International Development, Harvard University, Cambridge, Mass.

Phillips, Michael M. 1999. "The World Bank May Curb Power of Its Watchdog." *Wall Street Journal,* 12 January.

——. 2000. "Can the World Bank Lend Money without Hurting the Poor: Indian

Coal Project Shows Risks in Resettling Illiterate Farmers." *The Wall Street Journal Europe,* 14 August.

Picciotto, Roberto, Warren Van Wicklin, and Edward Rice, eds. 2000. *Involuntary Resettlement: Comparative Perspectives.* Vol. 2. New Brunswick, N.J.: Transaction.

Pincus, Jonathan R. 1996. *Class Power and Agrarian Change.* London: Macmillan.

———. 2001. "The Post-Washington Consensus and World Bank Lending Operations: New Rhetoric and Old Operational Realities." In *Development Policy in the Twenty-First Century: Beyond the Post-Washington Consensus,* edited by Ben Fine, Costas Lapavitsas, and Jonathan Pincus. London: Routledge.

Polak, Jacques. 1996. "The Contribution of the International Monetary Fund." *History of Political Economy* 28 (suppl.): 211–24.

Portes, Alejandro. 1998. "Social Capital: Its Origins and Applications in Modern Society." *Annual Review of Sociology* 24: 1–24.

Princen, Thomas, and Matthias Finger. 1994. *Environmental NGOs in World Politics.* London: Routledge.

Psacharopoulos, George. 1981. "The World Bank in the World of Education: Some Policy Changes and Some Remnants." *Comparative Education* 17 (2): 141–45.

Putnam, Robert. 1992. *Making Democracy Work: Civic Traditions in Modern Italy.* Princeton: Princeton University Press.

———. 1993. "The Prosperous Community: Social Capital and Public Life." *American Prospect* 13: 35–42.

———. 1995. "Bowling Alone: America's Declining Social Capital." *Journal of Democracy* 6 (1): 65–78.

———. 1996. "The Strange Disappearance of Civic America." *American Prospect* 24: 34–48.

Ranis, Gustav. 1997. "The World Bank near the Turn of the Century." In *Global Development Fifty Years after Bretton Woods,* edited by Roy Culpeper, Albert Berry, and Frances Stewart. London: Macmillan.

Rauch, James E., and Peter B. Evans. 2000. "Bureaucratic Structure and Bureaucratic Performance in Less Developed Countries." *Journal of Public Economics* 75: 49–71.

Rees, Colin. 1998. "Safeguards Update." *Environment Matters.*

Rice, Edward. 1998. *Recent Experience with Involuntary Resettlement: Brazil—Itaparica.* Operations Evaluation Department, report no. 17544. Washington, D.C.: World Bank.

Rich, Bruce. 1994. *Mortgaging the Earth: The World Bank, Environmental Impoverishment and the Crisis of Development.* London: Earthscan.

———. 2000. "Still Waiting: The Failure of Reform at the World Bank." *Ecologist Report* 30 (6): 8–16.

Risse, Thomas, Stephen C. Ropp, and Kathryn Sikkink, eds. 1999. *The Power of Human Rights: International Norms and Domestic Change.* Cambridge, UK: Cambridge University Press.

Rodrigues, Maria Guadalupe. 2000. Searching for Common Ground—Transnational Advocacy Networks and Environmentally Sustainable Development in Amazônia. Paper presented at Human Rights and Globalization: When Transnational Civil Society Networks Hit the Ground conference, 1–3 Dec., Center for Global, International, and Regional Studies, University of California, Santa Cruz. Available from www2.ucsc.edu/cgirs/conferences/index.html; INTERNET.

Rodrik, Dani. 1998. Trade Policy and Economic Performance in Sub-Saharan Africa. NBER working paper series, no. 6562, National Bureau of Economic Research, Cambridge, Mass.

Röling, Niels. 1995. *Mid-term Review of the Indonesian Integrated Pest Management Training Project.* Appendix 6. Jakarta: World Bank.

Roxborough, Ian. 1992. "Neo-liberalism in Latin America: Limits and Alternatives." *Third World Quarterly* 13(3): 421–40.

Sandstrom, Sven. 1998. Operational Policy Reform. Compliance with Safeguard Policies, World Bank internal memorandum, 20 May, Washington, D.C.

Sanford, Jonathan. 1988. "US Policy towards the MDBs: The Role of Congress." *George Washington Journal of International Law and Economics* 1.

Sanger, David E. 1999a. "China to Get World Bank Loans despite US Objections." *New York Times,* 25 June.

——. 1999b. "World Bank Beats Breast for Failures in Indonesia." *New York Times,* 11 February.

——. 1999c. "World Bank Rates Its Indonesia Performance as 'Marginal'." *Association France-Presse,* 10 February.

Sanger, David E., and Joseph Kahn. 2000. "World Bank Criticizes Itself over Chinese Project near Tibet." *New York Times,* 27 June.

Sanghera, Sathnam. 2000. "China Drops Pleas for $40m World Bank Aid to Fund Tibetan Scheme." *Financial Times,* 8–9 July.

Schiavo-Campo, Salvatore, Giulio de Tommaso, and Amitabha Mukherjee. 1998. *An International Statistical Survey of Government Employment and Wages.* Public Sector Management and Information Technology Team, Technical Department for Europe, Central Asia, Middle East and North Africa. Washington, D.C.: World Bank.

Schiff, Maurice. 1992. "Social Capital, Labor Mobility, and Welfare: The Impact of Uniting States." *Rationality and Society* 4(2): 157–75.

Schuh, G. Edward. 1993. "Involuntary Resettlement, Human Capital, and Economic Development." In *Anthropological Approaches to Resettlement: Policy, Practice, and Theory,* edited by Michael Cernea and Scott Guggenheim. Boulder: Westview Press.

Schwartzman, Stephen. 2000. The World Bank and Land Reform in Brazil. Environmental Defense Fund. Unpublished manuscript.

Scott, James C. 1998. *Seeing like a State: How Certain Schemes to Improve the Human Condition Have Failed.* New Haven: Yale University Press.

Sen, Amartya., and Jayati Ghosh. 1993. Trends in Rural Employment and the Poverty-Employment Linkage. ILO-ARTEP working papers, New Delhi.

Sen, Jai. 1999a. Of Mushrooms That Bloom: Critical Intersections in Washington, D.C.—Or, Why the World Bank's Inspection Panel Is Important to All of Us. Calcutta. Unpublished manuscript.

——. 1999b. "A World to Win—But Whose World Is It, Anyway?" in *Whose World Is It Anyway? Civil Society, the United Nations and the Multilateral Future,* edited by John Foster and Anita Anand. Ottawa: United Nations Association in Canada

Sender, John. 1999. "Africa's Economic Performance: Limitations of the Current Consensus." *Journal of Economic Perspectives* 13(3): 89–114.

Sender, John, and Deborah Johnston. 1996. "Some Poor and Invisible Women: Farm Laborers in South Africa." *Development Southern Africa.* 13(1): 3–16.

Sender, John, and Sheila Smith. 1986. "What's Right with the Berg Report and What's Left of Its Critics." In *World Recession and the Food Crisis in Africa*, edited by Peter Lawrence. London: James Currey.

——. 1990. *Poverty, Class, and Gender in Rural Africa: A Tanzanian Case Study*. London: Routledge.

Serageldin, Ismail. 1997. Foreword to *Voices of the Poor: Poverty and Social Capital in Tanzania*, by Deepa Narayan. Washington, D.C.: World Bank.

Severino, Jean-Michel. 1998. Correspondence from vice president East Asia and Pacific Region, World Bank, to Mr. Bruce Rich and Dr. Stephanie Fried, 17 December, Environmental Defense Fund, Washington, D.C.

Shannon, Amy. 1999. "Reform of International Finance and Trade: Investing in a Sustainable Future." *In Focus* 2(2).

Shepard, Daniel J. 1996. "Donor Countries Back Wolfensohn Debt Relief Plan, but Financing Still a Problem." *Earth Summit Times*, 29 September.

Shihata, Ibrahim F. I. 1994. *The World Bank Inspection Panel*. New York: Oxford University Press.

Shin, Jang-Sup. 1996. *The Economics of the Latecomers: Catching-Up, Technology Transfer and Institutions in Germany, Japan and South Korea*. Routledge Studies in Growth Economies of Asia. London: Routledge.

Shleifer, Andrei, and Robert W. Vishny. 1993. "Corruption." *Quarterly Journal of Economics* 108(3).

Simpson, Glenn R. 1998. "World Bank Memo Depicts Diverted Funds, Corruption in Jakarta; Report Contrasts with '97 Denials." *Wall Street Journal*, 19 August.

Smith, Jackie, Charles Chatfield, and Ron Pagnucco, eds. 1997. *Transnational Social Movements and Global Politics*. Syracuse: Syracuse University Press.

Spraos, John. 1986. IMF Conditionality: Ineffectual, Inefficient, Mistargeted. Princeton Essays in International Finance 166, Princeton University.

Standing, Guy. 1999. New Development Paradigm or Third Wayism? A Critique of a World Bank Rethink. Draft, International Labor Organization, Geneva. Mimeographed.

——. 2000. "Brave New Words? A Critique of Stiglitz's World Bank Rethink." *Development and Change* 31: 737–63.

Standing, Guy, John Sender, and John Weeks. 1996. *Restructuring the Labor Market: The South African Challenge*. ILO Country Review. Geneva: International Labor Organization.

Stern, Nicholas, and Francisco Ferreira. 1997. "The World Bank as 'Intellectual Actor'." In *The World Bank: Its First Half Century*. Vol. 2, *Perspectives*, edited by Devesh Kapur, John P. Lewis, and Richard Webb. Washington, D.C.: Brookings Institution.

Stiglitz, Joseph E. 1997. "An Agenda for Development for the Twenty-First Century." In *9th Annual Bank Conference on Development Economics*. Washington, D.C.: World Bank.

——. 1998a. Distribution, Efficiency and Voice: Designing the Second Generation of Reforms. Paper presented at the World Bank Conference on Asset Distribution, Poverty and Economic Growth, Washington, D.C. Mimeographed.

——. 1998b. Knowledge for Development: Economic Science, Economic Policy and Economic Advice. Paper presented at the Annual World Bank Conference on Development Economics, 20–21 April, Washington, D.C. Mimeographed.

——. 1998c. More Instruments and Broader Goals: Moving toward the Post-Washington Consensus. 1998 WIDER annual lecture, 7 January Helsinki.

——. 1998d. "Towards a New Paradigm for Development: Strategies, Policies and Processes." 1998 Prebisch lecture, 19 October, UNCTAD, Geneva.

——. 2000. "What I Learned at the World Economic Crisis." *New Republic,* 17 April.

Stremlau, John, and Francisco Sagasti. 1998. "Preventing Deadly Conflict: Does the World Bank Have A Role?" Carnegie Commission on Preventing Deadly Conflict. Available from www.ccpdc.org/pubs/world/world.html; INTERNET.

Suzman, Mark. 1998. "World Bank Accuses Itself of 'Serious Violations'." *Financial Times,* 7 January.

Taylor, Lance. 1997. "The Revival of the Liberal Creed—The IMF and the World Bank in a Globalized Economy." *World Development* 25(2): 145–52.

Thorne, Eva. 1998. The Politics of Policy Compliance: The World Bank and the Social Dimensions of Development. Ph.D. diss., Political Science Dept., Massachusetts Institute of Technology, Cambridge, Mass.

"Tibetan Tinderbox." 1999. *Economist,* 19 June.

Timmer, C. Peter. 1993. "Rural Bias in East and Southeast Asian Rice Economy: Indonesia in Comparative Perspective." *Journal of Development Studies* 29: 149–76.

Tjønneland, Elling N., Henrik Harboe, Alf Morten Jerve, and Nazneen Kanji. 1998. *The World Bank and Poverty in Africa: A Critical Assessment of the Bank's Operational Strategies for Poverty Reduction.* Oslo: Royal Ministry of Foreign Affairs.

Tobin, James. 1999. "Comment on Dahl's Scepticism." In *Democracy's Edges,* edited by Ian Shapiro and Casiano Hacker-Cordon. Cambridge, UK: Cambridge University Press.

Treakle, Kay. 1998. Accountability at the World Bank: What Does It Take? Lessons from the Yacyretá Hydroelectric Project, Argentina/Paraguay. Paper presented at the annual meeting of the Latin American Studies Association, 24–26 September, Chicago.

Treisman, D. 2000. "The Causes of Corruption: A Cross National Study." *Journal of Public Economics* 76: 399–457.

Udall, Lori. 1997. *The World Bank Inspection Panel: A Three Year Review.* Washington: Bank Information Center.

——. 1998. "The World Bank and Public Accountability: Has Anything Changed?" In *The Struggle for Accountability: The World Bank, NGOs and Grassroots Movements,* edited by Jonathan A. Fox and L. David Brown. Cambridge, Mass.: MIT Press.

Umaña, Alvaro, ed. 1998. Forward to *The World Bank Inspection Panel: The First Four Years (1994–1998).* Washington, D.C.: World Bank.

UN Conference on Trade and Development (UNCTAD). 1998. *Trade and Development Report.* Geneva: United Nations.

——. 2000. *The Least Developed Countries 2000 Report. Aid, Private Capital Flows and External Debt: The Challenge of Financing Development in the LDCs.* Geneva: UNCTAD Secretariat.

U.S. Agency for International Development (USAID). 1997. Strategic Plan. September, U.S. Agency for International Development, Washington, D.C. Mimeographed.

Useem, Michael, Lou Setti, and Jonathan Pincus. 1992. "The Science of Javanese

Management: Organizational Alignment in an Indonesian Development Program." *Public Administration and Development* 12: 447–71.

Van Arkadie, Brian. 1996. "Economic Strategy and Structural Adjustment in Tanzania." In *Governance, Leadership and Communication: Building Constituencies for Economic Reform*, edited by Leila Frischtak and Izak Atiyas. Washington, D.C.: World Bank.

Van der Eng, Pierre. 1996. *Agricultural Growth in Indonesia: Productivity Change and Policy Impact since 1880*. London: Macmillan.

Vianna, Aurelio. 1998a. The Panel Inspection Request as a Process and Not a Result: A Preliminary Evaluation from the Itaparica (Brazil) Case. Paper presented at the annual meeting of the Latin American Studies Association, 24–26 September, Chicago.

——. 1998b. "Statement by Aurelio Vianna (Rede Brasil) to the World Bank Board of Executive Directors." 3 February World Bank and Center for International Environmental Law, Washington, D.C. Available from www.ciel.org; INTERNET.

——. 2001. "O Painel de Inspeção do Banco Mundial para Itaparica," in *Banco Mundial, participação, transparência e responsabilização*, edited by Flávia Barros. Brasilia: Rede Brasil, sobre Instituições Financeiras Multilaterais.

Wade, Robert. 1990. *Governing the Market: Economic Theory and the Role of Government in East Asian Industrialization*. Princeton: Princeton University Press.

——. 1997. "Greening the Bank: The Struggle Over the Environment 1970–1995." In *The World Bank: Its First Half Century*. Vol. 2, *Perspectives*, edited by Devesh Kapur, John P. Lewis, and Richard Webb. Washington, D.C.: Brookings Institution.

——. 2001b. The U.S. Role in the Malaise at the World Bank: Get up, Gulliver! Paper presented at the American Political Science Annual Meeting, 30 August–2 September, San Francisco.

——. 2001a. "Showdown at the World Bank." *New Left Review*, 2d ser., 7 (January–February): 124–37.

Waldmeier, Patti. 1997. "World Bank Defends $570 Million Restructure Plan." *Financial Times*, 21 February.

Waldmeier, Patti, and Mark Suzman. 1997. "World Bank 'Fails to Learn from Past Mistakes'." *Financial Times*, 14 December.

Wall, Ellen, Gabriel Ferrazzi, and Frans Schryer. 1998. "Getting the Goods on Social Capital." *Rural Sociology* 63 (2): 300–322.

Wapenhans, Willi A. 1992. *The Wappenhans Report*. Portfolio Management Task Force. Washington, D.C.: World Bank. (Also published as *Effective Implementation: Key to Development Impact*.)

——. 1994. "Efficiency and Effectiveness: Is the World Bank Group Prepared for the Task Ahead." In *Bretton Woods: Looking to the Future*. Washington, D.C.: Bretton Woods Commission.

Wapenhans, Willi A., et al. 1992. Report of the Portfolio Management Task Force. Internal document, World Bank, 1 July Washington, D.C.

"Western Contractors Face Bribery Charge over Lesotho Dam." 1999. *Financial Times*, 19 November.

"What Are They Protesting About?" 2000. *The Hindu*, 8 October.

White, Oliver Campbell, and Anita Bhatia. 1998. *Privatization in Africa: Directions in Development*. Washington, D.C.: World Bank.

Williams, G. 1999. "Panchayati Raj and the Changing Micro-Politics of West Bengal." In *Sonar Bangla? Agricultural Growth and Agrarian Change in West Bengal and Bangladesh,* edited by Ben Rogaly, Barbara Harriss-White, and Sugata Bose. New Delhi: Sage.

Williamson, John. 1993. "Democracy and the Washington Consensus." *World Development* 21(8): 1329–36.

Wilson, James Q. 1989. *Bureaucracy: What Government Agencies Do and Why They Do It.* New York: Basic Books.

Winters, Jeffrey A. 1997. "Down with the World Bank." *Far Eastern Economic Review* 13.

———. 1999a. "The Determinants of Financial Crisis in Asia." In *The Politics of the Asian Financial Crisis,* edited by T. J. Pempel. Ithaca: Cornell University Press.

———. 1999b. "On the Mostly Negative Role of Transnational Capital in Indonesian Democratization." In *Financial Globalization and Democracy in Emerging Markets,* edited by Leslie Armijo. New York: Macmillan and St. Martins Press.

Wolfensohn, James D. 1998. The Other Crisis. Address to the Board of Governors, World Bank, October, Washington, D.C.

———. 1999. A Proposal for a Comprehensive Development Framework: A Discussion Draft. World Bank, 21 January, Washington, D.C. Available from http://www.worldbank.org/cdf/cdf-text.htm; INTERNET.

Wolff, Luciano, and Sérgio Sauer. 2001. O Painel de Inspeção e o caso do Cédula da Terra," in *Banco Mundial, participação, transparência e responsabilização,* edited by Flávia Barros. Brasilia: Rede Brasil, sobre Instituições Financeiras Multilaterais.

Women's Eyes on the World Bank Campaign. 1997. "Gender Equity and the World Bank Group: A Post-Beijing Assessment." 50 Years Is Enough. Washington, D.C. October.

Woods, Ngaire. 2000. "The Challenge of Good Governance For the IMF and the World Bank Themselves." *World Development* 28(5): 823–41.

Woolcock, Michael. 1998. "Social Capital and Economic Development: Toward a Theoretical Synthesis and Policy Framework." *Theory and Society* 27(2): 151–208.

World Bank. 1960. *Articles of Agreement of the International Development Association.* Washington, D.C.: World Bank.

———. 1981. *Accelerated Development in Sub-Saharan Africa: An Agenda for Action.* Washington, D.C.: World Bank. [Also known as the Berg Report.]

———. 1985. *General Conditions Applicable to Loan and Guarantee Agreements.* Washington, D.C.: World Bank.

———. 1992. Report of the Portfolio Management Task Force (Wapenhans Report). 1 July, Operations Evaluation Department, Washington, D.C. Mimeographed.

———. 1993a. Aide Memoire: Indonesia IPM Training Project. 11 December, World Bank, Washington, D.C.

———. 1993b. *Articles of Agreement.* Washington, D.C.: World Bank. (As amended through April 28, 1993.)

———. 1993c. *The East Asian Miracle: Economic Growth and Public Policy.* World Bank Policy Research Report. Oxford: Oxford University Press.

———. 1993d. Financial Reporting and Auditing Task Force. Internal report, 8 October, Central and Operational Accounting Division, World Bank, Washington, D.C.

——. 1993e. *Staff Appraisal Report: Indonesia, Integrated Pest Management Training Project.* Agriculture Operations Division. Washington, D.C.: World Bank.

——. 1993f. *The World Bank Inspection Panel.* Resolution no. 93-10, Resolution no. IDA 93-6. 22 September. Washington, D.C.

——. 1994a. *Adjustment in Africa: Reforms, Results and the Road Ahead.* New York: Oxford University Press.

——. 1994b. *1992 Evaluation Results.* Operations Evaluation Department. Washington, D.C.: World Bank.

——. 1994c. *Progress Report on Next Steps.* Report no. R94-154. Washington, D.C.: World Bank.

——. 1994d. *Resettlement and Development.* Environment Department. Washington, D.C.: World Bank.

——. 1995a. Address by James D. Wolfensohn to the Board of Governors of the World Bank Group, at the Joint Annual Discussion. Press release, 10 October, World Bank, Washington, D.C.

——. 1995b. *Midterm Review.* Washington, D.C.: World Bank.

——. 1995c. Wolfensohn Lays Out Future Direction of World Bank. Press release 96/S21, 10 October, World Bank, Washington, D.C.

——. 1996a. *African Development Indicators 1996.* Washington, D.C.: World Bank.

——. 1996b. "Aide Memoire: Indonesia IPM Training Project." Washington, D.C. July 3.

——. 1996c. *Annual Report.* Washington, D.C.: World Bank.

——. 1996d. *Effectiveness of Environmental Assessments and National Environmental Action Plans: A Process Study.* Operations Evaluation Department, report 15835. Washington, D.C.: World Bank.

——. 1996e. Meeting of President Wolfensohn with Senior Management. Internal document, 12 March, World Bank, Washington, D.C.

——. 1996f. Meeting with Jean-Francois Rischard. Internal staff minutes, 21 October, World Bank, Washington, D.C.

——. 1996g. Office memorandum from Myrna Alexander, OPRDR, to various Bank staff. 15 March, World Bank, Washington, D.C.

——. 1996h. Portfolio Improvement Program: An Update. Internal memorandum, 4 November, World Bank, Washington, D.C.

——. 1996i. *Poverty Assessment: A Progress Review.* Operations Evaluation Department, report 15881. Washington, D.C.: World Bank.

——. 1996j. *Poverty Reduction and the World Bank: Progress and Challenges in the 1990s.* Washington, D.C.: World Bank.

——. 1996k. Questions and Answers about the Networks. Internal document, 16 September, World Bank, Washington, D.C.

——. 1996l. *World Bank Participation Sourcebook.* Washington, D.C.: World Bank.

——. 1996m. *World Development Report 1996: From Plan to Market.* New York: Oxford University Press, for the World Bank.

——. 1997a. *Agricultural Extension and Research: Achievements and Problems in National Systems.* Operations Evaluation Department. Washington, D.C: World Bank.

——. 1997b. Aide Memoire: Indonesia IPM Training Project. 2 April, World Bank, Washington, D.C.

——. 1997c. *Annual Review of Development Effectiveness 1996.* Operations Evaluation Department. Washington, D.C.: World Bank.

——. 1997d. *Evaluating Development Operations: Methods for Judging Outcomes and Impacts.* Operations Evaluation Department, Lessons and Practices 10. Washington, D.C.: World Bank.

——. 1997e. Guidance for Communicating the Compact. Internal document for managers, February, vice presidency for External Affairs, World Bank, Washington, D.C.

——. 1997f. *Helping Countries Combat Corruption: The Role of the World Bank.* Washington, D.C.: World Bank.

——. 1997g. "Indonesia and the World Bank." Press release no. 98/1426/EAP, 28 July, World Bank, Washington, D.C.

——. 1997h. Portfolio Improvement Program: Highway Sub-Sector, Review of Projects at Risk, Phase I. Internal report, February, Quality Assurance Group, World Bank, Washington, D.C.

——. 1997i. Portfolio Improvement Program: Reviews of Sector Portfolios and Lending Instruments: A Synthesis. Draft internal report, 22 April, Quality Assurance Group, Portfolio Improvement Program, World Bank, Washington, D.C.

——. 1997j. Review of Technical Assistance Loans in the World Bank. Internal report, February, Quality Assurance Group, World Bank, Washington, D.C.

——. 1997k. *Rural Development: From Vision To Action.* Economically and Socially Sustainable Development Studies and Monograph Series 21. Washington, D.C.: World Bank.

——. 1997l. *Staff Appraisal Report: India Coal Sector Rehabilitation Project.* Report no. 16473-IN. Washington, D.C.: World Bank.

——. 1997m. *Summary of RSI Staff Views Regarding the Problem of 'Leakage' from World Bank Project Budgets.* Jakarta: World Bank.

——. 1997n. *World Development Report 1997: The State in a Changing World.* Washington, D.C.: World Bank.

——. 1998a. Aide Memoire: Indonesia IPM Training Project. 30 July, World Bank, Washington, D.C.

——. 1998b. *Annual Report.* Washington, D.C.: World Bank.

——. 1998c. *Annual Review of Development Effectiveness 1997.* Operations Evaluation Department. Washington, D.C.: World Bank.

——. 1998d. *Assessing Aid: What Works, What Doesn't, and Why.* World Bank Policy Report. New York: Oxford University Press.

——. 1998e. *Assessing Development Effectiveness, Evaluation in the World Bank and the International Finance Corporation.* Operations Evaluation Department. Washington, D.C.: World Bank.

——. 1998f. *Global Development Finance, Analysis and Summary Tables.* Washington, D.C.: World Bank.

——. 1998g. Human Resources Policy Reform. Internal memorandum, 6 March, World Bank, Washington, D.C.

——. 1998h. *Indonesia Country Assistance Note.* Operations Evaluation Department. Washington, D.C.: World Bank.

——. 1998i. The Initiative on Defining, Monitoring and Measuring Social Capital:

Text of Proposals Approved for Funding. Social Capital Initiative, working paper 2, World Bank, Washington, D.C.

——. 1998j. The Local Level Institutions Study: Overview and Program Description. Local Level Institutions, working paper 1, World Bank, Washington, D.C.

——. 1998k. "Partnerships for Development: Proposed Actions for the World Bank, A Discussion Paper." 20 May, World Bank, Washington, D.C. Available from http://www.worldbank.org/html/extdr/pfd-discpaper.pdf; INTERNET.

——. 1998l. *Recent Experience with Involuntary Resettlement.* Operations Evaluation Department, report no. 17538. Washington, D.C.: World Bank.

——. 1998m. *The World Bank Group in Africa: An Overview.* Washington, D.C.: World Bank.

——. 1998n. *World Development Indicators.* Washington, D.C.: World Bank.

——. 1998o. *World Development Report 1998/99: Knowledge for Development.* New York: Oxford University Press.

——. 1999a. *Annual Report.* Washington, D.C.: World Bank.

——. 1999b. *Annual Review of Development Effectiveness 1998.* Operations Evaluation Department. Washington, D.C.: World Bank.

——. 1999c. *Articles of Agreement.* Washington, D.C.: World Bank. (As amended effective February 16, 1989.) Available from http://www.worldbank.org/html/extdr/backgrd/World Bank/arttoc/htm; INTERNET.

——. 1999d. Attacking Poverty. Chapter outline for the World Development Report 2000/1, World Bank, Washington, D.C. Mimeographed.

——. 1999e. "Bank's Financial Risk." Questions and Answers about the World Bank. Fall 1998. Available from http://www.worldbank.org/html/extdr/faq/faqf98-64.htm; INTERNET.

——. 1999f. *Indonesia Country Assistance Note.* Operations Evaluation Department. Washington, D.C.: World Bank.

——. 1999g. Indonesia Country Assistance Review. Revised draft, January 6, World Bank, Washington, D.C. Mimeographed.

——. 1999h. Lending Retrospective: Volumes and Instruments: Issues Paper. Internal discussion paper, 19 July, World Bank, Washington, D.C.

——. 1999i. OED Participation Process Review. Draft, 21 April, Operations Evaluation Department, World Bank, Washington, D.C.

——. 1999j. "Operating Procedures, as adopted by the panel on August 19, 1994." World Bank, Washington, D.C. Available from http://www.worldbank.org/html/ins-panel/operating—procedures.html#annexI; INTERNET.

——. 1999k. "Report of the Panel Working Group: Second Review of the Inspection Panel 1998, Clarification of Certain Aspects of the Resolution." World Bank, Washington, D.C. Available from http://www.worldbank.org/html/extdr/ipwg/report.htm; INTERNET.

——. 1999l. Social and Environmental Aspects: A Desk Review of SECALs and SALs Approved During FY98 and FY99. Draft, 24 May, Environmentally and Socially Sustainable Development Department, World Bank, Washington, D.C.

——. 1999m. "World Bank Announces Debarment of Firm as Part of Anti-Corruption Drive." Press release no. 99/2116/S, 16 March, World Bank, Washington, D.C.

———. 1999n. "World Bank Announces Debarment of Individual and Three Corporations." Press release no. 99/2138/2, 8 April, World Bank, Washington, D.C.

———. 1999o. "World Bank Approves Controversial Proposal to Change Inspection Panel." World Bank Information Center and the Center for International Environmental Law, Washington, D.C., 21 April. Available from www.ciel.org; INTERNET.

———. 1999p. *World Development Indicators.* Washington, D.C.: World Bank.

———. 1999q. *World Development Report: Knowledge For Development.* New York: Oxford University Press, for the World Bank.

———. 2000a. *Annual Report.* Washington, D.C.: World Bank.

———. 2000b. *Annual Review of Development Effectiveness 1999.* Operations Evaluation Department. Washington, D.C.: World Bank.

———. 2000c. "Comprehensive Development Framework: Progress Report to the World Bank's Executive Board." World Bank, Washington, D.C. Available from http://www.worldbank.org/cdf/progressreport.htm; INTERNET.

———. 2000d. *Helping Countries to Combat Corruption: Progress at the World Bank since 1997.* Washington, D.C.: World Bank.

———. 2000e. "Poverty Assessments: A Follow-up Review." Operations Evaluation Department. Washington, D.C.: World Bank.

———. 2000f. *World Development Report 1999/2000: Entering the 21st Century.* New York: Oxford University Press, for the World Bank.

———. 2001a. *Annual Report.* Washington, D.C.: World Bank.

———. 2001b. *Annual Review of Development Effectiveness 2000.* Operations Evaluation Department. Washington, D.C.: World Bank.

———. 2001c. *IDA's Partnership for Poverty Reduction (FY 94–FY00): An Independent Evaluation.* Operations Evaluation Department. Washington, D.C.: World Bank.

———. 2001d. *OED Review of the Bank's Performance on the Environment.* Operations Evaluation Department. Washington, D.C.: World Bank.

World Bank Inspection Panel. 1999. *Request for Inspection—Argentina: Special Structural Adjustment Loan (Ln 4405-AR) Panel Report and Recommendation.* Washington, D.C.: World Bank.

Yeats, Alexander. 1990. "On the Accuracy of Economic Observations: Do Sub-Saharan Trade Statistics Mean Anything?" *World Bank Economic Review* 4(2): 135–56.

———. 1998. What Can Be Expected from African Regional Trade Arrangements? Some Empirical Evidence. Policy Research working paper 2004, Development Research Group, World Bank, Washington, D.C.

Young, Oran. 1999. "Comment on Andrew Moravcsik, 'A NewSstatecraft? Supranational Entrepreneurs and International Cooperation'." *International Organization* 53(4): 805–9.

Contributors

BEN FINE is professor of economics at the University of London and director of the Centre for Economic Policy for Southern Africa.

JONATHAN A. FOX is associate professor of Latin American and Latino studies at the University of California, Santa Cruz.

DEVESH KAPUR is assistant professor in the Department of Government and a faculty associate at the Weatherhead Center for International Affairs at Harvard University.

MUSHTAQ H. KHAN is senior lecturer in the Economics Department of the University of London's School of Oriental and African Studies.

JONATHAN R. PINCUS is lecturer in the Economics Department of the University of London's School of Oriental and African Studies.

BRUCE RICH is program manager of the Environmental Defense Fund (EDF) International Program.

JOHN SENDER is professor of economics with reference to Africa at the University of London's School of Oriental and African Studies.

JEFFREY A. WINTERS is associate professor of political economy at Northwestern University.

Index

Note: Page numbers in *italic type* refer to tables or figures.

Corruption *(cont.)*
financial accountability and, 101–2
fraud detection, 116–18
indices of, 167–68
judicial system effect on, 170, 171
loan-approval culture and, 46–50
at local levels, 177
power relations in government and, 108
rent-seeking and, 170, 173
in Russia, 47–48
sanctions against, 120
World Bank culture and, 121–22
World Bank legitimacy and, 101
World Bank response to, 101, 102, 105–6, 164, 168
See also Anticorruption strategies; Indonesia
Creditworthiness, 56
Criminal debt, 25, 107–8, 224–25
estimated amount of, 102
for Indonesia, 102
Inspection Panel and, 109n
international law and, 108–10, 125, 129
sharing the burden of, 102–3
World Bank knowledge of, 125
Crook, Richard, 178
Culture. See Social policy; World Bank culture

Dahl, Robert, 75
Dams, 149. *See also specific hydroelectric projects*
Debt forgiveness, 66, 71
criminal debt and, 109–10
Decentralization, 174–76, *175*
as anticorruption strategy, 174
corruption and, 178–79
See also Governance
Deflationary macroeconomic policies, 189–90, 197
Democracy, 75
Democratic Republic of Congo, 6, 72
de Tray, Dennis, 125, 126, 128–29
Developing countries
clientelism and, 165, 184
corruption in, 166, 168–69, 178
creditworthiness, 56
economics of transition, 181–84
foreign aid to, 5, 28
OECD capital flows to, 6, 7, 21
political stability, 183–84
private capital flow to, 6–9, 8, 28
public enterprises in, 190
service delivery in, 178
state capacity, 166, 167
See also Africa, sub-Saharan countries; Less developed countries; *specific countries*

Development
comprehensive approach to, 78
corruption and, 165
efficient markets/noninterventionist state model, 165, 172
market-based strategy of, 17
See also Comprehensive Development Framework
Development banks. *See* Multilateral development banks; World Bank
Devolution of governance, 174–76, *175*
corruption and, 178–79
See also Governance
de Vries, Barend, 204n, 209
Dice memorandum, 48, 49, 51, 128n
Dilts, Russell, 96n
Dollar, David, 193
Dominican Republic, 40
Downing, Ted, 145n
Dresdner Bank, 145

Economic Development Institute, 188
Economist, 29
Ecuador, 39, 139
Education
graduate students in economics, 209n
lending and, 207–8
and World Bank, 65, 207, 209
Edwards, Sebastian, 206
Egypt, 6, 18
Eichenberger, Joseph, 66
Elf Aquitaine, 38
Environmental Assessments, 34–35, 37
Environmental Defense Fund, 32
Environmentally sustainable development, 28–29
Environmental policy, 27, 28, 134
Bank versus client standards, 150–51
infrastructure mega-projects and, 20, 139, 152–53
See also Policy reforms; Safeguard policies
Environmental projects, sustainability of, 45
Environment Department, 33
Environment, Rural, and Social Development network, 33
Equity, 61–62
European Bank for Reconstruction and Development (EBRD), 65, 75
Evictions. *See* Resettlement
Executive Board of Directors, 53, 58–59, 61, 157
Inspection Panel and, 135, 156, 160
Exxon Corporation, 38, 153n

FAO, 88–89
"Fifty Years Is Enough" (slogan), 18–19